From Me to You, I'm Just Saying…

Volume 1

From Me to You, I'm Just Saying...
Volume 1

Lawrence E. Crockett

This novel is a work of fiction. Any references to real people, events, establishments, organizations, or locales are intended only to give the fiction a sense of reality and authenticity. Other names, characters, places, and incidents portrayed herein are either the product of the author's imagination or are used fictionally.

Copyright © 2017 by Lawrence E. Crockett

All rights reserved. No part of this book may be used or reproduced in any manner whatsoever without written permission except in the case of brief quotations embodied in critical articles and reviews.

ISBN: 978-0-9973712-1-5

I'm ready to be in conversation with the world:
This moment came once I realized...
No sacrifice is too great; nor endurance too long when you pursue your dream, especially if you're determined to succeed!

Lawrence E. Crockett

Lawrence E. Crockett

For Tanya Delissa Hughes Crockett

My Wife,

A source of inspiration and uncompromised support; couldn't have done this without you. So much love for you and between us.

Contents

Acknowledgement	v
A Cry for Love	1
My Little Princess	10
Baby Got Back!	16
Giving or Receiving Love on Valentine's Day, Maybe or Maybe Not!	49
Hopelessly Frustrated	53
Family, Friend or Foe…?	60
When Love Is Entangled With Deceit	66
Coping With a Loss	73
The Making of You	80
A Tribute to a Bugle Boy	84
Where Have You Been?	89
Graduation, a Time of Reflection	94
Mr. President, We Salute You on Presidents' Day	99
Farewell Mr. President, a Job Well Done!	104
U Can't Touch This	108
Run Kanye, Run	113
Hillary, Girl We Got A Big Problem!	119
Republicans What Happened to Your Party?	124
The Thrill Is Gone	129
Wait, Hold Up	134
The Morning After, You Da Man, Period!	139

America's Olympic Bluster	143
A Black Magic Woman, Part 1	149
Touched By An Angel	170
Benjie	176
Prince	181
A Tribute to Michael Joseph Jackson	183
Hello Cousin	185
Hello Fella	188
Anybody Seen Benny?	193
One Strong Memory	197
Thinking of Home	201
The Strangest Thing	208
Ms. Ora's Hot Tamales	211
Are You My Daddy?	220
Youthful Innocence	223
Hire Me Please	228
Music and the Business	234
The Internal Revenue Service Scam	239
From Me to You, I'm Just Saying	243
Facebook, Google+, E-mails, Direct Mail and Text Messages	251
Author's Biography	258
Other Releases	261
Coming Soon	263

Acknowledgment

Gratitude is priceless!

In the beginning, it was so lonely, sitting quietly in front of my computer deep in thought. Oh, how lonesome it was! Nina Shakes Harlem was my first novel, and just like a firstborn, it was such an enormous undertaking. At times feeling besieged and overwhelmed with so much doubt, I carefully contemplated the many challenges I faced. After taking a long deep breath, I continued my onward march. With an immense learning curve, nescience loomed large. In spite of this, I pressed on. Carefully weaving each thought into a coherent sentence, I wisely chose my words while pursuing clarity. There were so many random thoughts floating around in my head in search of meaning and truth. Although struggling a bit as I tried to make sense of it all, a few failed attempts aided me in finding a rhythm. Gradually I began to write, one word after the next. Eventually, it became easier once a spark illuminated a path forward. A new adventure had begun, writing a series of short stories for you.

Quite often it's just me, up early in the morning, sitting in front of my computer with a blank screen staring back. My determination is always relentless when I try to disappear inside myself in search of substance. Usually, it's such an awesome struggle but necessary. Most incredible challenges are. You see, I try to channel all of my energy into one purpose, creating something meaningful to share. It feels like an odyssey of sorts, constructing a bridge to a part of my consciousness rarely used and seldom shared. After spending so many precious years learning from my adventures, I find myself reviewing each success as well as my failures, vowing never to forget lessons learned. After considerable reflection, I choose which thoughts to share. Life's experiences have a way of shaping our sentiments, and in this instance somehow connecting us. At first, just a few of you took notice, but that quickly changed. Incessantly a few hundred more began reading and sharing their experiences with other like minds. Miraculously the numbers began to grow, quickly reaching several thousand. Now, over a million of you are reading my stories.

Does this sound too eccentric? More importantly, how did we happen? If you're anything like a few of my close friends, you're always busy. Living a contemporary life is extremely demanding. But somehow a door opened, and our connection was made. Stranger things have been known to happen you know. Regardless the circumstance, the introduction is now complete, and I'm glad; aren't you?

Time is precious. Too precious to take for granted. I certainly don't take yours lightly by any means. Fortuitous encounters have never been a part of my experiences. We were meant to happen, you and me. I feel certain of that! For so many of you, demands are placed on each minute of your day. Allocating time between work and pleasure can't be easy. Most days, finding some quiet time to relax a bit if only for a few minutes, can be an awesome challenge. At times, a desire such as this can be far too elusive to achieve. But occasionally you might still hope for a moment to take a brief break from your daily routine even when it doesn't seem possible. So what could possibly bring a moment of pleasure? Reading a few chapters from a book or a few pages from an article in a magazine? Or could you simply be intrigued by the daily news? Do any of these things capture your interest? Sometimes talking with an old friend could also bring joy. Our hearts occasionally requires such a coveted reunion.

Maybe a short story could be just as good, or possibly your smart phone. Playing one of your favorite games can be fun. Some of them are quite popular and very addictive you know. So many people do just that. But you chose to read something written by me. Was it a short story or my first novel? Okay, enough of my conjecture, perhaps a bit clueless anyway, right? Whatever the case might have been, I'm thankful you chose something of mines to read. Hopefully, you weren't disappointed. I'm honored to be a part of the moment that brought you a little pleasure. Share your experience with a friend. There's nothing quite like a good referral. Should you decide to share your comments, social media has made that very tempting and easy to do. I really do read your comments. Seriously I do!

So much of your support and encouragement has already reached me through Facebook, Twitter, Google+, e-mail, phone calls or texts. Occasionally, I meet some of you in person. Oh, what joy it brings when you share your experiences with me. Admittedly, I'm discovering so much about the world around us, and it's exhilarating. I love sharing most of it with you. You've become an integral part of this adventure, and I do feel your presence in both words and deeds. We're all unique creatures of consciousness, and occasionally a spark ignites a flame. When this occurs, our universe is expanded. Oh, what a difference this makes. Change sometimes illuminates such beauty in this wonderful world we call our planet. It magnifies our uniqueness offering an opportunity for us to share our differences as well as the things we have in common: love, joy, happiness, pain, and sorrow are all emotions which connect us as human beings. These emotions are unavoidable, and they are an essential part of our social fabric. Well most of them anyway! I love experiencing all of these emotions while writing. It engages me in astonishing ways causing such wonder making me feel so alive! Moments like these connects me to something larger than one person, a coalescing of sorts into a rejuvenating experience.

Uninhibited and unfiltered, these moments of discovery arrive bringing a new and exciting opportunity to embrace something larger than our singular existence. I can't fully explain this feeling beyond the words I've chosen. But I do often try. I know how it makes me feel. It's like breathing air after a hard downpour. The freshness becomes a catalyst awakening something new and special inside, a rebirth of sorts much like a usufruct. Much more could be said but stopping here seems right. Besides, I want you to know how much I appreciate your support. Your kindness and embrace have been inspiring, and the love is heartfelt. As your numbers continue to grow, I can't wait to hear from many more of you. Until then, I wish each of you success in life and sincerely hope happiness finds its way to your heart.

Oh, one final word if I might share just one more thought. Closing without responding to a few of your comments would be regrettable. Some of you have asked about my background and want to know how I landed in this spot as a writer. Well, I assure you it wasn't planned. I'm serious; really didn't see this coming. I believe some people measure their life by the things they wished they'd achieved while others measure theirs by the things they choose and then develop a passion while doing what they love. I chose the latter, and now that I've found this joy, I don't want it to end, not now, not ever. Writing is one of those things I love doing. It's my new love wrapped inside a big bundle of joy. Quite often, that's been the difference in my life between success and failure or happiness and sadness. Maybe this just might apply to your life as well.

I write because I love it. If you're anything like me, you've already faced some crucial circumstances in pursuit of happiness. By now, perhaps life has presented a few critical challenges in your journey. For me, my first challenge was discovering my talent and finding the passion for developing it. There are so many people in the world anointed with talent; for some, maybe more than one. However, it usually requires an enormous commitment to cultivate. That's where the separation occurs. So I took a chance to develop mines. An education was paramount. Don't cripple yourself by neglecting yours. It's an awesome responsibility and too precious to disregard. We need the knowledge to advance our talent, and there's no substitute for a good education. Without a doubt, this gift is too important to ignore and too valuable to neglect. I don't know where I'd be without mine.

The final challenge is learning how to recognize opportunities. They're all around us you know. Some require an effort to discover and a little kindness or luck to realize. Benevolence is the milk and honey that sustains a virtuous life. It's out there waiting for you. Treat others the way you want to be treated, and doors will eventually open even for you. Success, sometimes unpredictable, can come when you least expect it; quite often from the most unlikely sources. Maybe it doesn't happen when you want or need it the most, but success can be realized even by you. So don't sit around waiting, get busy and work toward it. Smart, hard work with determination and focus just might put you on a path toward a promising future. After all, it really does depend on you. Spend your time wisely and believe in yourself.

This is where your journey begins. With a commitment to that belief, you'll be ready to make a difference in your life. There's such a thin line between success and failure. Don't be afraid to try, go for it! Start by developing your talent. Get a good education, pursue opportunities and realize your dreams. Remember, it's never, never too late in life to try. So many attempts at success in life begin with a simple idea. However small, they can grow with discipline and persistence.

I leave you with this last thought: there's nothing greater than love, or the people in our lives that love us. We have only one world, and there's certainly only one you. I'm so glad we're here, especially you!

A Cry for Love

03/25/2016

To demand a love, flawless and without imperfections, is synonymous to attempting an unsuccessful flight to the moon…with a kite!

"I'm so tired of being alone." While looking through the sparkling sunlit window, the sunrays slightly obscured her skyward view. Once she found serenity, she released a deep doleful sigh. Briefly pausing to renew her courage, she fought back the tears before continuing to speak. Suffering from too many failed attempts in pursuit of love, lingering discords had weakened her resolve. A painful look covered her face as she began spewing words laced with the sour taste of despair. I watched in suspense as her painful words dripped slowly from her lips. Suddenly a glaring look of pain appeared in her eyes. Yet she continued with her scathing recitation straight from her heart. Having little hope for an antithesis, disappointment had obviously usurped her fate. Oh, what a dreadful combination these three emotions are—despair, discord and disappointment, those awful three D's. Steadfastly, she continued with animus, delivering an endless flow of heartfelt emotions too abundant to hide and certainly too painful to hold inside. Reticence had poignantly succumbed, ensuring a clear path for her solemn soliloquy.

"I don't want to grow old without love and sharing my life with someone special who loves me. Such a waste it seems, living all alone without love and romance in my life. Why…? I deserve better! There's nothing wrong wanting all of this and more, is there? My heart is big, I have that right. There's a lot of love inside me and living without love, ain't living at all." Consumed with a level of despair, unlike anything I'd seen before or since I wouldn't dare interrupt her testimony. After all, this was her moment, and she spoke as if I wasn't there. Usually, she cleverly conceals the secrets of her heart, perhaps like most women, tucking them away somewhere safe inside, hidden quickly before being noticed. But that day was different. Every single word touched my heart making our moment together incredibly memorable, yet slightly peculiar. Something triggered her horrendous foray; maybe her heart was full of emotions she just needed to release. Her anxiety was enormous. Years of lingering pent-up frustrations had finally surfaced. A friendship such as ours required sensitivity, no less, and my undivided attention was warranted. In her case, her heart resembled countless broken pieces scattered over the timeline of her life. Only my love and understanding was capable of yielding such empathy under the circumstances. I felt obliged to lend an ear, that was the least I could do for an old friend.

"Life has a true purpose when I'm in a committed relationship with someone who offers true love and appreciates the love I give in return. What am I doing wrong? Sometimes I find a nice guy, but it doesn't last. Most of the men I'm attracted to don't tend to notice me and the ones that do, well I'm not interested in any of them, not in the least. So many of them aren't about anything anyway; at least that's been my experience. See, I'm interested in real love, not drama or stupid games. Trust me; I don't need any of that crazy shit in my life! You know what I mean don't you?" So rare was the look I saw in her eyes. It felt as if I were staring deep into her heart.

"Yes, I do." What else could I say? I wasn't in any position to judge. She's my friend you know, struggling with life and the choices she makes with her heart rather than her head. Never been married, no kids and just shy of forty, she was feeling the pressure of time. Her biological clock was ticking, and the chance for love with a beautiful little girl she so desperately wanted was quickly fading. Her brown eyes sparkled from the sunlight penetrating the large framed window just a few feet away from our table. A lovely glow befell her face, spreading her beauty throughout. In spite of her mood, it was a stark contrast. A delightful ambiance filled the restaurant with warmth. Beyond the unpredictable elements of the season, it was a magnificent sunny day. A perfect afternoon in the spring for sitting in a cozy little restaurant in New York City just on the edge of Chinatown, not far from the courthouse on Centre Street. Such a festive day it was, as the locals were working the streets in pursuit of that tourist dollar and boy were the people out looking for a bargain.

I took the subway to Canal Street. It felt every bit like rush hour standing toe-to-toe on the downtown A Train. We meet every so often to connect and catch up with one another. Honestly, I love being in her company. She's my friend, and I love her dearly. Such a beauty, every inch of her; five feet, nine inches tall with lovely brown skin, long black hair with gorgeous sexy bedroom eyes. My, my, my... most men, including myself, would fervently compete for her affection if only for a rare moment of romance, the kind that lingers a while, maybe a lifetime with a woman like her. It's possible. I've had a few encounters like that. Not many, just a few. How about you?

"I don't understand," I said as I reached across the table to gently touch her hand. "What seems to be the trouble? You're the kind of women most men dream of falling in love with, and I can't imagine I'm the only guy in your life that notice how beautiful you are!" Once again, she focused her beautiful brown eyes on me and began to softly speak in a minor key with a melody bearing a sweet resonance only a Bach Sonata could bring in a seminal moment such as this.

"I don't know. It feels like I keep making the same mistakes, over and over again. You know, choosing the wrong guys and wasting my time for what? I'm not getting any younger; seems like my best years are behind me anyway. Since my thirties, it's been a steady decline. Now it feels like purgatory, a hopeless rut with no chance for love. I just want what most women want: a true agape love with longevity. Why can't I have a real life-long romance with a beautiful little girl to adore and be appreciated by a man who wants something out of life without the baby momma drama and all of that excess baggage from previous failed relationships? His crap is too heavy as it is to carry and I certainly don't need that kind of trouble in my life. Nope, been there and done that. That's not for me. It ain't worth it. Is that asking too much?" I didn't want to sound insensitive or too predictable, so I thought long before speaking. Cautiously, I sat there and measured each word before speaking.

"Well no, I don't think so. So what type of men are you attracted to?" Looking squarely in her eyes, I waited for a reply, knowing fully what she likely would say. Her answer, although predictable, was necessary to be heard. Like I said, she's my friend, and a good measure of diplomacy has kept us as such for many years.

"Well, I'm a little tall for a woman, and with heels, I'm just shy of six feet. So he has to be at least six feet tall or better, educated with a good job, and knows how to treat and please me in every way if you understand what I'm saying."

Oh, she began to smile with that sparkle returning to her eyes. I knew exactly what she was saying, I think. Okay, I knew for sure! But I played my part well that day. "I'm not sure what that smile means, did you think of someone in particular, like one of your old used-to-bees? I think I know the one. After all, we're friends with a history, and I've heard all about most of them." Usually, she's not a kiss-and-tell-type of girl. Well not exactly. What happens in her relationships, especially her bedroom, stays there. But there's one lover, in particular, she just couldn't help spilling the beans on. With that look in her eyes, instantly I knew exactly who she was thinking of, Melvin Watson of all people! According to her, that soft spoken silver tongue devil had all the right moves both in and out of her bed. According to her, he took love and sexuality to new heights.

"Oh, so you want a repeat performance with Mel, huh? Um, once wasn't enough?" She began giggling, briefly covering her mouth to hide her joy. After looking away to gather her thoughts, she began speaking in a whisper. Bingo, he's the one, the standard by which she measures all men- past, present, and future. I met him. He's a smooth brown skin brother, about six feet tall with an associate's degree from a community college up in the Bronx and that was good enough to call him educated by her standards. He had a good job with Verizon as a FIOS Technician up in the Bronx where she lives and also where they met a few years ago. The brother was old school, a sharp dresser with a nice ride and a great one bedroom apartment over on Fifth Avenue and 110th Street overlooking Central Park. The boy was bad, and he knew it. One problem, he was a player with moves. But she wanted a commitment plus a kid. After a year or so, Mel hit the brakes and broke off the romance. He went cold and cut her off, just like that. Without warning, their relationship was over. The pressure for commitment was obviously too much for old Mel. He wasn't about to change, not even for her, period. Stunned, her heart was broken into a million pieces. She never saw it coming. Even now, she's still not over him, and it's been a while. I read him like the Sunday's Entertainment Section of the New York Times. I knew his moves and his game. Marriage was nowhere in the cards. He's just not the marrying type, at least not before sixty, if ever. But she tried to change him. Oh, what a big mistake, not to mention a waste of time!

"Oh my God, he was so good." She just couldn't resist saying it one more time. "That man made love so gentle and nurturing. I never got enough, and I'll never find another like him, not ever. No one has ever loved me like that. Oh, I miss that. Boy, I'm here to tell you, he turned me on like a faucet. Honestly, I've never had sex like that... Just one touch was all it took!" With the mentioning of his name, the sparkle in her eyes glowed. But once reality crept into her consciousness, gradually it began to recede, forever sealing the realization of his absence. Couldn't say for sure what she'll miss the most, the love they shared or the sex?

The thought of Mel and his gentle touch lingered still, maybe lasting a lifetime. Was he the one for her? She thought so. But ladies let me say a few choice words regarding my dear friend and her desire for love. Now I'm not speaking out of turn here. You saw my story and decided to satisfy your curiosity by spending a few minutes of your precious time reading, so here's the deal. After many years of life, I've divided men into three basic and very distinct groups: Hunters or I call them Players; Settlers or the family type, a polite way of saying marriage material. And then, of course, the Half-N-Half, they're a dubious group with some promise, that is, if you have patience and don't mind gambling for a chance at love and happiness.

Now let's start with the Hunter or Player first, like old Mel. They're a creature of habits. Most of you women know the type. Usually, they're bold, smooth and assertive with endless confidence and equipped with a conversation for most occasions. He knows what, when and how to say what you want to hear. Usually they're good listeners in the beginning of the relationship at least, but of course, once they capture your heart, all that quickly changes. They aren't willing to make many compromises or concessions unless they fall for you, which is rare. Or at least pretend like they have. So if you meet one of these guys and fall in love know what you're getting into. They can break your heart, badly, into a million pieces like my friend and won't think twice about hurting you dearly. You can break your back trying to please them, but usually, that's never enough. Like a sweet summer breeze, they come into your life but can leave just as abruptly with the force of a tornado, leaving you and your heart in ruins.

They love variety and old habits die hard, if ever. At first, they're a lot of fun and will keep a level of excitement in your life, maybe too much if you know what I mean. The late night calls from other women, text messages, borrowing money and never paying you back, excuses-one after another and missed dates that you'd planned for a while. You see, most of them usually date a couple of women at a time just in case your relationship takes a sudden and unpredictable turn for the worse. They'll walk out of your life in a minute. Because they hate being alone, another woman is always waiting. You can waste a lot of good years of life on someone like them hoping they'll change but that rarely happens. No chance of that, unless you know how to tame a Tiger. So love them for the stripes on their fur because they're not likely to change unless they're tamed. If you're up for a challenge, go for it!

Now, if a stable family life is what your heart desires, choose the Settler. Not as flashy as the Hunter or nearly as exciting but he's a better bet. He may even have good credit, a saving's account with several Benjamins stored away. If you're having trouble figuring him out, meet his family, especially his mom. If he's still devoted to her and shows interest in her after all those years, you've got a good chance of having a good man and a good marriage. These guys love stability, routine and comfort. Seldom, if ever, would you think of them as flashy. But here's the deal, you become a second mother of sorts; usually he wants to be taken care of. If you run a good home, enjoy taking good care of the kids and control the finances, you got one good partner for life. It'll take all of that and more. But with the right man, ladies it's worth it. If you want someone to grow old with, he's the one. He'll be there when the sun goes down, and you'll have the security and hopefully wonderful memories to show for it.

Occasionally you might find a man trapped between both worlds. He's a Half-N-Half. They usually are indecisive and can't make up their mind which group they belong to. Always giving off mixed signals regarding their intentions, which makes them appear confused and very unpredictable. I know you know the type; their mixed messages can be a constant source of aggravation. Kind and considerate but hopelessly trapped in perpetual expiration. Their behavior could be troublesome, more like a whole lot of trouble! Get ready for one helluva roller coaster ride and be prepared to wait for love. It's in them somewhere. But you just might be the one to rescue him, from himself of course! It'll take a whole lot of personal attention from you, and endless patience may be required.

So if you're wondering what I told my friend, in between the Rice Cakes with Pork, Spicy Beef, Won Ton Soup, and Dumplings, I decided not to ruin the moment. She's a smart, beautiful woman and I'll always be there to listen. Sometimes that's all a good friend can do, listen and be patient. Usually, they'll figure it all out in the end, and you'll preserve your friendship by avoiding the sometimes unpleasant truth. Most people know how to fix their problems long before asking. Sometimes talking about it is a necessary first step before taking action. Once the pain becomes too much to bear, they'll get around to doing what's necessary to ease their suffering. Trust me, it never fails. A heart can only take so much abuse before it refuses to tolerate anymore. After she gets that last cry out of her system, I know she'll work it out without me telling her to erase the thought of Mel from her memory, forever! Well maybe not all of him exactly, because she said he had some helluva moves in the bedroom. Even I took notes, especially that position she described to me. Yez... I'm gonna use that one! I gave it a special name. What..? You expect me to tell that? No way! Call it just compensation for her emotional torment with a large dose of my empathy. You just don't know how hard it was to restrain my tongue because when someone loses hope, despair sets in. So please remember, the choices we make define who we are and the life we live!

If you live in New York City or planning a trip here anytime soon, Chinatown is where you need to go for real Chinese Food, anywhere else just won't do. The food is just that good. Up in Harlem the only Chinese people coming in or out of those take-out places are going there to work not eat! I'm just saying....

My Little Princess

02/26/2016

Always remember beauty is so unique and begins once you decide to be you.

"Oh, you're so beautiful." My heart was beaming with joy when I spoke those precious words so long ago. I couldn't help myself. Our only daughter was just adorable; at least I genuinely thought so. A little princess was she. At the time, she must have been five or maybe six. I can't remember exactly which. But surely she was more than a few years past three. Certainly, no more than four I believe. I can't really say for sure. But those words, my words, were so enduring and sweet. They felt special, especially coming from a proud dad like me! Of course, I thought she'd be so pleased to hear such praise. But once our eyes met, her little-perplexed face reflected something unusual, something never before expressed I dare say. Shockingly, dismay replaced the joy which once occupied my stunned face. Wow, what was that, I wondered? Before I could say one word, mysteriously she escaped, emotionally fleeing from my praise. Retreating to a place of doubt and disbelief, she fled so far, far, far from me. Suddenly I thought, what was she thinking? What was wrong with what I said? Did she not know every single word came from my heart rather than my head? But oh how I love her so because a proud father has that right you know.

Her look was too uncertain to know for sure. Feeling self-conscious with such a strange look, her eyes reflected her self-doubt she deeply harbored and mistook. Underneath all her pain, a little girl was drowning in a sea of shame. Apparently feeling unworthy, she dismissed my words without serious thought. Not one word was uttered, just a wall of self-doubt. She seemed overwhelmed by my expression of love. But her beauty seemed so obvious you see. Just looking at her was a reminder of all the love deeply held inside of me. Only her daddy could think or say such a silly thing; and besides, maybe she assumed a compliment was too biased coming from me. A huge measure of shame she must have surely felt. Absent of confidence, why didn't she accept the love my heart felt? After all, it came from her proud father blinded with glee. My expression of love seemed too meaningless to be; so she tossed it aside and watched it tumbled far, far away; well beyond the reach of any expression of love or any words I could possibly think to say.

How could she already have such indelible doubt stitched both inside and out? Her precious little head should be filled with laughter and joy, not self-doubt. A horrible cancer was eating her confidence away. Not once or twice but every single day. Just a mere few years past three, she hated how she looked. But, she looked so much like me. So young and so innocent how could this be? Where did it come from? Did it accidentally come from me? Did I do or say something terribly wrong? Clueless, so clueless not knowing what to do, I searched for answers sometimes all through the day. Looking for a reason, any reason to understand why. That moment was too profound to ignore, and to this day I still wonder why. Such confusion was bouncing around inside my head. Unpredictable, I hadn't detected it once; this enigma had arrived at our door all at once. Find a cure? Where would I begin to look? What could I do? Unprepared, what else was there to do? Does she not know she looked the same as me? With her mother's smile-so warm and sweet, and her grandmother's intriguing, sexy eyes, truly she should've felt blessed; such beautiful features she should wear with pride. Incredibly smart with endless talent too, but she can't see any of this. She doesn't have a clue. Her smooth, beautiful brown skin was a reflection of her Chickasaw, Caucasian and African kin, all gifts given to her from her mother and of course a little bit of me too. Oh her DNA is a splendid blend, proudly making her an apple of my beaming eyes. So how could she not possibly see all of this? Oh mercy, mercy why...? Didn't she know all of her beauty was a reflection given from her mother and me?

I was certain she must have heard something that awakened such wicked thoughts within. But what could have possibly shaken her confidence so violently leaving her scarred and hurt with so little pride? Her journey in life has forever been transformed, making more difficult her path forward as she searches for a future free of shame or scorn. She'll travel over rugged terrain: playgrounds, classrooms, puberty and dating too. They're all full of so many silly games. Some heartaches and moments can bring endless pain. But a life filled with happiness was surely our intended aim. With her spirit broken and the lack of self-love too, what will become of her? What will she ever do? Confidence is like protective armor, fortified with pride and strength. Strong enough to endure the torment she'll likely travel through. But her armor is weak. How will she ever survive? The cruelty from adversaries and sometimes family too will likely test her resolve. Maybe because she's my daughter or maybe just because: too short, too dark, too much of this or far too little of that!

I'm a man, and I know so little about filling a little girl's heart with pride. I've just tried to love her and give her what she needs to survive. Teaching her how to love herself was too deep for me. I thought she came to this world already programmed you see. Besides, isn't that a need her mother's love provides?

After taking her to ballet and piano lessons for years, I was sure it would teach her grace and shape her confidence and skills. Her self-worth is invaluable you see. It's part of her protective shield. After traveling the world enjoying the full breadth of its culture and beauty, she had it all but lacked a sense of her own beauty. We did it all, Broadway plays, and of course museums too, but that wasn't enough, it just wouldn't do. So we decided to let her become a model. The Ford Modeling Agency welcomed her among their privileged few. But even that wasn't enough to chase away her silly blues. It felt as if this only made matter worse, far too complicated or obscure to say. In her eyes everything about her was wrong: wrong color, wrong shape, wrong hair, wrong size, and most of all, wrong nose, lips, and eyes. Never mind whose features they reminded me of; none of it mattered. Whether they came from her mother or me, or my mother, or any other family, it made no difference. But her eyes are a gift from my mother so worthy of a gorgeous prize.

An early reader by the age of three, oh did she read: newspapers, magazines, books and a little bit of everything. A constant source of daily intake routinely she consumed. My, my, my did she ever gather all of this in such haste! Watching and learning what was considered beautiful, she obsessively took notice every single day.

Her deconstruction had begun in full, and she was well on her way, far beyond our reach before we realized what to say. She was convinced that the world would never accept her looks; after all, she looked too much like me, and that wasn't a part of the messages she took. Beauty was tall and thin, light and white, long straight hair with blue or green eyes; none of this did she possess. Oh, what a surprise! So she went in search of a solution without any advice, not from her mother and certainly not from me.

An idol she found in Michael Jackson whose physical transformation convinced her of his point of view. He didn't like the way he looked, so he bleached his skin. After changing his hair, face, nose, and eyes, he changed everything except his heart he held inside. He did whatever it took to pursue a beauty he felt necessary to match a certain look. He became unrecognizable to his kin once he left to pursue fame. His hold on our daughter was devastating, making his death both traumatic and a shame. She grieved for days crying inconsolably. I wondered why? Finally asking my wife, "Would our daughter ever grieve like that for me?" Well, I hope I'll never know the answer to that. It's far too frightening! Just thinking of it is very hard and saddens me.

Having studied marketing and advertising too, no case study prepared me for what we went through. Our society's influence is so powerful with our kids. Their consciousness is shaped at such an early age. Beauty has become too infamous to be underrated and too valuable to be overstated. Every day people go in debt searching for that perfect look. A dress or a pair of shoes, that bag to die for, with a little surgery too, is an endless pursuit for what some people will do. Fake boobs with some newly bought hair could perfectly accentuate an outfit to wear. Does any of this sound familiar? Do you know someone like this? Wow, what happens when the styles change, or they grow older? Back to the drawing board, I imagine, right?

I see beauty in all things because everyone and everything has its own. Sure, uniquely accentuate your beauty, absolutely. Makeup and style, has its place but don't do anything too drastic, okay? That kind of change is too much for most, more than you know. There's only one you, and that's what makes you uniquely so. Trust me, there's someone out there looking for that special someone that could only be you. So if you change too much, you may never find your true love willing to accept you the way you came straight from above. The one love you long for while waiting in haste may not recognize you if you change your body or face. So don't for God sake! You came into this world already beautiful for all to see. Let the world admire God's creation, one unique living original. You are God's masterpiece! One day, you just might decide to make another you. Don't you want her or him to see their beauty reflected in and out of you? Your hair, lips, nose, face or eyes could be a beautiful surprise. Only you can show your child this, no one else could possibly know your heritage better than yourself. So go forth and make the next princess or prince with a man worthy of you! Just be very, very careful who you pick or choose. He or she may not be the one, the one who will always be there for you.

As for our little princess, well I'm still working on her you see. She survived puberty and college. I'm not ready to give up; never, not me, not one little bit. I love her too much. Besides, she still has her mother's beautiful smile and those sexy eyes. Ooh her beautiful smile just melts me whenever she smiles. When I look at her, I see so much of me. But most of all, she just reminds me of my sisters Judy, Brenda and of course my baby sister Fen; maybe a little bit of my mother too. She would be so proud to see herself in her granddaughter too. As for her mother and maternal grandmother, let's just say they're so beautiful. Our daughter has a lot from which to choose, all original genes from a darn good pool.

So, ladies, I remember what my uncle once said many years ago, "There's nothing under the sun greater than you." Most importantly, always remember beauty is so unique and begins once you decide to be you. I love that!

Baby Got Back!

04/19/2016

"Oh shit…" she said. *"We gotta talk. That butt ain't real; I'm here to tell ya! You've been fooled. I know what I'm talking about."*

Early one morning in the spring, while briskly walking along Lenox Avenue toward 110th Street, I was just shy of the northern entrance to Central Park West when suddenly a street light abruptly halted my progress. I stood there, with a small group of people, waiting for the light to change. It was such an inconvenience on a beautiful day in Harlem. But when you're in a rush, it always seems to take an eternity for the light to change which was the case this particular morning. Running late for a meeting with an old friend, all the while thinking how good a cup of hot chocolate would spice up my day. As a child, coffee was so delicious and a preferred choice on a morning likes this. At the beginning of each day, a fresh pot brewed on our kitchen stove and the scent of Maxwell House Coffee filled the air with such an iconic smell. Good to the last drop, it was always a part of our morning routine. A cup was never too far from my mother or father's hand. But it hasn't been a part of my life for quite some time. Throughout my childhood, my mother, a beautiful brown skin woman, repeatedly told me too much coffee made me blacker and hard headed; obviously suggesting I was black enough and too hard headed as it were. Besides, I suspected too much of either was a very ominous thing. Eventually, I lost my taste for the stuff. Although my parents are deceased, the smell of Maxwell House still lingers, even after all these years.

Darker than my mother but lighter than my dad, for years I've instinctively refused to drink another drop of coffee. Silly of me right? Well, I'm still a bit silly after all these years. In sum, I no longer have a taste for coffee, of course for different reasons. As a matter of consciousness, I proudly wear my dark skin and intelligence with unbashful pride. It represents a lovely blend of my mother's color with a hint of my father's dark skin including his incredible common sense, at least I think so.

Anyway, forever vigilant, I noticed a cute little poodle just a few feet in front of me with a decorative pink collar and leash connecting her to her owner. Her shaggy brown hair was the exact color of coffee after a nice mixture of cream had been added, just as I remembered from childhood. But a cup of hot chocolate is now my preference. I must admit though, my flashback was a pleasant moment of euphoria. Remembering the smell of coffee from my mother's kitchen brought a hint of childhood nostalgia. Seems a little funny how the poodle conjured up such an enduring thought. But she waited like the rest of us for the light to change. With a leash severely restricting her movement, she had very little choice in the matter. Appearing slightly agitated, the light couldn't possibly change quickly enough. If only a pet could talk, what would she say right about now? Obviously, her patience was duly tested, and my thoughts were akin to a sidewalk therapist rendering an unsolicited prognosis regarding her disposition.

Evidently, she had already picked the perfect spot inside the park to do her business. I stood there; carefully observing her temperament and quickly concluded the urgency of the moment would soon give way to her stressful predicament overtaking any hope of expected obedience. Her feet were frantically moving while holding her place!

Traffic was too fierce at that hour making a crossing without the assistance of the light far too dangerous. Pressing business was at hand requiring immediate action. But for that stupid light impeding her progress, she wouldn't have waited. Nature was calling. With a full bladder, she increasingly became more impatient. Oh my... judging her behavior, each second added even more stress. Her barks were confirmation.

Finally, the light changed and off she went with her owner struggling to match such a brisk pace. For any on-looker, it was apparent. There was no contest. Between a poodle, desperately seeking relief after a long night's rest, and an owner's fervent desire for control, a conquest ensued in earnest for all to see. Clearly, I saw it if no other! That poodle literally raced across the intersection with her owner in tow. Determined to hold onto that leash at all cost, she struggled awkwardly with each step as they sprinted through the busy intersection. She was an attractive young woman, apparently devoted to her pet, yet unwilling or incapable of succumbing to her poodle's urgent request.

Innocently, my eyes focused on the woman, if for no other reason than to partake in a moment of empathy. Under the circumstances, most would agree. My assessment was spot-on. Then I noticed her butt. Oh my God, there it was staring back at me. Bouncing with each step, her cheeks were effervescent. Vivaciously, without grace or rhythm, they bounced from side-to-side inside her tight fitting red and gray stripped running pants. Captivation best describes my prolonged visual obsession.

Mesmerized... of course, I was. Such a rapid pace created quite the spectacle. For a woman of her shape and stature, she was uncharacteristically proportioned. Not expected for a typical female of her size, especially white with buns like hers, no pun intended. Wow, I thought, could her butt be the real deal...? It was so large. I mean, really, really large. But was it real? She had bumps like a truck and thighs like what... Remember the way Sisqo described it in his infamous hit, "Thong Song?"

Whoa... doggone it! Wait one freaking minute and let me back this thing up a bit. Such a distraction was hardly expected or warranted. After all, our polls were open across the city.   It was Tuesday morning, April 19th. When I woke up, I'd hoped for inspiration to write about the 2016 Presidential Primary given that it was our turn to participate in the democratic process. Unwittingly, was I guilty of procrastination? All week long, I struggled to write something on the subject. Now another beautiful day has arrived bringing grave doubt. Could this be a case of mere reluctance? Perhaps, because my thoughts were hardly refined and now my ability to focus on politics and articulate something meaningful had been severely compromised. Of all things, the anatomy of an unsuspecting pet owner taking her poodle to Central Park for a badly needed bathroom break had usurped the moment.

Come on, I thought to myself, get a grip and refocus. You've seen plenty beautiful butts in Harlem before, but this one was different. It seemed out of place on a white woman's body! After briefly debating this unseemly dilemma, I struggled for control of my thoughts while wondering if I could manage to share something profound about our primary or instinctively follow a silly provocation which felt like a mindless pursuit. Let's see, there's The Donald, an undeniable fake, and then Hillary, always a sure bet for a few good laughs but my primal instincts were uncanny, and like that poodle, they were racing out of control for a destination unknown with unforeseeable consequences.

But for a few thoughts maybe, I didn't have much to work with. What I felt was mostly too unbelievable or incongruent with popular opinion... I needed passion to write about politics and the theatrics, although courtesy of The Donald, just wasn't inspiring enough.

Between the influences of actual events and activities I've witnessed during the course of the primary, I was convinced our political process had been hijacked. After becoming a rogue in a horrible uncivil Reality TV Show featuring a clever Svengali, or even worse, a Drug Dealer posing as a politician, a dreadful nightmare had begun. As a nation, we were in shock. Now The Donald mischievously holds our fate in undeniable peril. We are at a precipice of sorts after being seduced, bamboozled, or hoodwinked, whatever..! This freak show is hardly describable. Just think for a moment, he could be our next president and leader of the free world. That would be untenable. Showing no mercy or shame for his antics, he lacks the integrity or moral compass to lead a parade much less anything else. The thought of him leading our great nation is a terrifying thought.

Will he ever relinquish his spell on us? Of course not, why would he? He's having such fun with us, and for most of us, it's too entertaining to stop watching as are most good Reality TV Shows. We've been beguiled courtesy of the Russians who will stop at nothing to destroy our standing in the world. Add white backlash to the equation caused by an undeniable foul reaction to an eight-year occupation of the White House by the Democrats, and that Barack Hussein Obama, a perfect storm took shape in America. Add the obvious disdain some white women have for Hillary, and we've got big trouble.

In spite of my early distraction, I managed to find a little rhythm to write. But then, suddenly my phone rang.

"Good morning Brotha Larry. How U be...?" She asks this question like no other. It was Katrina, one of my dear friends whom I call the 'Millie Jackson' of Harlem. Oh, you must remember Millie? Her beautiful lush, juicy lips and her provocative songs laced with sexuality from a black woman's perspective during the 70's and early 80's are legendary. To truly appreciate such an embellished juxtaposition, listen to some of her songs and you too might fully understand the endearing contrast between them. Katrina is all that and more, of course minus Millie's successful R&B career. Like me, she lives in Harlem. However, her roots run deep, much deeper than mine. She was born and raised here. Anytime I want to know anything about the neighborhood, I run it past her first. She's always on point and has an answer for almost everything whether true or false; mostly true I think. But rarely do I know the difference because she's so full of it most of the time!

"Hey babe, I'm sitting here in front of my computer just trying to write but it ain't happening. I'm struggling this morning."

"Excuse me, struggling..? That sounds nothing like you. What's the problem? Cause, one day babe we gonna make it big and have plenty money to spend." We, I thought? She was an enigma wrapped inside a reservoir of energy so early in the morning. But maybe just what I need. Besides, without writing one sentence, she insists on sharing the fruits of my labor! Huh, go figure...!

"A freaking poodle caught my eye early this morning, and I can't get past the thought."

"A What....? A poodle huh..?"

"That's right, now I've said it okay... But you wouldn't believe what I'm thinking so why should I even go there?"

"Don't be messing with me like that. It's way too early in the morning. So what's really on your mind? C'mon, out with it Brotha Larry! This is your girl you're talking to." I paused for a moment if only to silently debate the consequences of full disclosure, but before I could stop myself, I let the words fly right out of my mouth.

"A butt, Okay...?" After a deep sigh, I continued. "Now I've said it; can't believe it though. Saying something like this, around you of all people, crazy right?" I braced myself for her raw-Millie-Jackson critique. She's known for that you know!

"Hmm..., a butt this early in the morning..? Whose? It wasn't mine! That's for damn sure, because babe, you know I'm packing... One good look, I mean a real good look can f**k up a brother for days, maybe nights too. I've experienced it both ways you know. Whenever I'm in the streets, I notice all that. I can walk past some of them, and they'll stop their conversations in mid-sentence to take notice of my ass! I know they can't help themselves. A good looking ass like mine deserves special attention. I'm aware of that; that much I know. As long as they don't touch it, I don't mind. It brings out the dog in 'em, woof, woof..! Where that dog at? I'm just asking..." She was on a roll, and I wouldn't dare stop her recitation. "Boy, my shit is real! Hello George Clinton, Where's that "Atomic Dog"...Bow Wow, Bow Wow?" She just couldn't contain her vanity. After letting loose a long deep jolly laugh, I felt a reverberation through my phone.

"Okay, you're not joking, right? So a freaking poodle, seriously..? How can a damn dog make you look at a woman's ass? After all, all poodles are dogs, but not every dog is a poodle. She had some gold up in there, right? Or maybe some precious jewels hanging all over it? C'mon Brotha Larry, this is Harlem. We got plenty big ass women UP HERE! I'm here to tell ya. It's in our DNA. After years of eating those Red Beans and Rice, or that Chicken Fried Rice, a sister can put a hurtin' on a brother's eyes. Hell these days, I sometimes ask if it's a man or woman's ass we're talking about? Some of these brothers got some nice, smooth and tight looking asses. A lot of 'em are trippin' too. I don't know what's gotten into some of them. Half of 'em are confused, and that's a damn shame. They act like they're not interested in a woman anymore.

Take the other night, for example, I went to a bar with a few of my girlfriends and the men up in there were more interested in one another than us. We were some nice looking big butt bitches on the prowl. I'm here to tell ya. We were looking good too, especially me! You know your girl. I had it going on. I'd just got my nails and hair done. Plus I wore that brand new red dress from Macy's with my favorite fragrance. I looked and smelled good. You know I did. As usual, my scent was the bomb! I call it a man tamer. I had it going on. A brother couldn't help but notice! So you better come again with what you're saying. Keep it real-a hundred percent, okay?" She paused a few seconds after letting loose another one of her infamous laughs..., this time it was loud and deeper with plenty bravado to boot. I could feel her curiosity growing as she waited impatiently for a reply.

Proceeding cautiously, a large measure of diplomacy was required. I began recounting the events of the morning, but an incoming call interrupted our conversation.

"Wait one minute Brotha Larry, this is Bonita. Hold on a minute, don't go anywhere... I'll be right back." My eyes refocused back on my computer screen. I began to stare. After a minute or so, she returned before I could do anything with the thought I'd entertained briefly.

"Look, I got a situation here, and I need to straighten out this little heffa. She's on my last damn nerve with some dumb ghetto drama okay...! She owes me a buck fifty, and I put her big ass on hold. Rihanna's song is playing in her ear right now, Bitch Better Have My Money. You know I'm serious when I play that song. I'm getting her good and ready for what I'm about to say in a minute, and it's been that already. So let me take care of this and get back with you, okay? You know I don't play around when it comes to my money. This bitch better have mine. In a few minutes, Rihanna will sound like a Nun once I'm through with her crazy ass!"

"Whoa, calm down babe. Slow your roll, okay? I'll be here, probably still struggling."

"Well, I wanna hear more about the poodle and certainly that butt you saw this morning. After all, a poodle is a dog too, bow wow-okay?" Before she let me go, she asked. "A woman, right...?" I just had to let her know none of that other stuff was going on with me.

"Of course, but I didn't say what color. White, with a nice butt, and she was fine as hell too!"

"Oh, shit..." she said. "We gotta talk. That butt ain't real; I'm here to tell ya! You've been fooled. I know what I'm talking about. Do you know what they're doing? Let me call you back in a minute, okay? You need to hear every bit of this!"

"Okay, later..." After returning to my computer, I tried to pick up where I left off.

Back to politics of course; practically every day all of the major news outlets routinely gave The Donald free, unfettered coverage including ABC, CBS, NBC, CNN, MSNBC, and FOX especially. A coveted front seat was offered daily. Every broadcast featured him at some point as their lead-in story, on or off camera, it didn't seem to matter. They all competed for Donald's attention. His early morning tweets were intended to dominate the news cycle, and they fell for it. His unending teases were akin to a master tormenting a vicious Pit bull with a delicious treat visibly placed in front of him but slightly beyond reach. If you're wondering why he did and said such terrible things, wonder no more. He craved attention. Who wouldn't? If you're running for president and getting all that free coverage, why not tweet something ridiculous enough to arouse attention? After all, a sucker is born every minute. Besides, no sense spending any of his money for such nonsense when they freely gave it, right? Lord knows he couldn't help himself. But what does that say about our country and our news coverage?

America, our I.Q. just fell off a cliff. Let's face it; nothing else could explain such stupidity! Now, look what's happened. The Republican Party opened the door, and The Donald abruptly walked in and crashed their party. Maybe hijacked is a better choice of words. Their party and America will never be the same again. As bad as this sound, maybe Sarah Palin wasn't so bad after all. Hello Tina Fey, are you listening?

Sometimes I wonder if The Donald could be the Anti-Christ. He possesses all powers or so it seems. Maybe he's merely a wicked charmer with a criminal mind, filled with immeasurable deceit and mischief. With ease and amazing social media skills, he walked onto our political stage and hooked so many Americans with a populous slogan full of empty promises, "Make America Great Again." Sounds like something a six grader might say running for class president. But a grown man running for president should have been quickly dismissed.

Emphatically I ask great for whom? When, where or how will the fulfillment of this manifest destiny be achieved? Oh please, his product is neither national pride nor prosperity for any citizens other than his immediate family. Offering the worse kind of demagoguery not seen since the likes of Hitler who nearly destroyed an entire continent with hateful rhetoric and unbridled ambition, The Donald picked up where Hitler left off. His words, laced with an extract of finely blended Crack or K2 so potent and addictive with incredible effect has aroused the most horrific demons rooted in our nation's consciousness. Ask any Black, Native or Mexican- American and you'll get an earful. This behavior dates back hundreds of years. The Donald didn't invent this, he's just exploiting it!

Every one of his performances has been brilliant for a childlike mind. Befitting a first rate carnival barker, he's been incredibly successful. My thoughts at best represent a bizarre tapestry of moments over time, and it feels like an embarrassment for most Americans, if only the sane ones, assuming there are a few of us left. Hopefully, this addiction will soon pass, and maybe we'll find a cure for what ails us before we let him destroy our beautiful country, maybe the world. After all, he will have the nuclear codes. For some, his words feel damn good, like another famous German mentioned earlier. Should I mention him again? My God, help us, please!

Perhaps the legendary first high of a hopeless Crack junkie might be a more befitting juxtaposition. A feeling of exhilaration at first, but subsequently you'd spend every waking hour chasing the next high, with no success of course. Once sober, the carnage is undeniable and quite visible for all to see. Our nation's pain and suffering is so deep, caused by years of political gamesmanship and neglect. Both parties, I must admit, have watched the growth of our predictable hunger for jobs, education, and prosperity for our families for some time now. But my Lord, the whole world now sees the ugliness of our dark side. This petulant demeanor has fueled unrest and divided us by class, culture, ethnic origin, xenophobia, sexual orientation and a little bit of everything else. Senseless prejudice, discord, and violence are on the rise throughout the world.

Oh America, what are we doing? Moreover, what have we become? The whole world is WATCHING US, and for the most part, puzzled as hell by our erratic discourse. Is this what we wanted? Until recently, we were likely known throughout the world for having the fakest lips, boobs, butts and of course our real nuclear bombs. We have plenty! But oh my God, now and possibly forever, we'll be known for electing a FAKE President; a man who suffers from Dementia at best or straight-up lunacy at worse. Does it get any crazier than this? Maybe so, remember The Shining, starring Jack Nicholson and his favorite lines? Now imagine Donald Trump in the White House sleep-deprived. Unhinged by his bad political poll ratings and his foul affections for Russia, he aimlessly roams around that big house late at night or early in the morning in fits of rage after watching the latest news. He's so alone in that big place. A looming storm agitates him even more. The flashing lightning lit up the sky. It was so awful. The roaring thunder really did him in, especially that last thunderous burst. Frightened, with the nuclear codes written on a crumpled piece of paper he firmly held in his shaking hands, impulsively he does the unthinkable during the perfect storm for a lunatic to blow-up the world. And then, in a Schizophrenic episode he screams out, "Wendy, I'm home!" Just before pushing that button... "Oh shit, somebody stop him. DONALD..., get a grip man. Your wife's name is Melania. It's your freaking Dementia remember?" BOOM..., too late, he's blown up the freaking world!

Here's Johnny..! Seriously, like Jack in The Shining, The Donald has brought nothing but chaos to America. Jack only had an axe and one house to torment. But Donald has the nuclear codes and the entire world to torment. Lord, have mercy on us. He's a FAKE. Why can't all of us see this, including those who voted for him? Since I'm reserving most of my thoughts for another time, I'll share more when the time comes. I've said enough already since being distracted by that freaking poodle. I must warn you though; I didn't drink the Kool Aid nor take The Donald's product-wooden nickels or false promises. Oh no, I wouldn't dare. My sanity remains uncompromised and intact. My logic is solid, and my sight is crystal clear. People, he's a fake president!

After speaking with Katrina, my primal instincts usurped my political inclination, thus returning to my dominant thought of the morning. Upon reflection, her comments took center stage. The beautiful butt distraction was in full bloom, after being heavily influenced by her point of view. There are a lot of sisters in Harlem noticeably endowed with big, luscious butts. Sir Mix-A-lot famously stated this observation many years ago with his hit rap song, "Baby Got Back." Released around May 7, 1992, it became an anthem of sorts for so many black women, and apparently white women took notice. Should I dare go there? His song resonated in our culture. So many black men, at least 99.99% of them, worship a big butt woman, the kind only a black woman possessed once upon a time, at least according to Katrina. For most men, their primal instincts kick in, and that testosterone surge occurs at the mere sight of a sister's big butt, and Katrina certainly noticed this phenomenon a long time ago because of hers. They, or being blunt, we can't help ourselves. Our admiration is a natural proclivity, no matter the color! Forgive me; I must speak the truth here. Honestly, some white men like big butt women too but I believe a sister's breast holds a more impulsive place in their hearts and minds dating back to slavery and the wet nurse era.

Remember The Commodores celebrating a black woman's body with their hit song in 1977, "Brick House?" Oh, I remember, don't' you? Maybe most white men hadn't noticed our sister's butts until then. So, I'll lower their interest percent by let's say five points or so, give or take, alright? However, I still think their love affair with the breast of our sisters continues to occupy their minds. Some of them got hooked many years ago, and the spell was never broken. A sister's breast milk is some awfully powerful stuff! What..? Am I the first to state the obvious? Where do you think all that black talent comes from, especially the athleticism? It's not the shoes okay! Trust me. I'm just saying...

Suddenly my phone rang. Expecting a call from Katrina, but it wasn't her number. Just before it bounced to voice mail, I finally picked up. To my surprise it was her.

"Okay Brotha Larry I'm back; didn't think you'd answer your phone. What's up with that?"

"I almost didn't. What's up with this number? This isn't your regular one." She let loose one of her trademark laughs again before speaking.

"This is my Obama phone. Hell, it's free and those minutes come in handy, especially for a situation like this. My regular phone just died. Well, I haven't paid my Verizon bill, and they just restricted my service. I can get incoming calls but can't make one. You know we're on strike, right? Our CEO makes over 18 Million Dollars a year, and we can't get a contract with decent pay and benefits. That's a damn shame."

"Why didn't you warn me about the picket lines? I went over to Broadway and 109th the other day to pay my bill, and the strikers had that Verizon Store on lock down. The employees inside looked so stressed. Anyone crossing that line got screamed at, including me. It was difficult going in there. Why...? I just wanted to pay my freaking bill. It was a mess. All I wanted to do was take care of business and get the hell outta there."

"Yeah, I know. But what can we do? We gotta eat too. How many millions does a CEO need for himself before he shares with the rest of us? We're doing all the damn work!" She sounded frustrated with the strike. Their union demanded her participation, leaving her no other choice in the matter. The rage and hostility were on full display throughout the city. She just hated being caught-up in all that drama. After all, she just wanted to work and pay her bills.

"Is that why you haven't paid your bill?"

"Hell yez. You know I can't cross that line without being recognized, at least not yet anyway. And, the union doesn't pay much in lieu of lost wages."

"I see. Did you straighten out your girl?"

"Bonita..? You know I had to. She's got three kids, and they're all by different men. Her eldest child's father stole her tax return. That idiot sold two of her kid's IDs, and that messed up her taxes. When I e-filed her return last week, the IRS rejected it. That's a damn shame but that don't change what she owes me. I told her ass a long time ago to be careful with her personal information. That shit ain't my fault. She got weak and let that low-life brother back in her life, big mistake! He was no damn good then and never will be. He's a thief, and I don't care. I want my money. She gonna pay me for filing her taxes, no doubt about that! Now, let's get back to the big ass you saw this morning."

I settled in for a verbal onslaught. She repeated much of what I was thinking, with a few new twists here and there I hadn't considered. Usually, I include a summary of her thoughts somewhere in my stories, but this time I'm letting you in on our conversation, okay?

"Look, first of all, some of these white girls started with the pads, and then the Silicone, but now they got some new shit, and all of them are getting that procedure done. Even some of the Latino Girls are getting theirs done too, especially the Dominicans."

"What kind of procedure?" She had my attention, and this was something new, I was sure of it.

"There's a clinic over on the east side making plenty money. They're shooting the fat from the stomach of these women into their asses. It's like a Botox butt. I mean it's buzzing in that place. They're going over there in droves at $4,500 a pop. I'm here to tell you. One of my friends showed me what they're doing. She had a video on her phone and babe that shit ain't pretty. It's hard to watch, but it seems to work. They've gone from the face to the lips, the breast, and now their asses. None of that shit is real- fake, fake, fake, all of it. Some of them go to the DR., but it's much safer here. I've heard the horror stories about those DR. trips, and that's no joke. So many of them got their butts really messed up."

"Any sisters getting theirs done..?" I just had to ask. "Hell no, our asses are naturally big. We don't need all that. Wanna poke mines? Ain't no Botox or fat up in this. My ass is 100 percent genuine! But Nicki's butt..., well that's another story. I see some of those Dominican women up in the Bronx and Washington Heights with their big butts and tiny waists. Some of them are proud of their fake butts. From what I can see, they sure look good too."

"Wait, hold up! What did you say about Nicki? Tell me it ain't so! Her butt is real, right?" I was hoping I heard her wrong. Sure, that had to be it. Of course, I misunderstood. I had to. That just couldn't possibly be right. And then, she repeated what she said.

"Hell no, Nicki's butt ain't real. It's fake too." Oh my word, is anything real anymore? I was just out done. Fake hair, fake lips, fake boobs, fake butts, what's next?

But Nicki Minaj became the big butt goddess with her version of "Anaconda" released on August 4, 2014. Her version was just another raw take of "Baby Got Back." In your face, it offered an updated affirmation that a sister's big butt lock-down remained sacred, secure and intact, at least that was her proclamation. Her infamous music video even had Al Roker of NBC excited, and that's saying a lot! Such an empathic assertion gave renewed hope to most black women offering assurances that once again boosted their confidence, elevated their prominence and uplifted their standing among many desirable black men. Their companionship was still coveted. That is until the big butt explosion came like a tidal wave. That darn procedure was like gun powder or a nuclear bomb, a decisive game changer. Nicki's promise was short lived if not completely obliterated.

Just two short years later, the myth had been debunked, and a new anthem dominated: "All About That Bass," by Meghan Trainor. Oh my, my, Nicki look what you've done! Kim Kardashian arrived. By any stretch of one's imagination, she's now the new queen. After Meghan's song, Kim, with her alleged fake butt, came on the scene and stole the show. Have you seen her butt? With her super-size presence, how can any woman compete with that? She pushed Paris Hilton and her entire tiny butt entourage right off the front pages of most social media if not all. There was no contest. Have you seen Paris lately? Bam, just like that the era of big butt white women had arrived, and Kim claimed her throne. A Reality TV Show, plenty press coverage with and without Kanye, made it official. Don't think the sisters haven't noticed. My, my, Nicki look what you've done!

You know, there's a striking testimony embedded in Meghan's song and video; "I got the boom boom that all the boys chase; all the right junk in all the right places." Was she talking about that procedure? Well now, everyone took notice; or could she have been saying something more? Anyway, to whom exactly was she saying all this to? Was it her man or did it also include black men too? It's difficult trying to distinguish the difference. Was it for both? With her announcement, some black women must have felt like salt was rubbed in an old wound dating back years. The wound remains open and unhealed in spite of time. A sister's big butt status has been hijacked. Oh, Nicki why? How could you let such a thing happen? So many sisters depended on you!

That door has opened. Was it because of Nicki, or in spite of her? Could she be an imposter? Maybe so, because Nicki's song started a new era; a case in point, let's takes Iggy Azalea as a prime example. A sixteen-year-old high school dropout from Australia came to America in 2006, I believe I have her arrival year correct. In just eight short years, she grew a big butt or made enough money to buy one, hooked up with a few established rappers, learned to rap-if you agree with her version, got signed to a major record label in 2011 and had her first hit, "Fancy" by 2014. Once she hooked up with a new boyfriend, NBA Star Nick Young, her golden path to success was paved and complete. Ooowee, just like that, she was living the American Dream after using a few rappers along the way, mere stepping stones, including the likes of A$AP Rocky, one of Harlem's own and T.I. Oh, Nicki, you showed her how to do this with your fake butt!

As the infamous Don King might say, "Only in America." Why," I ask, would she have come so far in the first place seeking fortune and fame, if she didn't believe what worked for Nicki could work just as well, if not better for her? It seems so logical now. After all, they make music in Australia, don't they? I think so. So why else would she come to America, but for Nicki's obvious encouragement? You get the picture, don't you?

"Don't think we ain't watching all this shit. We see everything that's happening. Just because we ain't openly talking about it don't mean we're naive." Katrina chimed in stating the obvious.

"These white girls are taking all the good men and leaving us the scraps. What's left? Just the tired, worn-out and broke brothers, that's all. Do I look like the Statue of Liberty? I work with one just like this, and it's a damn shame!

Now, take out the locked-up and gay ones, there's not much to choose from. You know many of them got turned out in prison. Oh, Ben Carson was telling the truth. We just didn't want to hear that shit! Who wants to be bothered with that? How does a woman compete with that? Imagine a man lying next to you wishing you were another man? How does a woman compete with that shit? She can't."

I could hear the frustration embedded in her voice. Then she said:

"I heard a brother talking with one of his boyz just the other day. I fell out laughing after hearing what happened."

I wanted her to tell it all, and she kept going.

"He was making love to a big butt white girl uptown on the west side. He got her so worked-up her tongue slipped. Before she realized what she'd said, it was too late."

"What did she say? Tell me." Her brief pause was intended to be a suspenseful tease, just for me and it worked. Finally, she let it go.

"Goddamn Nigga, you sure know how to F**K. That orgasm got the best of her ass, and she blew her racist cover! He told his friend he stopped right in the middle of his down-stroke and smacked her in the mouth. He went off on her and told her to get the fuck out of his house. One big problem though, it wasn't his apartment! She reminded his stupid ass he didn't live there. SHE DID! That serves his black ass right."

"That's some crazy shit." What else could I say? But she continued without much encouragement.

"The other day, one of my co-workers walked behind me and asked for a tool. He knew I was carrying that big bag with a lot of shit in it. I had what he wanted in there somewhere. Of course, I had to put that heavy ass bag on the floor, bend down, and get that damn tool for him. It took a minute because it was all the way at the bottom of the bag. When I turned around to give it to him that S.O.B was all up on me. Looking crazy and acting like he couldn't control himself, I gave him one of my don't f**K with me looks, and he just stood there staring at my ass."

"Hmm, you don't know what happened?" I just knew she understood his moment.

"No what?" She asked.

"He had a conEd moment..."

"What kind of shit is that? What does conEdison have to do with my ass?" I had to explain.

"Look, a black man's blood flows to two distinct spots on his body. If you want an intelligent conversation, do everything possible to keep his mind off the coochie. His brain needs all that blood to keep him thinking straight. Whatever he's got up there needs every single drop. But the moment you bent down, his blood flowed straight to his Anaconda. When that happens, you can forget all about his intelligence. There's nothing left. Babe Elvis left the building once he saw your big round fat luscious butt. He had brain freeze. You know a conEdison blackout. His mind was gone just like one of our hot New York summer outages. His blood had reversed directions and headed to his snake. Even you said your ass is the real deal, right? Don't you think after looking at you like that he imagined you and him getting busy? Girl, he wanted to hit that ass."

"He can forget that. That ain't happening. He better be glad he didn't touch my shit. I would've fucked-up his crazy ass."

"Calm down Katrina, it's over now babe, okay?"

"It better be. Don't get me started; Nicki just f**ked-up everything."

Wait, all of a sudden, I had a flashback moment when she said that.

Just the other day, I was downtown on 5th Avenue and 53rd at a Microsoft Store. By the way, that's a very nice place. You should check it out sometime. One of their employees, a sister, of course, heard "All About That Bass" playing in the background. No sign of Nicki's "Anaconda" up in there! Oh, boy did she cut loose with a few of her best moves right in front of me of all people. For a moment, she didn't seem to care that the store was no place for moves like that. Must I remind you the store is next door to Trump Tower? Surely her performance was inappropriate for such a setting, but for a few minutes, it didn't seem to matter.

Then I began to wonder, is God trying to tell me something or could it be the devil tempting me once again playing with my mind? Sometimes only a fragile line separates these two powerful forces. With ease, this sister moved her butt in sync with that monster beat. Darn, for a second, I caught myself admiring her and wanted to join in. She knew how to move her body especially her nice bumps as one of my Dominican Sister's might say. Hers were too small to compare to Katrina's butt. But for a moment, she cast her spell with smooth and seductive moves in a language only an Anaconda could appreciate. You get my meaning, don't you? Oh yeah, he did. Why else would he RISE? Softness was transformed into hard, and the search began for a wet pool to land. Trust me. You can take my word. Wait now! I wasn't the only one captured by her spell... She had all the right stuff in all the right places, I'm just saying, okay? Of course not like Nicki, Kim or Iggy, even though theirs are fakes. She can't compete at that level, no way, that's a whole new stratosphere! And now, Katrina has burst my bubble with the news that Nicki's butt is a fake! What's the world coming to?

Think I'm sounding like a provocateur do you? Well, maybe just a bit. But after thinking seriously about this topic, it grabbed me a little. I know some of you might have to quickly catch-up to my way of thinking so stay with me for just a while longer, and I'll explain. Besides, Katrina was giving me an earful, and this chasm between the real and the fake was getting wider by the minute.

You see, in our culture, a lot of people often notice trends, especially black proclivities like ethnic beauty traits and fashionable flairs. Once detected, and thoroughly evaluated, oh boy, a quick assault becomes a game changer. Seems like every young white person gets the same message and change instantly occurs. Sir Mix-A-lot's video used a couple of women, white of course, to make a mockery of a black woman's big butt suggesting that no decent or respectable woman would dare have one that big. Have you seen Kim's? It's huge...

He knew he was playing passionately with fire, so deeply rooted. Long before big butts were fashionable, most black men worshipped them. All this rapper did was set the stage for his proclamation, "I like big butts, stuffed, fat, big, round and juicy." Oh my God! He was a genius and handsomely rewarded with money, fame and universal admiration from so many black women all over the globe. Can't say for sure what the demographics looked like for the average buyer or consumer of his song but there were many. It was a HUGE success after being played everywhere: radio, television, movies, boom boxes, music videos and maybe outer space too.

In his song, he referenced Cosmo Magazine while challenging their standards for beauty and even Jane Fonda, an attractive iconic figure during her day. She was the bomb! Her exercise video was an undeniable success. It was HUGE okay. Everybody bought one. After all, it offered the promise of looking just like Jane. Young white women got the message, and the seeds for a hostile takeover began.

For his role, Sir Mix-A-Lot got paid. He got the attention of young white females, and a new industry was born. Hello Botox and cosmetic surgery, especially for previously unthinkable parts of a woman's anatomy like the fake butts, breasts, and lips. Well, perhaps I'm a little too generous with the facts. Maybe a little bit too far reaching, you think?

Well now, let's not forget Bo Derek and the hair braid assault. Remember the movie "10" starring her and Dudley Moore? After seeing black women wearing their hair braided in LA, she took it to the big screen. Single handily, she redefined white beauty. Her beautiful braids were remarkable and drove most men crazy, me too... Until that movie, I'd never seen anything like her. Whoa, Nelly! Another assault on yet one more ethnic beauty trait, the black hair braids which most black women thought was uniquely theirs. Black hair has quite a history you know. Once Bo wore those braids, she cast a new light on white beauty, especially in the eyes of so many black men. You had to be there to witness the impact. Were you? Trust me, the movie and impact were significant. Now, there's no limit or boundaries for a white woman's pursuit of beauty. A war was renewed between her and her black counterpart.

Bo had successfully challenged one perception once considered unthinkable regarding black hair. Afterward, white women routinely began wearing braids or weaves like a black woman. Because of Bo, they discovered they looked just as good if not better than some of the most attractive black women. Now, with enhanced butts, nuclear dominance was once again in full effect. The reset button was pushed beginning a new era of white beauty. No longer will a size two be considered the standard. The hairs, along with the butts are now fair game.

"Okay Katrina, What about Angela Davis Afro? Was that real? Oh, I can't believe Tina Turner's legs or Janet Jackson breast are fakes. Don't forget

Beyoncé's butt, Millie Jackson's lips or Susan Taylor's famous braids. You think they were fakes too?"

Oh, Angela Yvonne Davis, where have you gone, my sister? Her Afro and style were iconic during the Civil Rights Movement. But our sisters lost the Afro war to Bo's braids and the weaves. And now, their butts have been hijacked by Iggy and Kim with a brand new anthem by Meghan. My, my, my, when will this invasion end?

After listening to Katrina, I decided to employ a little empirical research. Indeed some of my assumptions required testing. Now my scientific methodology is a bit shaky. I've violated a few fundamental principles in my evidence discovery, but sometimes one must cut corners to advance a new theory such as this you understand? Quite often the ends invariably justify the means, once again making Niccolo Machiavelli's theory preferable. I used at least three good solid sources. I'd already heard a Harlem's point of view from aka Millie Jackson. Like I told you before, Katrina is as solid as they come. A sister with a sensitivity that's raw and unfiltered is like gold. A perfect fit for such a topic; although sometimes her poignant views can be painfully honest. At times, perhaps she can be a bit much. But she's my girl, period. She never fails to give it to me just the way I like it, hard and real-a hundred percent.

On the other hand, another dear friend of mine lives on Long Island. Dee is a true New Yorker in every sense of the word. A sure bet for some honest intellectual dialogue minus the drama, most of the time. She usually gives straight honest answers. Almost like Katrina but in her own way of course. I called Dee after talking with Katrina, the perfect time I thought. It wasn't our usual time to have one of our predictable chats, but she was available, so I went for it. Like always, I came at her straight.

"Look, Dee, I got a question for you." She was a little caught off guard but quickly recovered after a brief hesitation.

"Shoot hon, what's up?"

"I'm trying to figure out something that caught my eye this morning, and I want to come straight with this; you know primal and raw. There's no political correctness anywhere in this conversation, so I'm going to lay it on you unfiltered okay?" I could feel her curiosity growing, but she instinctively got ready for whatever was coming.

"Okay shoot, what you got?" With her beautiful blonde hair and radiant, tanned skin, she strapped herself in like a savvy race car driver ready to go full throttle, if necessary on this ride.

"I saw a woman in Harlem this morning, and there was something about her that got me thinking. So much so, I need a second opinion before I attempt to write my thoughts."

"Oh," she said, "Bring it on!" I felt a sense of safety and comfort in her tone. Without delay, I continued.

"Well she had a butt like a black woman, and I couldn't take my eyes off her. Unexpectedly, I was taken by the way she looked. She was fine as hell too! Not to imply that there aren't a lot of beautiful white women, but I haven't seen many with a butt like hers, at least not here in Harlem. So after I noticed her, I hung out in Central Park for a while and was surprised to see a few more. I saw maybe three or four in a few minutes with big butts getting their morning exercise in. When and how did this happen? I mean they were fine too! Did spring bring a new phenomenon, unlike anything I've noticed before? Seems like, you know, a butt transplant happened over the winter for white women, and big butts are in vogue. Know what I'm saying?" She didn't seem surprised in the least by anything I'd said. If she were, I couldn't tell.

"Things have changed," she said. "I've notice this myself."

"So what's happening? I've known about the pads some women wear to firm things up a bit but what I saw was no pad, no way! I know the difference."

"For a long time, beauty for a lot of white women was a thin waist, maybe a size two and a tiny butt. But music videos changed all that beginning with Jane Fonda and Jennifer Lopez. Since then, the genie left the bottle. You wouldn't believe how hard some of these girls workout in the gym to shape their bodies including their buttock."

"Oh really...? How so...?"

"Oh, there are several workout routines to shape a buttock." She wouldn't dare say it, you know, their ass. "There's a Brazilian Butt Workout and several other routines like that to work those muscles back there. I can think of three or four others to be exact that gets those buns nice and firm you know, shapely and round. But of course, there's more to beauty than a big ass, you know what I mean?" Well, at least, she finally said ass!

"I know, but that's a part of a woman that invariably commands attention even if you don't like admitting it."

We had a lively conversation for a while. Actually, she had a lot of thoughtful things to say. After referencing Maslow's Hierarchy of Needs, so much of our discussion made perfect sense. Our Basic, Psychological and Self-Fulfillment Needs are indeed relevant in this instance. I feel incredibly overwhelmed trying to voice my opinions on such a difficult and sensitive topic. But Maslow's Theory holds a great deal of truth. Neither the white nor the black woman can escape this reality. Far be it for me, a somewhat irrelevant guy, to judge or suggest they'll honestly figure out this complicated relationship because they really do need one another on many levels: economically, politically and socially. It defines who they are and what they feel is equally relevant. Is all of this simply one gigantic enigma? After all, a need for love and their preferences play a huge role in each of their lives. Who's to say who's right or who's wrong? Or who has benefited the most from their entangled past? Love is complicated especially when each of them desires the same things: relationships, love from a significant other, families, happiness and careers. Dee is a dear friend and makes perfect sense with her point of view. Maybe that's why I love her so.

Later on, I found much of what she said on the internet. You'd be amazed what comes up when you google this topic: big butts, big asses or big buttocks, it doesn't matter how you type it. It's all there. She felt so uninhibited when it came to sharing her perspective on the subject. Everything was fair game with very few exceptions. No one and no limits could stop a woman determined to look good, period, including their butts-no matter their color.

I called a few more women I know, and some more interesting comments came up in our conversations. This being New York City, a good richly mixed gene pool has enhanced a genetic dynamic that's contributing to the eradication of a once common phenomenon, the white woman's flat butt. So I decided to talk with some women outside of New York City. Now a friend down in Texas blushed the whole time we talked, but I could sense her curiosity coming through the phone all the way from Houston in spite of their recent natural disaster. Water was everywhere. A huge storm had recently dumped an enormous amount of water. But she and her family were safe. Maybe my timing was off a bit with such a ridiculous topic to discuss, and she was noticeably restrained with her comments. After all, Texas is solidly in the "Bible Belt." Even she, a single white female, was aware of the trend and that butt procedure had reached Texas of all places.

Of course, my homegirl in Arkansas was a must. Indeed A life-long friend, who always have an opinion ready for me regardless the topic and a suitable match for many of my crazy thoughts with endless curiosity. No doubt about it, she's the real deal. A good southern sister with an ear for most topics such as this; she's an incredible source. Absolutely, I needed her thoughts.

"Peaches," I said once she answered her phone. "I'm working on something I want your opinion on."

"Okay, what's happening?"

I ran it all down to her, and without interruption, she listened attentively while I offered my thoughts. Of course, I shared some of the previous comments mentioned by others, especially Katrina's and Dee's. Then I paused and gave her the floor.

"Look, everything you've said is true. I've noticed all that and more a long time ago. I know I live in the "Bible Belt" but let me tell you one thang, they can copy our lips, breasts, and butts but they can't work their bodies like us. I know I put a hurtin' on my man just the other night. Sometimes a sister gotta let him know what he'll miss if he strays. He'll be cut off completely from my coochie if he messes thangs up here! Sure he might think about looking around, but I make sure he knows what's at stake. He won't get any more of what I put on him last night. That's for damn sure! He'll think twice. You can bet on that! I haven't seen a white woman yet that can move better than a sister, especially me. I'm here to tell you."

Wow, she wasn't holding anything back.

"Babe I keep my stuff together, and it's always nice and tight. My man knows it too. No doubt about that! I know a white woman don't have nothing close to my coochie."

She was ready for our conversation leaving no stone unturned.

On the other hand, my African and Asian female friends don't see themselves trapped in this struggle. They're standing on the sidelines watching everything. They want no part of this. It's not their war. Kim, an Asian friend, had a few chance encounters with a couple of brothers. Once she saw the hostility from the sisters, she left the party; too much drama for her taste. Oh, she heard the complaints from black men about the sister's fake hair, or this and that but not much else. "Sure," she said, "we like fashion, maybe a little light cosmetic surgery on the face, lips, and breast but not our butts." Some Asian women go to South Korea for their procedures. But our butts are off limits.

My African friend puts her Muslin religion before her color. She's Muslin, not black, and don't feel any kind of bond with her black American counterpart. But she's encountered her share of resentment when she dates American black men. Her black African butt needs no procedure. That Root is strong. Why mess with perfection, right?

Wow, let's see: Encroachment, vanity, insecurity, entitlement or privilege and absolute superiority are all elements at play here. I understand both sides of this equation, although somewhat imbalanced it seems. But what surprised me the most was a false assumption I had. First, the African females don't feel any kinship with her American sister. The only thing they share in common with the American Black Woman is color, without a bond. Latino Women of color feel pretty much the same way referring only to their geographical origin. So the American Black Female is all alone in this struggle. This whole label thing, being called an African American is a false narrative without meaning. Such isolation makes a black woman's struggle more painful and real.

Most mornings, I watch CBS This Morning with Gayle King, Charlie Rose, and Norah O'Donnell. How about you? Usually, I keep my score card at the ready most mornings, closely watching Gayle and Norah compete for the viewers' attention, and of course Charlie's affection. Most mornings their show is something to watch. Norah dressed in her killer red dresses while Gayle wears her stunning green or yellow is nothing short of a successful morning fashion show. Oh, their hubris is subtle, but sometimes maybe not. Their dress and demeanor say it all. Of course, I score them neck to neck most mornings but once in a while a home run is hit, straight outta the park. When that happens, Charlie can't control himself. His Anaconda... okay at his age, his centipede is surely awakened by Gayle or Norah. Now Gayle is the new Angela Davis, you go girl! Sometimes, you're simply irresistible but you better not slip-up because Norah got it going on too. Just remember, it's a morning show, not after six…. Those big necklaces she wears sometimes are a bit much!

I made one final call back to Katrina in case she had a few final thoughts. I kept hearing her words bouncing around inside my head.

"Look," she said, "we've been their maids, raised and fed their kids- sometimes with our own breast milk, made love to their men when they couldn't or wouldn't take care of his sexual desires-whether we wanted to or not. Sometimes we didn't have much choice. How do you think this light, bright and damn near white rainbow got all up in some of our families? We did what we had to do to survive!

Remember the movie Mandingo with Sandy Duncan and Ken Norton? She had her daddy buy her a black buck! I couldn't believe they put that shit in a movie. If we weren't directly affected by any of this, don't you know most black women have family or friends who were? I know what I'm talking about, I've heard the stories. Now, what does she want, our coochies? She can't take or fake that. No siree…! Some of my boyfriends have told me many times my stuff is damn good. I believe them too because when they go and do something stupid, I cut them off cold Turkey and they get real crazy."

Oh boy, she'd said a mouthful. But was she right I wondered? You can't sell water to someone who prefers wine or silver when they prefer gold, so if white women don't naturally have what's desired, they take what they want, including a black man. For example, isn't that just what Sandy Duncan did? If a black woman possesses anything she wants, she may feel obliged to take it.

A black woman can be an unwilling participant in many of these transactions. She suffers, yet ages so gracefully, in many instances without the assistance of cosmetic surgery. She's watched, imitated and taken for granted by so many, including her kids, family, friends and their men, both black and sometimes white. Of course, her white female counterpart hardly acknowledges her burden.

I remember walking past the statue of Dr. J. Marion Sims on 5th Avenue and 103rd, ever heard of him? Of course, Katrina would be disturbed if I revealed to her his true identity. In some circles, he's a legend. Some call him the father of gynecology. But only a few will admit what he did to achieve such recognition. He exploited, some might say tortured black women to death in the mid-1800s to advance safe and proven procedures for the comfort of white women. After all, it was said, he believed a black woman's tolerance for pain was superior to that of her white counterpart. So weren't those procedures pursued for their benefit? With unimagined medical experiments, without sedation, of course, his medical practice in Alabama and South Carolina established his leadership in the medical field. And yes, he likely studied the black woman's vagina. Oh lord, what would Katrina say if I shared this bit of information with her? Don't think for one minute that there aren't scientists somewhere in the world using Dr. Sim's research to advance science. Once again I ask, for whom?

It was seemingly rather easy to duplicate the braids, weaves, lips, and finally the butt. But a black woman's vagina might take forever unless Dr. Sims made a discovery. You think so? I really don't know. That African DNA hasn't been easy to decode or replicate. Remember the story of Henrietta Lacks? Without consent, her cells advanced worldwide medical research for the polio vaccine, cloning, gene mapping, in vitro fertilization, and more. Henrietta's cells have been bought and sold by the billions. They named her cells Hela. That's all the credit this poor black tobacco farmer received. Born in Roanoke, VA, poorly educated with no health insurance while living in Baltimore, she died poor in a county hospital from Cervical Cancer in 1951 at the age of 31.

So many people have benefited from this woman's cells. After all these years, no other cells are able to grow outside a human body like hers. Henrietta and so many other black women like her feel largely ignored in spite of their enormous sacrifices, contributions, and hardships for the greater good of others. Such a shame don't you think? And now, she fights daily for respect and acceptance. Ouch, that's gotta hurt!

Anyway consider this, for years black women have been making huge sacrifices and reaping very few benefits. In most cases, all they ever see is the short end of the stick. But remember, they're raising so many of these successful black men. For some, once they get a nickel above breakfast, look out white women, here they come. You know I'm speaking the truth, the part largely unspoken.

If you're expecting any brilliant answers from me, I'm fresh out of solutions. Melancholy has such a firm grip on my emotions. While I hope for the best, a polarized world poses an incredible challenge. A treaty like Détente or something between the white and black women could be reached or how about a quota system of sorts to restore parity? Maybe the sisters should have a say in who they take? It's a thought at least.

I'm just going to take a seat and watch this thing play out. Katrina will likely sound the alarm. I don't have a clue how this will end. But this predicament won't end anytime soon. All I can say is this situation is HUGE, and something's gotta give.

I have a daughter, and I see the impact of her struggle and frequently hear her mounting frustration. Recently, I attended her college graduation, and there were so few young black men walking across the stage receiving a degree. As far as her finding a mate, the future looks rather bleak. Only God knows how this story will ever end. I sure don't.

I've seen and experienced you frustration first hand. Once I was in Los Angeles on business many years ago having lunch with a beautiful black woman. After a few martinis, she looked at me and said:

"I feel like a white woman trapped inside this black body. Why can't I have what she has? All of it: a successful career, financial security, unlimited pleasures with a good man!" How do you respond to something like that? Wanna know what I said? "Waiter... over here, bring the check please; we're done here!"

Giving or Receiving Love on Valentine's Day

Maybe or Maybe Not!

02/13/2016

Sometimes the greatest question of all is will we ever find love?

Wow...I'm here to tell you, it's been a long day. Somehow I got through it. Not one of my better days but I'll take it. I got a lot done. However, it did require an enormous effort. In spite of the unexpected interruptions, I did okay. So I stopped for a moment, collected my thoughts and began thinking about the next day. After all, time shouldn't be wasted regardless, even if you feel the need to do so, no matter the circumstances. Besides, time keeps moving with or without our consent. Looking over my shoulder, I noticed the calendar. Tomorrow will be Valentine's Day. I needed a few minutes to get my thoughts together. After all, it's a special day, comes once a year, and could mean so much to the one you love, especially a lover, or if you're fortunate, a beautiful spouse.

Oh, my wife may not say so, but I know she watches to see if I remember to do something special for that day. It marks yet another memorable year of our life together. Making another year better than the last can be an awesome challenge. We've shared so many good years together. Raising our kids and finding time for one another is never easy. In a marriage, you learn a few things about love and happiness. So how does celebrating Valentine's Day enrich a life shared with the ones we love?

Here's my usual check list year: A card, oh please, that won't do anymore. Flowers, although beautiful, don't last very long. Candy, my wife usually stays away from sweets. These are all typical choices that offer nothing new. For the past few years, it's been an iPhone, clothes, shoes, and trips. But this year, I'm fresh out of ideas and feeling a little frustrated.

A clear mind was needed. So I sat down at my computer and tried to block out all competing distractions. Of course, If I could get a little work done, I'd come up with something spontaneous and heartfelt. I began to write something special for the occasion. But it's hard today for some reason. I felt an enormous distraction. Could it be the call from an old childhood friend earlier today that took my mind in another direction? She wanted to know if I mailed her autographed copy of my novel, Nina Shakes Harlem. It takes a while for mail to reach Arkansas where she lives. Mail from New York City to London travels further but much faster than service to Arkansas, I wonder why? Or could it have been the conversation with someone else I've known for a few years wanting to know what pages in my novel did I read to her that really sparked her interest? That chapter is a must read if you want to spice up a romantic evening like Nina's when she got the upper hand in her relationship. Oh, man did her trick really work! You might learn something from Nina's experience. That encounter with "C" was off the hook, and pure honey took on a new meaning in intimacy.

Neither one of those conservations could outdo the last one I just had with a friend that was in an entirely different situation. Unthinkable trouble was caused by this Zika Virus. Besides causing deadly harm, travel restrictions ruined a perfectly planned vacation for a lovely couple destined for Cancun. Trust me when I say his wife wasn't too happy when she learned I helped her husband get a full refund for the trip she was looking forward to taking. I thought she'd be pleased, boy was I wrong!

Then I began to wonder why or how do we choose the ones we love? Could love possibly choose us? What influence our choices? Is there any certainty that the ones we choose to love will love us the same or more in a relationship? Maybe or maybe not, who's to say for sure until we take a chance with love? Relationships can be complicated. But I couldn't say it any better than Randy Crawford in one of her hit song many years ago, One Hello. "One hello is how it starts; you might win it all or lose your heart." If you haven't found someone to love, one hello is a beginning.

I've been blessed to have someone special in my life for over thirty-two years. A mutual acquaintance introduced us. Who would have thought back then our introduction was the beginning of a new beginning. Love sometimes holds mysteries. Maybe that's what makes Valentine's Day special, learning new and mysterious ways to profess your love.

It's late, and my wife fell asleep several hours ago. I love watching her like that, at peace with no worries in the world; it makes my heart jump for joy. She's just locked inside her dream being entertained by a beautiful situation that's bringing her a loved filled moment. I see the peaceful smile on her face. Hope I'm somewhere in there! When you've been married for quite a while, you learn to enjoy the unspoken moments of tranquil happiness that love sometimes brings. Some of you might know what I'm talking about. Remembering their touch or the sound of their voice when they call your name is heartfelt. Or the way they look at you when their heart needs to know your love is forever more! Are you worthy of this kind of love?

Whenever I think of love, real love, I don't think it ever dies. What's safely stored in your heart should last until the end of time, or at least until your spirit takes flight destined for eternity somewhere in the sky. Once I came to this realization, some of my choices became apparent, bringing clarity after many years of obscurity. I've learned how to love from watching others and actual experiences from previous relationships throughout my life. My mother was my first teacher, followed by friends, girlfriends and eventually my wife. Now for the past thirty plus years, it's been our children. Figuring all this out hasn't been without a few heartaches along the way. Some of my experiences could be good source material for one heck of a novel. Maybe one day I'll have the inclination to write it. But it'll take a whole lot of courage and medication!

So on each Valentine's Day, love like it's your last because it could very well be, maybe or maybe not. Who knows for sure? Nothing here on earth last forever you know. As for my choice this year, it'll be a trip to somewhere my wife, and I will find joy and happiness, creating new memories in another chapter in our life together. Hope you choose wisely and have a great moment with the one you love.

By the way, so many of you have connected with me through social media in the last few weeks. I hope you've enjoyed a few of my short stories. They're just samples of my writing, and perhaps you might enjoy my novels as well. Check them out.

Happy Valentine's Day

Hopelessly Frustrated

08/26/2016

"My seventeen-year-old son is driving me nuts. He's out of control, and I don't know what to do."

"You busy?" Calm and softly spoken, her mysterious and unexpected words reached my ear. At first, I was surprised and barely recognized the voice. Sounding distraught and confused, unlike any other time before, I knew something was wrong. A powerful volcanic force containing unspeakable frustration was hidden underneath the calm, just moments before an inevitable eruption. Struck by her disposition, it had a rather usual intrigue. Admittedly, her timing and circumstance caught me slightly aloof. So I waited. Unable to restrain her emotions, the wait couldn't possibly be long.

Our romantic rendezvous was scheduled hours ago. From the tone of her voice, any chance of that was lost. She sounded like the weight of the world rested squarely on her shoulder. In the middle of some drama, her sanity was being tested. I could feel it. A safe harbor was needed. Perhaps that explains why she reached out to me in duress. After listening to her measured long deep breaths, expected from someone in distress needing both oxygen and time to calm their nerves, I prepared for the worse. Apparently, her day had been hijacked by unpleasant news.

"Maybe," I said after failing to conceal my disappointment from a failed attempt to connect earlier in the day. "What's going on?" Her silence was unnerving and only fueled my impatience. "Why are you calling now? What happened to you earlier?" Her silence continued with her call coming several hours late. With mounting agitation, I struggled to sound concerned. My mood had changed from exuberance to indifference. A no-show, without a call, what did she expect? Besides, I'd moved on. I had other things to do. Thanks to her a few of them will be neglected.

"Meet me in the park at our usual spot okay? We need to talk." It was Friday afternoon, and when she didn't show hours ago, I got busy doing something else. After a long week of struggling with the usual stuff, I finally settled into a calm and peaceful flow. Briefly hesitating while thinking of all the reasons why I should deny her a second chance at ruining my day, what's left of it at least, my stubbornness had a firm grip on me. Several hours of my time had already been wasted. Why should I let her waste more? She's never stood me up before but once is one time too many.

"Come on, you're my friend, and I sure could use one right now; I'm serious. Meet me in the park so we can talk, okay?" Hearing the slight desperation and regret in her voice left me little choice but to reconsider. After further thought, I reluctantly agreed, if for no other reason than to satisfy my curiosity regarding her pending crisis. Calling me a friend in many ways was correct. Although we met six months ago, she and I share a lot in common. There are some people you meet in life and things just click between you. She's one of those people. After adjusting to a new reality, I cast aside my hostility allowing my anger to dissipate.

"Alright, I'll see you in fifteen minutes. You better be on time 'cause I'm not in the mood to wait like before. It's been a long week, and I've got things to do, you understand?"

"I do darling. You just don't know what I'm going through right now. It's crazy trying to get a grip on things, and I'm about to drown in this crap if I can't see you okay. With that said, I'll be there, and I'm so, so sorry about before.

Standing you up was wrong, and I apologize. I couldn't help it. Forgive me okay? I'll make it up to you I promise. It's just I've got a situation here, and it's driving me crazy. I'll tell you all about it. I'm a few blocks away. Right now, I'm walking past the liquor store on Lenox and 111th. Can I get you something to drink?" It was a hot afternoon in August, and the streets of Harlem were full of sweaty people dealing with the heat, a cold beer sure would be nice.

So I said, "Pick me up a Miller, 24oz can. I'll pay you when we meet."

"I got it babe; this one's on me. See you in fifteen minutes."

I quickly got myself together and headed for the park. It was so hot; sweat was all over my face after walking a couple of blocks. The north end of Central Park was a few minutes away. On a hot, humid summer afternoon, it's doubtful that our bench will be available. Perched on a shady hill-top overlooking the Harlem Meer, it's a beautiful view straight out of a good movie. On any given day, especially a day like this, I can sit there for hours, waiting for one of those memorable sunsets. So peaceful, there's nothing else quite like it in all of Harlem.

As I got close to our spot, I saw her sitting alone on our favorite bench. Just like she promised, she was waiting for me. Once our eyes met, her face lit up with a beautiful smile. In spite of her looming drama, she looked great. After standing up, she began to wave. Her five-feet-two-inch frame swayed vivaciously side to side expressing her joy. Wow, all this just for me? What is this all about? Turning sideways to greet me revealed her beautiful body. Seductively curved, she's a perfect fit for sexual intimacy. Just looking at her sparked a hormonal rush like you wouldn't believe. Damn, I can't let her get inside my head like that, not now anyway. So I struggled to compose that part of me that she'd awakened, but with tight jeans, it won't be easy. Whoa nelly..., down boy, not now. She can't see you just yet!

"Hello darling, it's so good to see you. You look good as always. Give me a hug I need one." She opened her arms wide and just waited for me to walk straight into her embrace. Once her arms were firmly around my waist, she gently rested her head on my chest. We held each other for a moment without speaking. Her eyes were red; obviously, she's been crying. But that didn't stop me from saying what I felt inside.

"Damn you sure turn me on you know that right?" She held me closer. I could smell the scent of her favorite perfume. Honestly, since meeting her, it's mines too. But I wondered if she really knew how much I wanted to be with her earlier. She'd been on my mind all week, and I was really looking forward to being with her. Finally, she let go, looked into my eyes and then said;

"After listening to your heart, I feel connected to you. I think I'm in there somewhere and that's good enough. It sure makes me feel special. Besides, you know a girl gotta always look her best and smell good. I wore this just for you. Here, sit down and drink your beer. Cool off and rest a minute, okay? Wow, you're really sweating..."

She had a few napkins and began to wipe the sweat gently from my face. Sitting on our favorite bench, with a cold beer on a hot summer afternoon, it doesn't get much better than this. It goes without saying this woman sure knows how to treat a man. Few women do you know. It's not about dominance but more like choreography. When you're with someone special your interactions are like a sequenced dance. Each thought, word, or action brings a corresponding response. When successfully executed, it brings out the best in both of us; not only in words but incredible foreplay as well. Someone has to lead, and someone must follow with equal power in the exchange. Depending on the two personalities, the decision is made without much debate. The roles are instinctively assumed. When it's done correctly, pure love is summoned, and endless pleasure becomes an instant addiction. Instinctively the love flows. Not ordinary love, but the good stuff you've savored for the perfect occasion. I couldn't help imagining what it would be like making love to her that moment on a fantastic sunny day. It would be magical with spectacular fireworks!

She was wearing an eye-catching yellow Pink Lipstick, slinky seamless mini dress with a super sexy back slit. Yellow is definitely her color, at least I think so. With her honey brown complexion, she's like a Sunflower nested in a lush green meadow effervescently revealing her charm. Showing plenty cleavage with a beautiful necklace hanging slightly above her split breasts, she was irresistible. With breasts like hers, she didn't need any accessories. She was simply gorgeous no doubt about it. After a while, she began to share her troubles.

"My seventeen-year-old son is driving me nuts. He's out of control, and I don't know what to do. If I don't get help soon, he'll be dead or in jail inside a year."

She had a faraway look in her eyes. They were red from crying. At that moment, I felt her pain. With frustration raging inside, her heart was adrift. If she were a ship at sea, she would surely sink. Her crisis had no quick solution. Like a treacherous tide, big and powerful, it was too much to bear alone.

"Where's his dad in all of this?" Although the answer was obvious, it needed to ask.

"He's missing in action. I don't know where he is. It's been years since we spoke. One of those things, you know? My head was in a different place back then, eighteen years ago when he and I hooked up. Now I have a son that needs a father, and he's MIA. You think he gives a damn? I know he doesn't. I'm all alone in this and don't know what to do."

Now, I couldn't tell her exactly what I thought. I've seen this situation so many times before. But I just felt the truth wasn't appropriate, at least not now. So I just continued listening. Some women get out there in the world, and their bodies and looks draw all sort of interest from all type of young boys and men. The smart ones understand this hormone thing, and usually, their dress and manner support the notion, when or if they're ready to play the game of love. Or should I dare say sexual activity, because more often than not, that's what it boils down to. You see, there's love, and then there's sex, and it's happening all over the world regardless the age every single day, 24/7. When it's about sex, you got to keep it real and know that's all it is. Don't expect that young boy or man to be there if a baby is the end result. That's not a part of the contract or arrangement. What you do together is about instant gratification, plain and simple. Free love unattached and without responsibility, whoa nelly! Sounds good right? But if something goes wrong like creating a life? Will she be left all alone? Raising a kid all alone is not easy.

Even with two parents, it can be difficult. But all alone, ill-equipped or woefully unprepared, her journey will be a struggle with much heartache. Usually, most women want love with the sex, but if they can't be with the one they love, they'll love the one they're with. Those hormones can set the stage for some crazy drama. And that my friend, is a Pandora's Box with a heap of trouble for a lot of women!

I see this all the time, a young woman trying to raise her children alone, especially their sons. It's tuff. Watching them reprimand or correct inappropriate behavior in public is like burning resentment slowly but surely growing each year of their young life before bursting into a huge flame. When they reach their teens, the fights and struggles can escalate beyond a single mom's control. Trouble comes to their homes, and there's no place for them to go for help, until after the fact. Sometimes the grandparents or extended family might reach out to lend a helping hand.

For some, if they have talent, smarts or athletic ability, a safe nurturing haven could emerge. This could make all the difference in the world for some. But if it's a hit or miss proposition, the streets and trouble are where they usually land.

She had a young warrior, and he was out of control. A war against his mother was waged. The consequences were dire, against insurmountable odds it seemed. Invariably this war will likely be lost, in most cases at least. A young mother is clearly at a disadvantage.

So I continued to listen because her heart was full and in so much pain. Just letting her talk was like thinking out loud, as she searched for answers. That's what a real friend does, listen not judge. Judging wouldn't help her or change anything, anyway. From time to time, while speaking, she'd wipe the tears from her eyes. I'd show my concern for her suffering by holding her hand or rubbing her shoulder, and it seemed to help a little. She's a good woman, and I'm sure she'll come out of this okay, but it's going to be a bumpy ride, leaving a trail of tears and heartache. Regrettably, jail and lawyers await her. Maybe her prayers will be answered. I sure hope so. I know she believes in the power of prayer. She made that perfectly clear. However, I made a few suggestions just in case her prayers need a little help from some useful resources. A timely 311 call might give her more options. Sometimes they can be a useful source.

So, for all of you young women out there reading this story, remember if you can't be with the one you love and decide to love the one you're with, be careful and smart. That Pandora's Box is a B****!

Family, Friend or Foe...?

08/05/2016

I treated each word like a precious raindrop destined to innocently fall to earth. Before the inevitable transformation, I was determined to catch every single drop.

Just the other day, as I sat at my computer, my phone rang before I was too involved with my work. The caller was an old friend. Her voice magically awakened a part of my spirit filling my heart with such joy. Oh, how fond those memories are, the kind only she knows how to summon. We've been close friends since college. As always, I give my complete attention, blocking out all distractions whenever she calls. You see, she's a part of a very special equation in my life, and without her presence, my timeline is both incomplete and without balance. In many ways, we recognize the essentialness of our friendship, and I'm thankful to call her a lifelong friend. Imagining life without her is almost unthinkable. Well, it really is just that, unthinkable!

As she began to speak revealing events and circumstances she'd experienced since our last encounter, I knew it was time to catch up on all her adventures. Another chapter in our friendship was about to be written. Naturally, I was all too willing to record this special moment in my heart. Like most family or friends, especially her, I've learned over time when to listen and when to speak. On this occasion, it was clearly evident. It was time to listen. Every single word was connected to an emotion embedded somewhere deep inside her heart. To fully appreciate our conversation, an uncanny knack of empathy with my special brand of sensitivity was required. I treated each word like a precious raindrop destined to innocently fall to earth. Before the inevitable transformation, I was determined to catch every single drop. After all, once they fall, their uniqueness is forever lost. Just like a heart without a beat or love without a home, I felt determined to respond to this defining moment. After listening for a while, her words revealed a huge fault line running straight to her heart. She'd been betrayed by people close to her. They weren't just anyone but close family. To her, their betrayal felt like a Tsunami with a force sufficient enough to break her heart. I couldn't help wondering if she'd ever trust them again. Have you ever had such an experience in your life?

Hers could best be explained and expected had it come from a foe, but certainly not family or a close friend. With family or friends, deep emotional ties usually form after years of interactions which usually cement enduring memories that can last a lifetime. That's what makes them worthy of our love and trust. Quite often these experiences earn a special place in our hearts. But what happens when time brings about a change? For some people, circumstances sometimes bring incredible change. A person's needs or love is hardly static. Change often challenges constancy with force great enough to alter perspectives and impose consequences. I've seen this happen first hand and experienced it as well. Oh, it was painful. When it happened, I took notice as should you. Otherwise, your heart will invariably be at risk, presenting the perfect situation for your heart to be broken.

Once my friend chronicled her experience, it was clear. The line of betrayal was drawn straight to her heart. When you place something you hold dear in the hands of someone unworthy of your love or trust, this could also happen to you. But without thinking, she did. I could only imagine what I would have felt or done had I been in her shoes. It can be an emotional Tsunami.

Like most Tsunamis, a warning occurs long before the egregious event takes place. It doesn't require an unusual intellect to detect. Remember in 2004 one occurred in the Indian Ocean? So many people were killed. The devastation to property throughout the region was catastrophic, especially in Thailand. Oh, it was horrific, so much life was lost. But the animals escaped largely unharmed. They headed for high ground after detecting the early warnings. The difference between them and the people was apparent. Once the change was detected, they took decisive action. But so many people didn't. Had they heeded the same warnings which both received, a great loss of life would have been averted. Instead, the warning signs were largely ignored, and thus the consequences were deadly for so many. On that faithful day, change came, but the animals were spared after safely fleeing to higher ground before the devastation.

During our conversation, my friend began to think back and recalled the many subtle warning signs once ignored from family members she blindly trusted. The signs were all around her in both words and deeds. But just like the people in 2004, she largely ignored the warnings.

I knew that re-characterization was a word which would be quite familiar to her. If you're an investor, tax consultant or accountant, like her, you've heard this word many times before. The word is frequently used to describe an IRA Transaction. The difference between a Traditional and Roth IRA can be subtle. Now, let me paint a slightly different picture by using this comparison in a different way.

Let's say you chose a Traditional IRA rather than a Roth-an option to consider but not as attractive for tax purposes, and for several years, you set aside five thousand dollars a year for retirement. Your job was safe, and it was a good way to lower your tax liability because your contribution is untaxed or deferred taxable income. So for several years, this was the perfect arrangement for you. Now the catch is you can't access this money before you reach 59.5 years of age unless it falls within the IRS Guidelines without paying a ten percent penalty as well as federal, state and local taxes. But the market has changed, and your fund manager is losing your money like crazy. So you frantically decide to get your money out of the market. That's a huge change, and now there are consequences. By the time it's done, you've lost money in the market, paid the penalty and taxes on your distribution.

Once my friend saw the warning signs, she wouldn't have continued operating with the same assumptions. Long before the disaster, she would have taken decisive action. The prospect of losing her hard earned money would have been unbearable. Taking action was necessary.

The whole experience was bad but could have been much worse. Dealing with a stranger managing her money is just like dealing with a foe. She would have taken no comfort in him or her protecting her financial interest. After all, she worked hard for her money. The fund manager certainly wasn't family or friend, more like a foe. They're rewarded with gains when they make money using yours. But nothing happens to them when they lose your money. She has always been decisive with her money, and her heart requires the same decisiveness no less.

Now let's apply the same criteria, re-characterization, to a more personal situation like relationships between family, friends or foes. This is where I'll inject my friend again. Remember nothing stays the same, change is inevitable. If this were a matter concerning investments or managing money, she would have been far more decisive. Her training and skills would have been utilized. But most people are less inclined to react the same way with matters of the heart, as was she.

Over time, love and trust can form bonds. Enduring sentiments can affect your judgment and obscure warning signs. Not so much with a foe because there's very little trust or love invested in these relationships. But a friend or family is entirely different. When people don't feel the same as you, they behave differently, just like the water in a Tsunami. Their feelings gradually recede sometimes beyond view before a sudden and drastic change occurs. So if we ignore the signs, our heart will be broken. Just like my friends! I've had those moments in my life also. The pain can be deep. Deeper, if you ignored the warning signs; and just like that Tsunami, when the water returned to reclaim its place, all hell broke loose. Lies, deceit and being taken advantage of are just like that water, painful and devastating.

I love friends and family. They are an important part of my life. But I'm always aware of change. Forever vigilant, I constantly keep an eye open for it. Time or circumstances bring about change. For better or worse, no matter how hard we try to ignore or resist, it happens.

As for my friend, I told her a story that was once told to me by a cousin. He was a hardworking family man and was so devoted to his wife. One day he came home unexpectedly and found a close friend in his home playing house with his wife. He's a rather big guy, physically imposing, and had he lost his temper, it would have gotten pretty ugly. His friend and wife were nervous, and they both tried to explain their obvious indiscretion. He stood there and listened. Once they were finished lying. He extended his hand to shake the hand of his friend for the last time. "Thank you," he said before turning to his wife to address her. "I now know you don't deserve a good man like me, bye." He packed his things and left. That's the best example of re-characterization that I can ever make. Things changed, and so did he.

My friend is a very smart Christian woman. She will, if she hasn't already, find the compassion to continue loving the family members who betrayed her. Oh, you can love someone without trusting them. If she doesn't, my heart is big enough to replace the love she lost. After all, she's my lifelong friend!

Peace.

When Love Is Entangled With Deceit
09/05/2016

"Stop...don't you touch him. You're not his father!"

"Stop... don't you touch him. You're not his father!" Her words were uttered in a moment of rage. Stunned, he paused and wondered if they were true. "What did you say?" He asked. Refuge was sought with silence. At that point, silence was the only remedy once she realized what she had said. For years, the man she married thought he was the father of her child. In an instant, she destroyed their relationship with a shocking revelation, forever casting a cloud of doubt over the true identity of the father of her child.

What happens when deceit is entangled in love? Is a collision inevitable? With matters of the heart, sometimes opposites attract with imposing consequences. Long ago, he fell in love with her. They were such an unlikely couple, but he loved her so and felt compelled to make their relationship work. For five years, three months and twelve days, he labored in their innocent romance. In his heart, he was certain of his love. Yet, there were profound differences between them. Their expectations for a life together were miles apart. Such an enormous chasm divided them; it was too enormous to overcome. Nonetheless, he was ambitious and knew their education and careers were essential ingredients for any chance of having a successful marriage. After all, a child's fate was at stake. He understood and knew the value of a traditional family. Without stability, there would be no chance for success. Both of his parents were central figures in his life, especially his father. It was unthinkable for his child to be raised with less.

After the birth of her child, and miles away from their humble beginning, they married and started a new life together. He was already in college and wanted her and the child to join him there. More than willing to pay for childcare and her college expenses, he hoped she would pursue her education. Instead, she was unprepared for such a drastic change and conflict was the unintended consequence. She didn't want or shared the same vision of their future. This troublesome burden became too much to bear. Besides, for years, she had hidden a heartfelt secret until that eventual moment in a fit of rage.

He was shattered but remained devoted to the child. After all, it wasn't the child's fault! He had become a father to a child who knew no other. While his mother clearly indicated otherwise, he felt there was at least a fifty percent chance he was the father. The child deserved the benefit of that fifty percent chance. Faced with her repeated infidelity and deceit, love wasn't enough. When trust is eroded, a tender love has no chance.

Think about this for a moment, in many ways this is the kind of situation that some lives are made from. Love, lies, deceit, and hate have destroyed many families, including the couple previously mentioned. A situation like theirs can define who we are. Oh what a tangled web we weave when at first we try to deceive.

I've had my share of ups and downs in life, like most people I imagine. Love has been a constant companion with a few occasional encounters with hate. With love in my heart and hate in my head, rarely equated, but they are equal in both passion and power. Actually, love cannot exist without hate; its antithesis. When my heart desires are incompatible with my expectations, the stage is set for conflict, much like my friend. In many ways, these two passionate forces are the core of our intellect and being, invariably influencing the choices we make. Equally powerful yet amazingly different, the consequences are almost never predictable. So when the heart and head converge, is an emotional conflict imminent? Of course, no one goes around looking for emotional upheaval. Life is hard enough without conflict. But it happens, far too frequent it seems. Is this an unfair juxtaposition? I think not and here's why.

When a personal conflict erupts, causing an unpleasant discord, it's war; no doubt about it. With the example given earlier, does hate replace love? Or can love overcome hate?

Our frame of reference often creates the circumstances by which our preferences are ultimately made. By most accounts, the opposite of love is hate, and the opposite of peace is war. Therein lies many of our conflicts. When these moments come, what influence our thinking the most, our heart or head?

Usually there's no peace without love, and certainly, there's no war without hate. You agree with this logic? War is usually waged against an identifiable adversary or foe in an overarching conflict. It has ruined countless relationships, including my friend's. Your head and heart can face challenging circumstances if you're attracted to someone whose differences create conflict in a relationship. When hostility creeps in, trouble soon begins.

Wrong choices bring dire consequences. Just like the one my friend faced. Oh, this happens more than you know, as far back as the beginning of oral or written history and beyond. For example, in Greek mythology, much has been written about Helen of Troy. In her day, she was considered the most beautiful woman in the world. Black or brown skin women were largely ignored, at least in most of chronicled history. But a daughter of the God Zeus demanded no less. She was married to Menelaus, the king of Sparta until Paris, a prince of Troy, came for a visit. Paris was so smitten by Helen. He refused to leave

Sparta without her. After slipping her aboard their ship, they set sail for their return voyage home. Of course this enraged Menelaus, after all, she was his wife and the mother of their two children, a son, and daughter. The Trojan War was fought because of Helen, a classic example of deceit causing one of the most infamous love wars.

Although it was years ago, the fall of 1987 to be exact, I clearly remember sitting in a movie theater in Atlanta watching Fatal Attraction, starring Michael Douglas and Glen Close. Michael, a married man, had a weekend fling with Glen Close, a single woman. For him, it was just sex; but for her, it represented something entirely different. She wanted more, love and a future with him, after discovering she was pregnant with his child. Just as the movie ended, I overheard a couple's spirited conversation from a few rows ahead of us. "That shit is real," he told her. He went on to say, "What she did ain't no joke, I'm serious." Sounded like a personal testimony by all accounts. Frankly, I agreed with his sentiments although I would have stated it somewhat differently. Once Glen Close was discarded and largely ignored by Michael, love was transformed. Suddenly hell was unleashed! He and his family were regrettably targeted. Once again, love at its worse.

Some other movies have thoroughly addressed this subject including a popular romantic comedy, The War of the Roses with Michael Douglas and Kathleen Turner. Personally, Love and Basketball is one of my favorites with Sanaa Lathan and Omar Epps, released in 2000. She waged a battle for his love. So full of himself, he couldn't see her love until an injury sidelined his career as a basketball player destined for the NBA like his father. Frustrated, she challenged him to a game of basketball offering the highest stakes of all, her heart. A game of One-on-one was played with her heart as the prize. Winning meant everything. Although she lost the game, in the end, she won his heart. I suppose living happily ever after was worth the try but it could have just as easily gone the other way.

So, if a situation like this happened to you, would you listen to your heart or head? Think about this for a minute. How many times have you been attracted to someone or already in a relationship and things take a drastic turn creating a dilemma? Aw, are you curious as to why I chose the word dilemma? Simple, attractions involve your heart and head; rarely does the object of your affection meet all of your preferences. Perfection while often sought is seldom achieved. He or she might have some of the physical attributes and pedigree that attracts you, but there might be shortcomings in other areas like intelligence, annoying habits or behavior, old girlfriend or boyfriend baggage, children from a previous relationship, jealousy, career choices or no career at all, lack of education or ambition, personal choices inconsistent with your values, etc., etc., etc.…

So a dilemma of sorts is set in motion. Do you try to change him or her or do you compromise? In other words, do you settle for less than what you desire? If the attraction is strong enough, your mind is influenced, and eventually, a decision is reached. Now if you're totally honest with yourself, at this point in life, your preferences are starting to emerge. The type of person you're most attracted to becomes recognizable. Look, right now, if you're reading this, it's just you and my words exploring a part of you that you may or may not openly share with others. So let's pretend for a moment that we're having a private chat. Oh, I won't tell! Your secrets are safe with me...

At this point in your life, you've had all sort of images flashed in front of you. Television, movies, social media, magazines and newspapers are a constant source. Thanks in large part to the internet; it's nonstop, 24/7. Now I'm a good listener, at least I'm told that quite often. Over the years, I've maintained friendships with several people dating back to childhood. So many of these relationships have become my yardstick by which I compare most of these assumptions I'm about to share. Not only do I listen but I pay close attention to what people do versus what they say. What attracts you to someone is not accidental but rather a protracted yet subtle mental programming that began long before you understood its glaring significance. For years, you've been collecting visual images and internalizing social preferences. Your behavior is influenced as you absorb the values of the world surrounding you. Height, weight, complexion, ethnic backgrounds, hair, style, cultural influences-especially from parents, older siblings or friends, are all strong factors shaping your programming. I am no exception. By no means was I spared from this process. I have my own set of preferences associated with this reality as well.

So what should a person do? If you want stability and longevity in life, a head decision is a clear and obvious choice. Using logic, after considering your preferences is a very measured, sensible and safe choice. For many people, this is not an easy thing to do. For example, I have a very close friend who married her classmate. On the surface, it appears to be a good marriage. Longevity and stability are reflected in their life together. Several children and grandchildren are the center piece of their life, and in many ways, they appear to be a happily married couple. But I know her so well, and there are times I hear in her voice fragments from her heart left behind many years ago. Does she regret her marital decision? Maybe, but her garden is filled with flowers from her life's work created with the partner she chose many years ago.

As for my friend, he stood up after his failed attempt at love. With a fresh start, he's living an amazing life without an entanglement. Deceit and love are never a good fit.

We all need love, and a healthy heart is an essential part of a happy life. We've all had our occasional encounter with hate and deceit. But I chose love and truth... In my garden, I prefer Lilies; love not hate. No matter the season in life, Lilies always make me smile. So in the end, love is a healthy feeling. I just love the idea of love without entanglements. Each day of life, I consider it to be a perfect day for planting, Lilies of course. Love, sweet love, creates memories that never fade away...!

Peace.

Coping With a Loss
07/25/2016

When your heart is full, cry out!

"Come home, it's time we talked." His voice was solemn and strong. I knew instantly what that meant, a trip to Dermott, Arkansas for a week no less. A sudden trip home would be awful difficult to do, but time well spent because my father wanted me to. I just needed time to finish some urgent business at hand; a week perhaps, but surely not more than two. So I told him, "Daddy time will quickly pass I promise. Believe me; you'll see me soon. I'll come and sit a while. I can see us on the front porch with you in your favorite chair. Just like we always do. We'll laugh and talk just us two. Remembering all those crazy things, oh our laughter will fill the air. Joy will dance and sing such praise once our hearts rejoice. Just give me time, oh I swear, I'll be there real soon! We'll summon the spirits of our loved ones and melt our loneliness away. We'll reclaim their memories and declare our love we share each and every day. Because of me and you, our love and memories will never fade away."

After agreeing on a date, two weeks or so in June, I assured him once, maybe twice, I'd be there real soon. Unfortunately one week later, daddy passed away. After folding his arms across his chest, he took his very last breath. Calmly closing his eyes, he offered his soul without despair. He was ready for his journey, destined for heaven; our love surely guided him there. My heart was broken leaving such pain. So awful, my unhealed wound remains. He knew his time was near and wanted to say goodbye. But I was too busy to rush to his side. Now I wonder why? How could I disappoint him? So stupid and blind, I'm guilty of a painful moral crime. After all, it was such a reasonable request. When I think of that moment, it's hard to admit no less. Why...? I'll never know. I misunderstood his urgent request. One last visit was all he had asked before he took his last breath.

It's been a little over seven years since his call. A mere 104 years of life, his legacy still stands tall. He was alert, full of energy, always joyful with a perfectly sensible head. I never once thought he was so close to death instead. Except for an occasional complaint, a picture of health was he. After living a long healthy life, he earned the right to a peaceful sleep. Twilight, oh gentle twilight, you now possess his soul.

Never much of a big eater, he worked an awful lot. Living a clean country life can guarantee that, maybe once or twice with God's grace in your life. He loved his way of living so well; trust me, surely I know. Seldom did he ever use a phone. It was such a useless pursuit unless he really had something important to say to you. I lived many miles away, a good distance between us two. But that day in early June, he reached for the phone with a final request.

Has death ever claimed someone close to you? Did you really love them too? Have you ever received a dying request? Were you able to say goodbye? Is it possible we share this in common both in our hearts and in our minds? Are any of these questions bouncing around inside your head destined for a solution or something else instead? How could each question seem so dreadful, more dreadful than the next? Does it make you think or wonder much more or less?

I've experienced this situation on a few occasions it seems—first my grandmother, and then a cousin, uncle, mother, aunts, father, brother, and several close friends. All of them have been claimed by death over many years. Lately, I've struggled with a recent loss of a close friend. Adored for such a long time, she's sorely missed. Another like her will be hard to find. Of course, life goes on, but it's hard. When their spirit comes and stirs up memories, my tears sometimes flows. Oh, how I miss them so.

Let me share a few, maybe three, but certainly no more. Okay, only a couple of thoughts, I'll share no more. Remember my heart has many, so, for now, let me share the ones I can't ignore. You and only you will know what's in my heart. Deep inside of me is where I'll start. Special, indeed you are. Why else would I say so?

I couldn't bear seeing my daddy in that coffin. It was too chilling for me. All at once, my grief roared, a mighty ocean of tears existed deep inside of me. My tears flowed, there were too many to hide. His words and memory were so powerful, and I knew why. He was my dad, a seventh son, you see. He often shared this fact many times with me. I'm his seventh son; he believed the wisest of all his kids, at least that's what he told me over and over again. Sometimes, I can't believe he's dead. Really, I know he's gone. Oh, I keep him close in my heart. Forever, that's where he belongs.

Daddy, as a child I remember sitting on your foot while you sat in your favorite chair. I clung to your leg expecting a joyous and playful ride. Back and forth you moved your foot bringing excitement for a while. Long after fatigue claimed your strength, the memories are still alive; they're so precious and sweet. You held me high and taught me how to reach. Reach for an education; reach for my dreams. They're out there somewhere scattered among the stars and in the spaces in-between. If your spirit is there, catch me should I fall. I know this heart of mine was shaped by you most of all. Your hands guided horses, plowed fields, carried railroad ties, and drove spikes, and they also taught me how to work, and even how to fight. Fight for justice; fight for my place in the world. Protect and fight for my children's future while rejoicing as they excel. I remember it all so well; the sacrifices you made. The knowledge you possessed is a treasure worthy of praise no less. Forever grateful, I am to you. I've needed all of that and more as I've struggled through and through.

Will you remember what you wanted to say before death closed your door? Will you tell me when we meet again? Can we sit, laugh and talk until our minds are separate no more? Until then, forgive me for not being there when you were called. I cannot forgive myself you see. I should've been there at once when you received God's final call.

One year after my father's death, a dear friend called with a similar request. Her situation was more ominous. Stage 4 Cancer had claimed her body reducing her life to a few precious weeks. We were friends for many years and vowed to say goodbye before death claimed one of us. Enduring as she was, her life eventually had to end; saying goodbye was the final act for such a sweet, gentle friend. Remembering the experience I had with my dad, I couldn't bear making the same mistake twice. But by the time I reached her side, she was struggling to stay alive. I seriously doubt she knew I was there. Her suffering had reduced her to mere skin and bones. With very little life remaining, her dignity was almost gone. It was hard seeing her that way, and my heart felt her pain. I was glad I came to be with her during her time of sorrow and pain. After all, she would have done the same for me. Within a week of my return to New York, she took her last breath.

Losing her wasn't easy. Death seems so final when it comes. It drew a very distinct line in my heart bringing about change. The past becomes the past, but the present and future remain. So hold on to those precious memories that time will never change. The present and future will never be the same. It'll take time without them all. But adjust, we must. Our love still remains.

At first, the pain and emptiness might totally consume you. It attacks the heart like a horrific storm. Bolts of lightning, stir your emotions like a painful callous on your hand. I have a dear friend experiencing this very situation right now. She lost her husband a few years ago. Her grief lingers still. In many ways, I completely understand. Besides time, there's no solution for a heart trying to heal. But now memories are all that's left and oh what a treasure possessed. Sadness can consume you when this peculiar struggle begins. Sometimes those precious memories can be punishing if regret fills you within. Broken promises can be vicious too. But fond memories can soothe a troubled heart if you let them through. Much like healthy food for a troubled heart, joy can rescue you from an awful lot.

Bitter disputes rob so many of us of so much joy. What once seemed important somehow doesn't seem relevant anymore. Once you realize there'll never be another conversation or family gathering with that special someone coming through the door. Have the sense to settle a dispute; your heart need not suffer more.

When we lost our mother, the pain was deep. She died so young, just a few months past sixty. However, daddy lived a full life, and before his death, I believe he made peace with God and was ready for his final rest. Although I was sad, his death seemed easier to accept. However, my failure to see him before he departed remains unreconciled, stifled with regret. My memories are like a window to my soul, and my parents left so many for me. When I need to be consoled, I gladly pick a few sweet memories. Then I call on them, although sometimes it's hard for me to do. Change is hard, but the future has its place.

I fight through the pain when I miss them the most, their spirit sometimes touches me and makes my heart overflow. The thought of never seeing them again or hearing their voice seems devastating and strange. However, life does go on. The Holy Spirit is powerful, too powerful to ignore. Have you ever had one of those moments coping with the change death brings? There's an agitation inside that's hard to ignore. Such a useless pursuit it seems, trying to fight for something that will never be anymore. It's hard to accept. After all, all of this and more is a product of death's awesome touch. A noticeable difference occurs in the way we see, think or feel. Everything seems different when your heart tries to heal. Our Lord has an imposing will, and our hearts must obey. A non-negotiable halt comes to our heart when I love ones pass away.

His work comes first in spite of what we want to do. Anything inconsistent with his will becomes useless until God's work is through. The order of business is changed with new demands imposed. Urgently, the clock begins to tick with so much to do; procrastination is not an option, and so we struggle through and through. Reaching out to family and friends, pulling it all together, seems such a daunting task but the right thing to do. After all, a place of worship, a funeral home, a burial and a repast is expected. A final chapter must be written for a life that ends. A splendid ending indeed is needed for someone you loved and called family or a dear friend.

In a conversation I had with my father shortly before his death, I asked him a few personal things about his life. Longevity, I thought, was such a blessing and I wanted just a little insightful reflection from his wisdom. He had a deep look in his eyes, paused for a while before speaking and then said, "A long life can be both a blessing and a curse too."

I was puzzled by his statement, so I asked why he felt that way. "Lawrence," he said, "it's hard watching so many of your loved ones die. With each death, a little bit of you dies too." Knowing his journey as I do, I understood. Upon reflection, that explained so much about him. He didn't go to many funerals. It was too painful to see a lifeless body lying in a coffin creating a lasting memory too haunting to forget or accept. So he found a way, his way to accept God's Will instead.

His wisdom, I will use for the rest of my life. Now I know I feel the same as he. A part of me died with each loved one I've lost. Over the years, I've learned to live with the grief when I suffer a loss. Maybe there's a better way to deal with it. But until I discover one, I'll keep holding on to my daddy's way; his gift he gave to me.

Peace.

The Making of You

08/05/2015

So much of who I am is from the making of you.

From our mother came the Turner, Carter, and Brown. In a special pan, a pinch of Watson was finely sprinkled in. A generous cup of Locks, Watson and Kelly added our father's DNA. With a healthy cup of Crockett, a splendid recipe finally took shape. With a free hand, it was mixed altogether; a perfect blend was at hand. Some nine months later to be exact, an incredible prospect began to rise. His edges were smoothened as he rose; a boy soon took shape and form. Once a cup of pride was added, his spirit awakened and found its place. Mother Whitfield was summoned to stand by our mother's side. Finally, it was time for him to arrive. So she pulled him from our mother's womb. On January 31, 1953, his life began, not one moment too soon. He was named James David Crockett; junior was taken years ago. His journey lasted a mere sixty-two years. Oh, where did the time go? How could it end so soon? Will I remember him...? Of course, I will because I was made from the same root.

So much of this recipe was needed for our dear cousin too. With a few minor changes here and there Dorothy was produced. The eldest great grandchild of our great grandparents, Joshua and Anna Brown Turner, she stood tall. Her mother, Aldonia was a proud grandchild of Joshua and Anna Brown. Ivelia was one of their three daughters who died way too soon.

A wonderful fiery spirit, Dorothy was never short of words. If she ever wavered, I simply don't recall. In the summer of 2015, James and Dorothy died fourteen days apart. Was their untimely departure coincident? Only God knows most of all. Maybe they needed one another for their journey they had to endure.

Dear brother and cousin, your deaths crippled my heart with grief, the loneliness lingers still. Sometimes I struggle through the days when sadness holds me until... A feeling of something peculiar deep inside of me summons the things that bind us, our hearts and love in thee. So much of who I am are from the making of both of you. When the Holy Spirit comes, the flowing tears run down my face. There's a noticeable difference in the way I think or feel I can honestly say. I'm through trying to figure out why. When that moment comes, it halts all activity inconsistent with his plan. In an instant, a new order of business is demanded. His will must be done. Urgency is required, there's no time to waste.

So on June 25, and July 9, 2015, at precisely 11:00 a.m. two churches and extended communities were entrusted with the task of two funerals, burials and repasts for James David Crockett and Dorothy Ann Baldwin Hoston. Much could be said about both. Perhaps in time, I'll find a way to say more. But then, the challenge before our friends and us were to carry-on with their memories forever more. Many acts of kindness came our way making our transition easier with each passing day.

In the Book of Matthew 18: (Verses 19-20) it is written: "Again I say to you, that if two of you agree on earth about anything that they may ask, it shall be done for them by My Father who is in heaven. For where two or three have gathered together in my name, I am there in their midst." On both days, our gathered numbers not only were greater than the required two or three but substantially exceeded the count and I trust everyone wished both of them safe passage to our father's house.

Before leaving Arkansas, I went to visit one of my cousin's, Reverend Jesse Lee Turner of Dermott. We had a good visit. Our laughter and fellowship, as always, was heartfelt. Like a good home cooked meal, it does my spirit good when I connect with family and old friends like Jesse Lee. The next day, he saw me walking. I was headed to his sister's house, Carvie Callion. But he stopped and asked me to get in his car. He wanted to take me back to his house and show me something he forgot during my visit the day before. It would have been unthinkable not to see his sister during my brief but expected trip home. Only after I promised a return visit emphatically did he relent. Later that day, I went to his home, and he eagerly greeted me at his door. After taking me straight to his bathroom, he bristled with pride while pointing to his wall and said, "Your brother did this for me! Look at it; a job well-done." It made me feel proud as I stood there admiring my brother's work.

Suddenly my mind flashed back some fifty years earlier. It was a hot summer day in Dermott; so hot I could see the heat from the Sun blowing across the fields where we worked. The scorching Sun was beaming down on my head, and the hot air was blasting my face with such intensity it was as if the gates of hell were open and the furnace was working at full capacity making air too hot to breathe. It was such an unpleasant day, but the work was necessary and needed to be done. I was about six or maybe seven years old, chopping cotton on our farm in that heat with my mom, dad, James and a few other people I don't remember so well. Unable to keep up, I fell behind. The heat had exacted its toll. As the distance grew between us, the more discouraged I became. Behind, with no help, my frustration only grew more with each passing minute working in that hot blistering Sun. My eyes filled with tears and I wanted to just give up. Quitting would have certainly not pleased our father. After wiping sweat from my face and tears from my eyes, I saw my brother James chopping on my row working back toward me. He had left his row to help me catch up, knowing we could rest in the shade and drink cold water once we reached the end. His love boosted my spirit and helped me through a moment of frustration and despair. Not one word was spoken between us, just his expression of love and care. To this day, tears come to my eyes whenever I think of that seminal moment buried so deep inside.

Perhaps our heavenly father will remember as I do, and have a similar moment, once he reviews James' and Dorothy's work as he surely must do. Hopefully, as they stood in front of God awaiting his judgment, they were not disappointed. Their deaths were fourteen days apart, increasing the likely chance of their swift reunion in heaven before they stood in his presence.

"Glory and praise for two faithful servants," God might say to both with a smile; "a job well-done! Welcome home, my child. You have earned a place with me. Here is where you'll stay. Come and rest now, for my Will you have obeyed." I'm sure my brother and cousin said to God after hearing this astonishing news, "hallelujah, glory hallelujah." And then they smiled and embraced.

I say glory hallelujah as well in his name for his judgment and grace! Farwell James and Dorothy, God's grace is sanctified and magnificent in thee I truly pray. Give a heartfelt greeting to all of our friends and kin. Save a place for me until we meet again. Amen, Amen...!

In memory of James David Crockett, January 31, 1953 – June 17, 2015

And

Dorothy Ann Hoston, December 09, 1943 – July 01, 2015.

A Tribute To A Bugle Boy

January 31, 2016

Your mystique represents the very best of memories my heart holds still...

Early Saturday morning, while sitting at my desk, an unexplained distraction caused such unusual duress. My wife had left for a morning run. Central Park is a perfect place to see the rising Sun. Now she's home. Nothing is taken for granted where danger often lurks. The park is usually safe most mornings, but danger sometimes dwells. With one less worry, my mind was eased. The smell of breakfast announced her safe return. My head was filled with ideas, enormous deliberation was required. But something was gnawing at me causing the strangest distress.

"Breakfast is ready." She said. "Come get it while it's hot." Curiously I wondered should I take time and stop. So much time was already spent before the break of dawn. Searching for a story required persistence and will. There was no time to play or waste, a good story needed all my skills. There'll be plenty time for eating, once the story is done. Chasing perfection is very hard and never easily found. Pursuing excellence is an endless quest when the words slowly drip out. I mumbled once or twice, making her aware of my egregious plight. Notice was finally received with an unlikely thought. Me... sitting in front of a plate simply had to wait. My obsession had taken control, well beyond the thought of food.

All morning long, I listened to my favorite songs. Lyrics, the good ones, embedded in a sophisticated song are all the magic I need especially when I sing along. Such amazing chord progressions inspire the will in me. With headphones on, I surrender myself to Miles Davis' Bitches Brew, Jim Croce-I got a name or Donald Byrd- Lansana's Priestess, Places & Spaces, and of course, Flight Time, one of my all-time favorite songs. All were gifts from my brother James who loved so many good songs.

I'm not entirely old school when it comes to good music and such. Although I can't resist the memory of Flight Time blasting from a dorm window while walking across campus at the University of Arkansas in Fayetteville many years ago. But every now and then a new artist stumbles onto the stage with something surprisingly good and new. The Weekend's-Can't-Feel- My-Face is recent proof of that. Funny I mention this one, maybe it's because of a recent conversation I had with my Mother-In-Law who likes the song but not the artist's hairstyle. It is a bit much, I must confess. When I told her he wasn't singing about a beautiful woman, but rather the cocaine he fell in love with as a struggling and aspiring artist in Canada. Of course, his addiction likely came long before being discovered by Drake, another one of Canada's great artist. He would have had her as a fan before this minor detail ruined her brief love affair with both the song and the man.

In her mind, his hairstyle was appalling enough, and the drug abuse was too much even for her to bear. A good Southern Catholic, God fearing Christian woman, even they have limits too. Thanks for the gift Lil Wayne and Drake. After all, who else would have discovered or signed him all the way up in Toronto? The Weekend would be just another shining talent laboring in obscurity thus sparing my Mother-In-Law one more disappointment all the way down there in Georgia.

Then I began to wonder. Why of all days would those thoughts command my attention like that? Not just random thoughts, but prominent and unique memories of my brother and his horn. Indelibly carved in my brain, I couldn't resist the songs, especially that particular day. The music was actively bouncing around inside my head bringing focus to his memory, and all the time we shared.

Wow, suddenly I remembered it was his birthday. He stood five feet seven inches tall. Possessing the color of our father's skin, he had a deep passion for music. Perhaps a gift sprung from our rich gene pool. Our father had shared many stories of his Uncle Hamp and his grandfather's musical skills too. They traveled among the many plantations up and down the Mississippi Delta spreading their music and their DNA throughout the south.

My brother, Rev. James David Crockett was born on January 31, 1953, in Dermott, Arkansas. He lost his life to cancer on June 17, 2015, but not his spirit. I hold that inside. I remember all the music I listened to during our youth. It was his gift to our family and our small community too. The Christmas Parades and concerts were joyful events to see, especially for our family, the musical talent runs so deep. We were so proud of him. I remember listening to him play. The very first time he blew his horn I remember like yesterday. Daddy bought it from a pawn shop while visiting an old railroad friend. All the way from St. Louis, Missouri his first horn came. It didn't matter to James that it was a second-hand horn. Our father was quite the bargain hunter, but James felt no scorn. Once our father saw his talent, his next trumpet was brand new. That spoke volumes about the confidence our father bestowed and held on to. He obviously saw the musical genius in his son with every successful parade. Joyous they were, he played his horn with unending praise.

I miss the sound of rehearsals coming from our garage. James spent countless hours honing his musical skills. Before long, he and Charlie Clark were known all over town. A local treasure, they were admired by many for miles around. Such pride was spurred in our community; a fund raising drive soon began. Uniforms were a must for our high school band. Our mighty Chicot County High School Tigers deserved nothing less. Two fine band directors, Mr. Blunt and Mr. Scurlock, led the valiant charge. After several years of robust fund raising, the PTA bought the band their first uniforms. This was a crowning achievement for our father as president of the PTA. The band earned and deserved our sacrifice. The countless bake sales for the best and brightest talent in our small town were deserved. They were worth every single cent. Some three thousand people rose up, in spite of our segregated school and town. The band proudly wore their uniforms until the two schools became one. Sadly, those coveted uniforms were relegated to boxes and never worn or seen again. The former white school colors became the new symbol for our segregated town. Just like that, a monumental achievement had been erased from our minds. Those blue and gold uniforms with our mighty tiger mascot were gone forever without a lasting trace. The only remaining vestige of our school was pride. Some of us will never forget our Alma Mater we sang with pride:

"Should dear ole Chicot be forgotten?

No that is not our aim...,

We'll always boast of C.C.H.S.

Because we love her name...

Remember dear ole C.C.H.S

We love thee and you'll be

Always our guide to lofty skies,

And a path to nobler deeds.

To be sure, the principles for which this school stood for slowly begun to fade. Oh, what a shame. In the hearts of a few, I believe the sweet memories will always remain.

Whenever I listen to Donald Byrd, Miles Davis or Hugh Masekela I think of my brother and all the special memories he created with his horn. He was an aspiring musical talent with a good ear for music. So forgive me if you've noticed I'm a little sentimental right now. I just want to hear one more of his rehearsals, watch another parade or concert with him proudly wearing his CCHS Uniform like he used to. I want to hear that tiger roar again.

I long for the time, so long ago it seems, when we were young, full of life and death was a distant unthinkable dream. Time and again, he allowed me to drive his first car, a red Volts Wagon Beetle and his second one, a brand new green Volts Wagon Beetle with that Rolls Royce front hood. While driving, I'd let the music play loud. Not just any music but the good stuff.

Brother if you can hear me, once you've thoroughly rehearsed the scales, prepare to play your favorite song. The one we love so well. Securely tuck and rest your lips gently on your mouth piece. Your bulging cheeks full of air are just waiting to be released. Thrust it all inside your horn and let your power flow. Imagine that Geyser at Yellowstone National Park, rushing through your veins. Let that sparkle flash in your eyes when you play your favorite note... Unleash your joy and loudly play each note. After all, it's your birthday. Of course, I know you know. I long to hear you play. We'd stand and shout, Cotton Candy, Cotton Candy, once we heard our favorite song. I know you still have your horn and the magic from yesterday too. So blow it, one more time, one more time today. Be the proud, talented bugle boy, the one who loved to play. Oh, how I miss you and your horn. Now let your spirit play. Just like before; oh please, just one more time I must say. Just for little old me! Your mystique represents the very best of memories my heart holds still. Forget you... of course, I won't. Not now, not ever, and even not until...

Where Have You Been?

02/20/2016

God, you have one incredible sense of humor!

I've been looking for you for quite a while, I think. Were you hiding in plain view or standing in someone's shadow too dark even for me to see through? Why did it take so long for us to meet? Now, my mind is full of so many questions and thoughts. They're just racing around inside my head, but you hold all the answers instead. After all, you chose me or did I choose you? You see, I wrote three maybe four short stories within the last few weeks, thinking perhaps a handful of special people would take notice of me. Unknown, I imagined not much more than that. Finding time to read when there's nothing else to do, well those moments are rare for most, maybe this includes you? Don't know why you came or how you found me, but thank you for coming and reading something from me.

At last count, over one hundred and sixty-thousands of you came to my Facebook Page and spent some of your precious time reading thoughts posted under my name. Wow, that's fantastic! You know, without a doubt, we're the most complicated species of God's greatest creations. Oh what a genius he, maybe she is. Personally, I think God is a woman, just much too smart and clever to be anything but! I see a nurturing and comforting force whenever God is near; kindness not vanity, empathy not bravado, and a deep, sincere love is often felt. But for the bible and places of worship, you won't see a woman's name branded on planes, a stadium or any giant skyscrapers either. Nothing like a man, you know I'm telling the truth. Come to think of it, I've never seen a plane, a stadium or a building bearing a woman's name. Have you?

Do you really think a man would have chosen a woman, assigning childbearing responsibilities to her? This is such an awesome responsibility in the circle of life. Why would any smart, bold and daring creator place this critical task in the hands of a weaker sex? I don't think so! The right decision was made by that woman we now call by a different name, God; after all, it rhymes with girl, right? So she gave birth to our world and decorated it with such amazing feats like great canyons and mountains, and vast rivers, streams, and peaks. Now I'm no scientist, but it seems obvious to me, very clever clues she left don't you see? Birth and earth sound like something a woman might say. Once again, this kinda rhymes; what can I say? And to think I figured this out all by myself. Okay, with a lot of help from my wife alright? Oh, she'll never say! Now if you're a man, I mean no disrespect. I am a man too. We're left with incredible challenges: running, most might say ruining the world, occasionally building things, frequently fighting wars and destroying our precious planet. Of course in between football, basketball and soccer seasons when there's not else to do. Such a huge responsibility, don't you think? No time for small talk or civility. Whoa, we're so much better than that; it's really true! Let's step up our game, please for God sakes. Why don't you? Doggone it; it's such a shame to miss this opportunity in God's name.

It's nothing short of a miracle watching a woman as she gives birth. The journey a child makes with their crowning debut, at any time of day or night, this is a source of great wonder. Oh the pain and suffering brought unto the mother is awesome but soon passes, replaced with joy. Born so innocent and free of all worldly sins; wrapped in a bundle and given to a deserving mother and/or man, well most of the time. It humbles me to think about it all; just watching her replenish our planet is a miracle. If only we could read a newborn's mind. Oh, what a discovery we might find. Their memory is pure, filled with all of the knowledge imparted during their last thoughtful dialogue with our creator. I can only imagine what was said:

I've given you a beautiful planet, unique in substance, space, and form; admire it. I took extraordinary precautions and filled the world with beauty and so many amazing things, like the rivers, oceans, and seas. I filled the waters with fish and diverse marine life. The soil is home to plants, animals, and trees. Of course, the Stars, Sun, and Moon are my epiphanies; all of it, just because of you. You will not find any of this nowhere else. Your stewardship of earth must be sincere. You're responsible for its upkeep, all of you. So take good care of it, please. The difference begins and ends with each one of you.

By far, your planet is a masterpiece, my finest work for every good eye to see. A precious gift from my heart to yours; treat it well, treat it kindly and show respect for me. I created one race; human you see. Despite what they say, there is only one voice, one people I often listen to. No other variations exist or will ever take the place of you. So take heed, white, black, brown or red are all distractions instead, all adjectives not nouns, enough already said. So how can an adjective ever take the place of you? Human is what you are just like me, and now you are too. I don't think you understand what you really are. Sure I spiced you up a bit. A little diversity is good for your soul. I'm far too intelligent and talented to make one mistake. So get over it, there's only one race.

Love your fellow man and do good work for me. One day soon you'll return and answer only to me. Humble yourself when you find my gifts of brilliance, talent or leadership, it will appear among a few. Don't ask me why I do what I do. Just join in when possible and do something good too. Remember

I gave you a billion stars and a planet full of life. Don't just stand there and watch without doing work in my name. Resist vanity, ego and your selfish ways; for this is the devil's work I dare say. He can't be me, not even on my worse day. I banned him from heaven a long time ago, but there was no other place for him to go. So I sent him far from here to the earth below. Even now, I pray for his lost soul. Every day I continue to pray he obeys my will, until then, the earth is where he'll remain forever or at least until. Oh, he'll remain there, he must, until he changes his wicked ways in pursuit of his selfish stuff. He's smart and part of me too. One day, he'll find his way back. With a changed heart, I'll likely let him stay.

That brain of yours has unlimited powers you see; find good deeds to fulfill your desires don't destroy. Anyone can destroy, but be like me and build; maybe the next great masterpiece. Be a creator of beauty and happiness and fill the world with love. I've freely given to thee. Of course, I made it special just for you to see. See the glory. Look, it's inside of you, a gift all from me.

Bam, just like that, before the child realizes it, they're off, sliding through a birth canal and on their way into the awaiting arms of their mentor, their protector, and their teacher. Their life will be forever changed. We call them parents and that's the most important job they'll ever do in Jesus name. Raising one of God's finest creations, a masterpiece and a work of art, is slow and steady work, but ever so precious when you're a parent.

I didn't intend to write anything this morning. But my mind was racing while lying in bed and I had to get these thoughts written down instead. So I'm sharing them with you while making room for my rest, just a little while longer, at best. My Uncle Cleon once said, "I've never seen anything under the Sun greater than me." At first, I didn't understand what he meant until after his death many years later. A bit late but thanks, uncle, I finally get your meaning, and now I'm sharing it with friends. There's nothing greater under the Sun than you. Until next time, I wish you happiness and love for all of humanity. So necessary it is, to save our unique planet.

Graduation, a Time of Reflection

05/25/2016

"Lord let me not die until I have done my work, for no one can do my work for me."

Those words, powerfully spoken with eloquence landed on my ears a long time ago. From a pulpit in a little church in Dermott, Arkansas a proud Howard University Alumnus stood, the late Reverend Samuel M. Taylor. Seven Star Missionary Baptist Church, where he pastored, was my church home during my childhood. Our mother was devoted to him and our church. No Sunday Service would be missed without a real good excuse. His love for education was evident by a late enrollment to Howard at the age of 26. Imagine a 26-year-old freshman entering college today? Well, I've never seen such a thing, but he did in spite of his late start and humble beginnings in Oklahoma. A smart, thoughtful husband and father, he could have chosen a different location or career with his talent. Instead, he chose the ministry and teaching at Morris Booker Memorial College bringing his unique skills to our small community in Southeastern Arkansas. How could he have possibly known the seeds he planted would one day grow inside the head of a little child like me becoming a dominant force in shaping my life? Dare I say, I think not, but those seeds he planted really grew inside me!

    As far back as I can recall; I began repeating those inspiring words to myself, searching for meaning and looking for a useful purpose for them in my life. Perhaps this was unavoidable because I can't remember a Sunday Sermon without them; along with, "it's not the quantity-how much, but rather the quality-how good!" Was it he who connected these profound comparisons or did I innocently connect them in my impressionable young mind? Time has erased the details of this enduring combination, but somehow I found strength and purpose in both. Growing up in the Jim Crow South, I needed all of that and more to survive. Living under the weight of segregation and limited opportunities, I searched for anything that could assist me in my journey.

Upon graduating from high school, I found my way to the University of Arkansas after applying those words to my daily routine. With a lot of hard work, I achieved success in a career, a marriage and raised my four children. That prayer was a constant companion in my struggle. So it came as no surprise to each one of my children as I insisted they not only learn it but made it a center piece of their preparation for life. They found their academic success with the admissions to four Ivy League Schools: Columbia, Cornell, University of Pennsylvania and Dartmouth. Two other Ivy League Schools, Princeton, and Brown offered a place on their waiting list. In the end, Dartmouth, Syracuse and the University of Texas at Austin were their final choices. As a parent, I am so thankful for their success.

Our daughter recently surprised us by including very personal and enduring remarks in a speech at her graduation ceremony at Syracuse University. She was one among a few who were chosen to speak on this occasion. When they called her name, she gracefully walked to the stage. Standing tall and erect, she showed confidence instilled from the many years of Ballet and African Dance Classes. Once she approached the microphone, she paused for a moment, as if she were waiting for someone or something before speaking. Her eyes were closed; perhaps she was collecting her thoughts because she held nothing written in her hands. Somewhere in my mind, a prayer was silently being spoken, from my heart to hers, intended to express my support and confidence in her for the moment at hand. "Lord let me not die until I have done my work, for no one can do my work for me." Over and over again I whispered the prayer.

Then she opened her eyes and began to recite the words of the prayer I taught her as a child. "Lord let me not die until I have done my work, for no one can do my work for me." Spoken in rhythm so much like her favorite Bach Sonata she usually plays with tears rolling down her cheeks. But this time, there was a glow about her, and she looked so different to me. Why I wondered? Why did she look that way? Suddenly it was apparent. She had summoned the spirits of her ancestors. Lucy Turner, Phebie Carter Turner, Martha Brown, Anna Brown Turner, Virgie Lee Turner, Charlotte "Shirley" Ann Watson Crockett, Sylvia Locks Crockett, Harriet Watson Crockett, Emaline Kelly, Emily Kelly Crockett, Lillie Abrams Dooley, Esther Dooley Hughes, Velma Louise Hughes, Mattie Mae Camp, Helen Camp Hughes, Era Mae Turner Caruthers, Annie Mae Watson Williams and Sammie Williams Sutton, they all came. All of these strong, beautiful black and brown women are part of her lineage, and she insisted on their presence. A coronation had begun. With dignity and pride, their spirits surrounded her. I felt their loving embrace, the kind that a mother would give a child to remind them of their uncompromised love. They stood there, by her side. Shoulder to shoulder they stood and formed a circle of love. After all, but for their sacrifices, she wouldn't be standing on that stage in the first place. Her words and delivery reflected their contribution. Not just any words, but unique words befitting her testimony. Their spirit ran through her. She spoke of her struggle and their apparent sacrifices which paved the way for her success and the celebration of their crowning achievement.

A chill came over me, and I began to cry while praising his holy name. I could feel their spirits. Although I tried, I couldn't hold back the tears of joy;

they were too powerful to stop. When I looked at my wife and other family members, I knew they too felt the same. Her words were so touching; spoken like a lawyer, presenting her testimony with grace and pride. As she chronicled her experience while expressing her deep appreciation for the endless support she received, I felt proud. She touched our hearts provoking great reflection.

In that moment, I felt the presence of Rev. Taylor and all those people who had been a part of our personal journey. She lifted up his prayer sparking a transformation; a new planting season had begun. Standing in a packed hall in Syracuse, NY at the beginning of a new planting season, so many young and old eyes and ears were in the audience. For a moment the gates of heaven opened for Rev. Taylor's words to find new fertile soil for his seed to be planted and germinate. Oh, how wonderful it must have been for him to watch the beginning of a new season; there's nothing quite like planting a new crop. With a perfect view from heaven, he'll recognize his field. It'll be the one with a high-quality stalk and beautiful green leaves. I'm confident he'll keep a watchful eye on the entire field until harvest.

Under a harvest moon, in early October, a perfect night will appear for the harvest, and a glorious celebration will ensue. I have so much to share and thank him for. He gave us such an excellent seed for planting. We owe him so much. For without his prayer, I couldn't have made much of myself or raised the four children God sent here to me.

So I urge you to try his prayer. Repeat it a few times each day. You just might discover the power I've used through the years along the way.

"Lord let me not die until I have done my work, for no one can do my work for me."

In loving memory of the late Rev. and Dean Samuel M. Taylor, Charlotte Watson-Crockett-aka Shirley, my mother, and all the other strong women in our family; may you continue to rest in eternal peace until we meet again under that magnificent harvest moon!

Mr. President, We Salute You on Presidents' Day
02/15/2016

Naysayers are without optimism or compassion. To them I say, just keep on living. Change comes quickly...

Same face, same smile, but he looks a little older now. For seven long years with the weight of America strapped squarely on his shoulder, his hair seems much grayer too. Was he too young or too ambitious to know what he really signed up for nearly eight years ago? Loneliness and disappointment have likely been a constant companion. Sure his family and friends have constantly supported him, but no one can know his heart better than he. Living in the big famous White House, surrounded by staff, Secret Service with cameras everywhere, and all those critics just waited for him to stumble or fall, but he didn't. He stood tall. Stumble..., well maybe a time or two but nothing catastrophic, he was just way too cool.

He traveled around the world and represented our great nation so well. A stellar ambassador for peace and good will, he rose above the pettiness to speak. The Nobel Prize for peace he earned, among many nations, America stood tall. Overwhelmingly prestigious, it's an honor he deserves most of all. But was it really worth it? You think he'd do this all again? Be our President I mean, knowing where we stand? The drums of war were never silent. American Exceptionalism never rested nor stalled, not once, if ever at all. In nearly two terms as president, he resisted many war calls. World dominance was demanded by our high and mighty elites. There was no harm or shame felt while drinking from the well of exploitation and greed.

Mr. President, I vividly remember your first election in 2008. I've never seen anything like it before. In my life, so far this takes the cake. Nothing else comes close. Any other comparison would be a dreadful mistake. The lines at the polls were incredibly long, especially in Harlem too. Never before or since have so many people come to cast their vote for hope and you. Not for president, and especially not for someone called Barack Hussein. Some voted for the first time after surviving our nation's devastating financial crash. It left our economy in shambles, crippled by greed and excess. Food lines were everywhere, and it felt like the end no less. We were at a precipice. With your guidance, our long cataclysmic struggle began; so much like what John Hanson faced as President once before. The Continental Congress endured this struggle early in our history, but of course, I know you know. During our struggle for independents, while we yearned to breathe free, I'm sure he felt the same as you with all the pressure you've seen. All alone when the stakes were high, he shouldered an awesome task. Saving our country from falling apart with Old Glory pressed against his chest. A steady hand was needed and a deep love for country too. Of course, you and I know this, but how many others do?

Our country was nearly broke once, and soldiers demanded their pay. Somehow through our struggle, John Hanson found a way, much the same as you. He too was a man of color yet forgotten by history it seems. Does the average American really know who he is? I doubt it. If you're lucky enough to see a two dollar bill, look for him, he's there. Oh, you'll need a magnifying glass to catch a small glimpse I swear.

Barack Hussein Obama today is Presidents' Day. You stand among 43 predecessors who share this distinguished privilege with you. Your name is now synonymous with George Washington, Abraham Lincoln, Franklin Roosevelt, John Kennedy and Bill Clinton. Despite your critic's subversive attempts, you'll be remembered too. For your service, alongside these other proud men, you'll stand. I'm getting a little sentimental because I know as president your time will soon end.

Someone else will take your place and sit at that awesome desk. But will they labor as hard while searching for what is right as often as you did? Long into the wee hours of the night, you sat and toiled with pride. A part of me, well a part of us Arkansans, Dermott in particular, were so proud when one of our own stood by your side. She served as a member of your staff. Beside you, she stood with pride; helping as best as she could when you needed help the most. Won't call any names but her parents were so proud when you singled her out to praise. Raising a capable, intelligent and professional child deserves an occasional applause.

Her dad's pride was unmatched by any proud father the day you held her high. You may not know this, but her grandmother's brother was a career soldier too. He served our nation with distinction after many tours of duty. Vietnam of all places, he served our nation with pride. Oh, he was a proud soldier, the apple of his mother's eyes. With dignity, her Uncle Jacob Benjamin Caruthers served our country too. I was especially proud to call him my uncle as well. A gifted translator was he. He spoke many languages including Vietnamese. You see, he married my mother's big sister. Oh, man did she sometimes protest his call to duty and the country he loved so well. Choosing a military career with a family was hard, but he was devoted to our country and flag. They are both deceased now, but I still remember and always include them in my prayers.

Hold on a little while longer Mr. President, I imagine some of your remaining battles will be hard fought. Your journey hasn't been easy, but we've been watching and praying for you. With every step you made, many prayers were uttered for you. I have many friends and acquaintances that depend on you to hold America to its Creed:

"I believe in the United States of America as a government of the people, by the people, for the people; whose just powers are derived from the consent of the governed, a democracy in a republic, a sovereign Nation of many sovereign States; a perfect union, one and inseparable; established upon those principles of freedom, equality, justice, and humanity for which American patriots sacrificed their lives and fortunes."

I believe it is our solemn duty to our country we love, to support our Constitution, to obey the laws, to respect our flag, and to defend her against all enemies both foreign and domestic. So for those who say they want to take their country back, I say it was never theirs, to begin with, but rather ours, now and forever. All of our blood is in this soil; one race, different colors but one blood-red!

History will be kind and show much respect for you. Long after the roar of the snake oil salesman or reality show personality, television and radio celebrities and political pundits have all faded, you will be remembered. But I must tell you when Congressman Joe Wilson of South Carolina called out to you a few years ago during your State of The Union Address calling you a 'liar,' this was a dark moment in our nation's history, and I will never forgive nor forget the shame he brought to our great democracy. For this is the land where my father died, my mother cried, and my children were born. Our children are watching, and from this discord, a new America shall be born. It'll happen I'm certain of it, making us better and stronger and a great nation once again.

So for today and for years to come, I'll celebrate Presidents' Day with renewed pride. You'll be standing among them, proud as our 44th President of the United States.

God bless you, your family and especially America. We sure could use some more leaders just like you. Perhaps a divine intervention will come again real soon. Amen!

Farewell Mr. President, a Job Well Done!

01/05/2017

And now one door closes while another opens. But it won't be the same without you.

Within a few weeks, the 2017 Presidential Inauguration with be held. One political chapter will close as we begin to write anew. The history of our great nation will continue on its path. Choices have consequences and bring about change; this will inevitably determining if we are better, worse or remain the same. What a stark contrast between the previous eight years and the legacy of our past. Now we're faced with uncertainty. Anxiety obscures our future unsure of what lies ahead. Never in my lifetime has such a drastic unparalleled antithesis gripped our country so. Oh, there have been previous attempts: Senator Barry Morris Goldwater from Arizona was the Republican's Presidential Nominee in 1964, but his message of hate was rejected. Then Governor George Corley Wallace, Jr from Alabama attempted three times unsuccessfully. His first attempt was as an Independent Candidate in 1968 followed by two failed attempts in 1972 and 1976 as a Democrat. Like Senator Goldwater, his hateful vision of America was soundly rejected three times. Their message, like our next President, Donald Trump does not represent our best. The Donald's slogan is Make America Great Again, but the subtle inferences are clear. They're filled with demagoguery, xenophobia, classism, sexism and the exploitation of our social issues. Oh no, this kind of politics should never ever stand.

The voters rejected these messages and the messengers four times before. They chose unity over division, love over hate and peace over hostility.

Oh America, we fought such a heroic fight to preserve and protect our great democracy. So how did we let Donald come into our lives?

Now let's review the message President Obama championed for the last eight years: Hope and change, unity over division, inclusion over exclusion, education over ignorance, opportunity over despair and reasonable gun safety over gun violence, global unity instead of wars, and health and wellness over sickness for all. These themes were hard fought and admirable; so much of the world agreed. The Nobel Prize for Peace was won by him in 2009. His vision for Make America Great was embraced by many, of course, this includes me. A sense of decency and hope is a good thing for America, on this, I fervently agree. These ideals for good are what our children truly need. With each new birth, a seed of goodwill grows inside a child. The next four years will likely challenge us with darkness and gloom abound. A national robbery is in progress while justice and joy sleep. Oh God, have mercy. Will America stumble, bend or fall?

Mr. President, I've admired your work and good deeds from a distance. You truly have a good heart. I watched the wolves gathered and mount their relentless attacks. With animus and vitriol, unlike anything I've ever seen; all of this was endlessly directed at you. Not since Jim Crow at least, have I seen such a thing. Without your belief in God, they surely would have destroyed you. Remember their countless attacks on the First Lady and even your beautiful kids? Too many to recount I'm sure, but you stood strong and never gave in. You didn't take the bait, and that certainly made them mad. You aimed high when they went low. God must have held your hand! I'm certain of that, for, without him, they would have destroyed you and your family too.

We've watched you struggle and weep in agony after each senseless shooting: Sandy Hook, Charleston, San Bernardino, Aurora and Oak Creek, the list never seems to end. Such madness has swept across our nation, one by one we fall. How much madness must we endure? Will we ever demand a change? Time and time you tried but failed. No place is safe anymore. The killing and violence must stop before it reaches another door.

In spite of it all, for eight long years our sickness you tried to heal. The time will come for your reward; your blessings will come soon. Fret not, you planted good seeds and oh what a beautiful harvest we shall soon see. A new generation will come and pick up where you left-off. Hope, the same hope you spoke of, will soon find its place. It will be so beautiful when our children come and decisively take your place. A new stewardship will soon come again. Because of you, a mighty harvest will come soon.

We just need to be patient and keep our faith in God. So when you stand on that inaugural stage, don't think for one minute your successor will succeed with hate. If he chooses darkness and hate, it will die like a horrible weed. We are a nation of planters, builder, and dreamers who depend on a good seed; that's what America needs. There's no room for Strange Fruit: Demagoguery, xenophobia, classism or exploiting social disputes. Weeds wither and die once we choose Sun, hope and the mighty blue skies. A good farmer knows how to protect his crop. Darkness and despair have no place with a harvest close at hand. A good harvest is hoped for when the seeds are planted with care.

Perhaps you already know how much we will miss you. It will be hard, very had to say goodbye. As a child growing up in the south, most of our homes, if not all, had a bible, a picture of Jesus, John F. Kennedy, and Martin Luther King, Jr. Some even included Bobby Kennedy along with Ebony or a Jet Magazine. Now you will likely be added to such an awesome collection. Being the forty-fourth president is an honor. Your sacrifice was enormous. Many lives were lost for the right to cast that vote. But vote they did twice for you. Now you join Jesus Christ, John, Martin, Bobby and maybe an Ebony Magazine too.

On behalf of a grateful nation, if I should be so bold to say, thank you, Mr. President, a job well done I must say. Farewell Barack Hussein Obama oh how we love you so.

U CAN'T TOUCH THIS

07/28/2016

Every closed eye ain't sleep, and every goodbye doesn't mean you're gone...

Stop, it's Obama Time! On July 27, 2016, in Philadelphia, Pennsylvania, the city of brotherly love hosted the last night of the Democratic National Convention and President Barack Hussein Obama stole the show, hands down, no doubt about it! Stanley Kirk Burrell, aka MC Hammer, unwittingly wrote the theme song in 1990 for the best pep rally I've ever seen televised, "U Can't Touch This." So why didn't they play his song? Beats me! Man, he's a genius and clearly was ahead of his time. A pep rally...? Yes and oh what a show those Democrats put on. Oh mercy, mercy me! The Republicans and the Fox Network only wish they had the flair those Democrats had during their convention last week. Let's see, the Republicans had the Donald plus his three kids, Ted Cruz who was an unwilling participant but not much else. Even Governor Kasich stayed away. Do I need to remind you he's the Republican Governor of Ohio, a swing state they badly need to win in November? Perhaps that explains why they held their Convention in Cleveland. Where were their former Republican Presidents and Senators? Most of them stayed home after refusing to attend or participate in their convention party's lineup; there are two former Republican Presidents you know, both Bushes' and the Donald destroyed Jeb Bush during the primaries. As you know, he's a brother and son to the former presidents of their party. But of course, I'm sure you knew that!

I passed through Cleveland on the second day of their convention heading back to New York City after a brief visit to Arkansas. I could hardly feel their presence. They did everything thinkable to convince us that the Republican National Convention was on the same par with those Democrats. Come on now, who's foolin who? If you put lipstick on a pig, you may fool maybe a few Republicans, but everyone else in the whole wide world knows it's still a pig. The Donald, they wanted him, and now they're stuck with trying to sell a pig to the American voters, a losing proposition I believe come November 8th. I'm a New Yorker, and we can spot a con from a mile away. The Donald, we see him coming from a greater distance; a snake oil salesman can usually be spotted with very little effort by a true New Yorker.

I can only think of one other person who could prepare the world for a new leader better than what the president did last night for Hillary. One, yes only one other person comes close, John the Baptist. Excuse me for a minute; I need a moment with Jesus. After last night, would you replace John for Barack? I'm just asking okay.

Surely Barack gave Jesus pause, you think? Only Michael Jordan, Magic Johnson, Kobe Bryant, Tiger Woods, Kareem Abdul-Jabbar, Mike Tyson, Steph Curry, LeBron James, Kevin Durant and maybe a few others know this kind of feeling; maybe you think? For a moment, they know they're the best in the world at what they do, and no one, I repeat, no one can possibly do better. Not one of the previous 43 presidents, including Bill Clinton and certainly not another politician could have done it better than Barack last night. Sound the bell, school is over!

After the President's speech, I went to the Fox Channel to see how they would spin what I just witnessed. Mind you, they live in an Alternate Universe, full of magic, deception, and lots of smoke and mirrors. You see, there are two parallel visions for America that juxtapose our democracy. Remember 2012 on election night when President Obama was declared the winner in Ohio and Carl

Rove was in complete denial sitting there staring at his oversized writing board? Well, Sean Hannity with Newt Gingrich served up the red meat to their audience last night. Newt had to admit it was a great speech and went on to say there was no one on their side who could have done better. Their convention proved that and he had no other option but to admit the obvious. But he quickly went to their talking points. "America is in crisis. While he's been president, over 3,400 people have been killed in the streets of Chicago; his home town. There are a record number of people on food stamps. We've got high unemployment among the blacks and the reason why the unemployment numbers are so low, people have given up looking. Libya is a mess. ISIS is a threat to America and Hillary has the blood of Benghazi on her hands. Let's not forget those deleted e-mails either."

Is that all they've got? For months, a long list of Republicans, including Joe Scarborough, Bill O'Reilly, Sean Hannity, Charles Krauthammer, Rush Limbaugh, William Kristol, George Will, Carl Rove and so many others have recited these talking points. Guys, let me give you some advice, you need new material. That stuff is all played out! With Roger Ailes of Fox gone, they're without a leader. So the Donald looks to Russia for help. Maybe losing Roger wasn't so bad. After all, he gave them The Donald, big mistake! Will somebody please help them? Jesse, could you find time to give Fox and the RNC a call? That's Jesse Williams, not Jackson!

Why do I say this? The Donald has taken out their entire political lineup for the next four to eight years. He destroyed Jeb Bush, Ben Carson, Ted Cruz, John Kasich, Jim Gilmore, Marco Rubio, Rick Perry, Scott Walker, Bobby Jindal, Lindsey Graham, George Pataki, Mike Huckabee, Rick Santorum, Rand Paul, Carley Florina, John McCain and Chris Christie. Their entire bench of viable candidates has been wiped out. What he did is tantamount to taking out an entire NBA Team. He's given the White House to the Democrats for the next eight years or maybe longer, thank you, Mr. Trump. If he had slipped a Trojan horse inside the Republican Party, he couldn't have harmed them more. The damage he's done to the Republican Party is lethal.

They continue to whine and complain. Now they are fighting among themselves. I've seen Bill O'Reilly, and George Will go at one another. Rush Limbaugh fights anyone who tries to take down the Donald. Sean Hannity even tries to serve that dangerous Kool-Aid to anyone willing to come on his show and drink, at least a gallon before speaking. If you refuse to think the way he does about the president and Hillary, It'll be a short interview. They're going down folks, fast.

Oh but last night, President Obama had that crowd in his hands. I could have sworn they were playing "Jump" by Kris Kross in the convention hall. They were clapping, jumping, cheering and crying. Look like they were having church up in there. The Holy Ghost took over; hallelujah Jesus-somebody scream! Darn, this feels good just writing about it. I need to find somebody's church come Sunday morning, hallelujah Jesus, Amen...

The president had SWAGGER and CHARM. He was in a zone with the flow of a polished rapper spitting his rhymes with magic on the mic. Pickup on this, he came hard. Larry Wilmore's famous line at the end of his White House Press Dinner speech was likely repeated all over America last night, especially in Philly. Sorry Rush, you still can't repeat it, "You did it my N***a!" So go on to your next show and wine some more.

No, I can't bring myself to say those words but here's what I think he should have done: looked around, and then brushed off his shoulder. You know like he did in 2008 when Hillary was sweating him, then drop his mic and walk off the stage, stage right of course! Bam... that would have brought down the house for sure. Ring that bell, the pep rally is over. Now go win this election and teach those awful Republicans a badly needed lesson! By the way, The Donald, if you're wondering if President Obama threw any shade your way last night, wonder no more. He did, plenty of it! You earned every bit of it too. His eyes are wide open, and he'll not say goodbye anytime soon.

Run Kanye, Run...

03/04/2016

A chicken ain't nothing but a bird!

After watching the Republican Debate last night on the Fox Network, words, mostly cynical, were beating a pathway through my head stimulating my fingers in such bizarre ways. If only for a chance to be seen or have their say, I jumped at the chance to write. I wanted to capture what I witnessed in words being said on stage by four presidential hopefuls. All of which was good old American Politicians, all except one, of course, The Donald. Initially, I tried to resist these thoughts, but they just wouldn't let me be. They constantly gnawed at me until I began to write.

Pushing all of this aside, I started my day by heading to the post office to send a fan her autographed copy of Nina Shakes Harlem. "Hey Jenine babe, I sent it first class; it's on the way to Virginia, okay! So much love for you and thank you for your support."

Walking through the streets of Harlem, I heard the chatter all about. Most were quickly dismissed, but some of it resonated, and the raw Harlem character took hold inside my head. I heard one proud Harlemite say, "Did you hear what that idiot Trump said on TV last night? He got it all wrong. It's the feet, not the hands. Hell, every black man in America knows that, and he says he's smart. Hell no, that dumb mothafucker oughta go somewhere and sit his monkey-ass down. He should get the fuck outta here okay before he does to America what he did to Atlantic City," Oh, I thought. So I wasn't the only one watching the debate in Harlem last night after all.

I went to Rite Aid on 8th Avenue and 117th Street to pick up a few things. While standing in line, I saw a tabloid staring back at me. The headline was screaming right at me, "Kanye You Need Therapy!" Allegedly the quote came from his wife, Kim. Suddenly I began to wonder, "Is God trying to tell me something?" What, you might ask, does any of this have to do with Kanye West of all people and the presidential debate? Well, I remembered a little while back he expressed his aspirations of running for the highest office in our land, President of the United States. Yep, he sure said it. I read that somewhere with a reference to his wife Kim Kardashian becoming America's First Lady. Wow, I'm not making this stuff up. Reality TV is the new Crack for Americans, and The Donald is the King of all dealers; there's no difference you think?

Now let's connect the dots. Last night, I heard The Donald defending his manhood. Apparently one of his presidential adversaries accused him of having unusually small hands for a man of his statue. Oh, The Donald proclaimed he was well endowed with his male extremities. Don't make me say it... Okay, ladies, he said he had a big penis! Potentially the next President of the United States wanted you and the rest of the world to know how big his Johnson is; HUGE okay. Oh please, this man needs his meds adjusted and more therapy! Then it hit me, Kanye would fit right in on that stage. He was ahead of his time when he expressed interest in the presidency. Now, I believe his time has come thanks to The Donald. If asked, he'd quickly say he has the balls and a big Johnson to man-up for the task. The only difference between him and The Donald is color, height and maybe a few dollars but everything else he's got covered. Both of them claim to be smart with HUGE egos, plenty money or so they both say. Each of them has beautiful wives that love attention, perfect for a first lady.

The Donald is making a mockery of our democracy, and the whole world is laughing, most of the time at least, but some are wary. Several world leaders are thinking the worst of America's leadership after taking a good look at The Donald. After the thought of The Donald, why not Kanye? Could he be a better choice? I imagine he could rap his way out of this dilemma. You think so? After listening to The Donald, he'd fit right in.

President Obama saved us from economic despair eight years ago, and Kanye can save us from The Donald and ourselves. If not, we'll become the butt of all jokes for four long years in the entire world; that is if The Donald succeeds with his hostile takeover aided by the Russians no less! Unbelievable, this is a national crisis of epic proportions. But as his friend Don King might say, "Only in America!"

Run Kanye Run, we're with you man, all the way to the White House, babe! So here's a little advice, not like you need a lot, but here goes. Keep your campaign slogan real and simple okay? "No silly wall can keep the Mexican's out." Hell America was once a part of Mexico anyway. Besides, who would take their place in the labor force? Not us, we work for doe, not pesos. We're free at last, remember? "No damn Muslim ban." That is a veiled shot at our president, Barack Hussein Obama-Assalamualaikum, my brother! After all, they want to kick him out of the White House and the country anyway. Besides everybody knows a large number of Republicans are convinced he's one of them; Muslim I mean. So what if he is? America was founded with a solemn belief of religious freedom. What happened?

By the way, Kanye stop them from taking their country back! Wait a minute; this is a false premise in the first place. Remember the Natives were here first. They've been waiting so long for a man like you to come along. You know what I mean? To be sure, they need someone like you to set the record straight. Are you up for the task? Do we need a man like you to take Obama's place? This is our country, right? For a pluralistic society, we need someone to fight. Where was The Donald when the Natives needed a wall? The country will finally hear their side. For all Native Americans, our history has not been kind or fair. A National Powwow is needed in Washington, DC. But Kanye they need one of your mad beats. It's time we celebrate. I got my eye on a great outfit I recently saw in Henning, Tennessee. My Chickasaw blood is ready and red hot. And last but not least, make sure you keep them from erasing President Obama from our history books. An asterisk by his name is about the same.

Remember, he's a Manchurian Candidate/President, and that shouldn't count. So they want to adjust the presidential count by skipping his number slot, forty-fourth will be left out. Some say this serves him right. How dare he give Americans an Affordable Care Act allowing poor people access to healthcare? Or food stamps to feed the hungry and poor. Or what about those free cell phones and those low-interest student loans? Why would he address police brutality and the inequities in our criminal justice system? How dare he talk about gun control? Haven't there been enough mass killings in our country? Nope, not according to the NRA; the shoot 'em up wild, Wild West is just fine with them as long as their kids are not the victims. After all, everything was just fine the way it has always been before Obama messed things up with his foolish hope. "We are choosing hope over fear. We're choosing unity over division and sending a powerful message that change is coming to America." He must be crazy to think such silly thoughts in America.

How dare he talk about gun violence and lecture our nation about too many gun deaths in our nation? The Second Amendment to our Constitution gives us the right to keep it real, wham bam thank you, ma'am! America, just keep killing one another okay, why stop now? Please, pretty please don't let them take all of this away, especially that Obama cell phone. Why that's criminal and unthinkable you know!

I think I've made my points quite clear enough. America needs another black man to save the day. Will you help us Kanye please, and Run Kanye Run...for President I mean!

Before I go, I must clear the air about The Donald and this hands thing. All my life, I've heard black men lie about their shoe size. Some of us even buy our sneakers a half size or so larger to prove that very point to the sisters. Well, including me once upon a time. So I made a call to my best friend down in Arkansas to voice my disdain for The Donald's comments hoping she'd set the record straight. Oh, boy, did I get an earful. After a brief moment of silence, she cleared her throat and began her post-mortem on my point.

"Now you know I love you and we've known each other since the second grade, but The Donald is partly right. He's good and stupid, but he's got this one sort of right. It's the fingers, not the hand. I'm here to tell you, babe! Those feet are a false positive, you hear me? It fooled the hell out of me a couple of times before I wised up."

I'm the one who called her for the truth, so I wouldn't dare step on her moment. "Let me tell you one thang, I've been with men with big feet, at least their shoes were big when I met them. But babe once we got busy, the truth was revealed. One guy with big feet had a penis the size of a Vienna sausage! I wanted to get up, put my clothes on and leave. He couldn't satisfy me with that. A Tic Tac can't satisfy a whale! I've been fooled once, maybe twice, with them feet but never, I mean never with those fat, long fingers. If he got big, long fat fingers on those big hands, babe, he's the one. You hear me? Oh babe yeah, he's the one. You know I wouldn't lie to you now."

I was speechless. In all my years, I'd never heard such a thing. For so many years, how could all of these brothers, including myself, be so wrong? Think of the number of Air Jordan's that were sold oversized, too often I might add. So naturally, I mentioned this conversation to my wife before finishing this story. After listening, she replied, "Even I knew that it's the fingers!" Oh damn, The Donald, look what you have done. God help America, please! That may be the only thing The Donald got right, and he just might end up in the White House after all! Oh mercy, mercy me...

Hillary, Girl We Got A Big Problem!

03/08/2016

Don't try to win tomorrow's race with yesterday's dreams!

Look, I'm not a worrier, but it's time we had a frank conversation about Hillary and this 2016 Presidential Election. So to all you Hillary naysayers, here goes: Now, I've been trying real hard to avoid this conversation about our girl, a reference of endearment no offense intended. Yeah, I said it; I want to declare my bias upfront making it clear where I stand on this issue from the start. In light of the many conversations I've had lately with several women, my wife, in particular, I'm coming clean with my HUGE concerns.

Why be sneaky about it? That's sort of like going to the fish market to buy your favorite fish, and once they see your choice, they put their thumb on the scale to make sure to charge you just a little extra because you want it so bad and will buy it anyway even if it cost a little bit more. What's the harm, right? Uh, that hasn't happened to you? Pay attention next time you're in the market. I catch them all the time. So smooth, most of them frequently get away with it unnoticed. Besides, it's a win, win for both. You get your fresh fish after paying a little extra to the proprietor and leave happy with your favorite entrée, and they make a bit extra on the sale. If my money is right, even though I catch them, I'll let them slide because I understand the game; taxes, wages and the rent in the city is a killer, but you might say that's the price they pay for doing business. Well for me, it's all about economics and convenience. Having a fish market so close with fresh fish is a must, and most of the time, I consider the transaction a fair trade. Convenience with a little extra cost is like a built-in tip of sorts, you agree? But when my pocket is a little light, I weigh-in right away and ask for a do over serving notice I caught them in the act of cheating. Once they realize they're caught, the price is corrected, lower of course. No harm no foul right? Competition you might say causes this whole scenario to frequently play out time and time again. Advertise low, then cheat to make a profit; standard practice in most cities, especially New York!

Now having said all of this let me get to my point. Anyone watching Bill and Hillary knows they've had their thumb on the scales for a long time like so many others past and present. It should have been Hillary's turn in 2008, but Obama messed up the coronation causing Bill to lose his cool and momentarily go nuts. Cashing in on their celebrity and connections was expected by most after many, many years of waiting while paying the ultimate price for this privilege i.e. one year after another of constant scrutiny, impeachment, humiliation, and attack after attack with no let up in sight, even now. So she's ready for the big dance, President of the United States. Anyone in this game knows what I'm talking about. And of course, Bill paid the ultimate price for his proclivities. Hello Monica, your service to our great nation is legendary; you surpassed Fanne Foxe! Now if you're too young to know that name, Google her; she's still famous after all these years.

We're all complicit because we allowed our political system to become corrupt. Evolving over time into something other than a democracy, now we have reached a tipping point. Time to hit the reset button you think? But most of us have been happy with this system for some time. Until recently, everybody got a crumb or two, but now the food chain is no longer yielding crumbs. So we are on the verge of anarchy in some of our cities, and food lines are a constant reminder. They're scattered throughout our cities. Oh excuse me, Bernie, A revolution is needed. We can't look the other way any longer because the thumb on the scale is too heavy and devastating for so many of us. So much so, some of us can't provide shelter for our families or feed and clothe our children; even educating them is beyond reach for so many without incurring a mountain of debt. That's the way this game has been played for years, and now it's time for a reset! But wait, change to what? The rich are still getting richer, the poor getting poorer and wars are being fought with a mountain of debt placed on our nation's credit card in the trillions. Of course the rich don't want to pay their fair share so who's left with the bill? You and me, who else?

So now there's a cry for fairness in the system they say, right? After all, how many billions does a billionaire need to live well while keeping greed from destroying the very system they routinely exploit? From inception until now, trade deals have benefited corporations, not the people. For a long, long time, our politicians, companies and business schools sold this concept to us. But if we had refused to buy those cheap products made off-shore in some foreign land in the first place, we'd still have good paying middle-class jobs in America. Our government was a willing conspirator. Wall Street, the money maker, has been out of control for years.

For instance, if you get in a financial tight and need to use some of your 401K, mind you, this is your hard earned money, you pay a ten percent penalty for the privilege. But, to ease your financial hardship, you elect to pay the penalty anyway because your circumstance requires it. Our government imposes this ten percent penalty for one reason only, for Wall Street Fund Manager. They can lose it all with no such penalty or consequence. Who do you think engineered this cozy deal, Democrats, Republicans or Independents? The answer is they all did; Bernie included. He has known of this for years. So why did he wait until now to make it an issue? Hillary too okay, there's enough blame to go around.

Bill actually opened the flood gates during his watch after revoking Glass-Steagall which was a part of the Bank Act of 1933 that kept us safe from financial ruins for many years. But if we go there, what about our dear Ronald Reagan, considered a God by most Conservative Republicans? His hands aren't clean either; remember the Savings and Loan Scandal? It happened during his watch. John McCain was one of the five senators complicit in the Keating Five, but no one brought that up during his presidential bid. Now some of us stand politely and quietly while Hillary's adversaries question her speaking fees and demand to see her speeches. Oh please, I don't get it! People lost their life savings in that scandal. Don't get me started here because I could go on and on. Reagan is a hero even after the Iran-Contra scandal that resulted in his administration being tied so close to drugs being sold in our cities which destroyed lives and ruined entire communities, especially urban.

So after several conversations with my wife and some of my other friends who are also women, I couldn't help but put this in proper context. Some of them are so upset with Hillary, complaining about every little sin she's committed, especially during the 2008 campaign against President Obama. Is Hillary guilty? Yes probably but so is Bernie and all the rest of our politicians we've elected over and over through the years. Bernie is a part of the same hypocrisy as her. Our system is broken and needs to be repaired. The only difference between Bernie and Hillary is this, she thinks like a man and acts like a man too.

Well, she could use a refresher, after being around all of that testosterone for so long. Too much rubbed off on her over the years. Hillary, that's the title of a movie, Steve just wanted to get paid, okay? That's all, period! So ladies, give Hillary a chance, please. Consider the alternative; The Donald is your worst nightmare. On the other hand, Hillary is ready to serve, agrees to keep hope alive and advance President Obama's agenda, prosperity for all. To my people, she's included your free Obama cell phone, low-interest student loans, health insurance coverage and free community college for anyone who wants to continue their education beyond high school. A vote for Hillary gives you all that. To my cousin in Milwaukee, everyone here in New York knows The Donald and if there's nothing in it for him, no more stuff for free, period. He's selling snake oil and Kool-Aid, Jonestown-style.

Have you seen his rallies? Not a pretty sight to watch especially if you look too different from the person standing next to you if you know what I mean! He wants to get paid too, okay? So he'll say and do anything to claim the White House, even eminent domain. He owes the Russian too much money and needs a HUGE payday. Besides, my friend from Detroit went to the debate in Flint this week, and if Hillary were planning on reneging on advancing President Obama's agenda, she would have called her out and informed me by now. Everyone should know the Obama phone is still in the package so spread the word. She got it straight from Hillary's mouth. But Hillary if you wanna win, you gotta earn it!

Gotta run, there's a headline on the morning news about a woman on top of a semi-truck in Houston on the Interstate dancing nude in that hot Texas morning sun. All the traffic has stopped, as Don King would say, "Only in America." Hello testosterone, come on let's get this show on the road; Oops, I wonder if she has a pole too, bye!

Republicans What Happened to Your Party?

05/11/2016

You fool around with trash; it'll get in your eyes.

Once upon a time, there stood a vigorous and revered grand old political party. They were invaluable to the success of our great democracy. Not just any system of government, but ours, the United States of America. Frederick Douglass, Abraham Lincoln, Teddy Roosevelt and Colin Powell once were proud members of this great party called Republican. Since the party's inception in 1854, their contributions to our country have been remarkable. With a rich ideology promoting freedom for all its citizens, free market capitalism, a strong national defense, and fiscal conservatism were just a few of their admired principles with broad appeal. Judeo-Christian beliefs were deeply embraced within the party making social conservative values a centerpiece of their moral standing. One hundred and sixty-two years later, I wonder if Douglass, Lincoln, Roosevelt or Powell would recognize their party or even be a welcomed member.

Barry Goldwater's 1964 racial assault on Black American's Civil Rights nearly fifty-two years ago deeply scarred their image. Now another brutal assault by Donald Trump is underway. Beginning with the birther movement and a persistent blatant assault against Mexican-Americans and Muslins, I think the Republicans have lost their way and here's why.

During the last eight years, they have lost two presidential elections after failing to appeal to a majority of our nation's voters. So desperate to reclaim the White House, they've become unrecognizable after using political tactics unbefitting a major party. I noticed their transformation some time ago, but these last eight years have been by far their worst. What happened? Was the two term election of Barack Hussein Obama a tipping point? His success was an obvious game changer, driving them into a painful deep seated rage! He brought out the worst demons imaginable among their ranks after beating them twice. Obstruction, hatred, self-destruction and questionable tactics have been employed to impose their will with devastating consequences. Badly needed work, although expected, has been largely ignored. Animus has blocked advances in our nation's infrastructure, our decaying schools, health care and government leadership in science and technology have lingered. Oh, what a shame!

They have been so willing to do just about anything to usurp the will of the people. This is coming at a great cost to our nation, especially the middle class.

If a third term were possible, President Obama would win again. I'm certain of it. He could probably serve as long as he wanted if our Constitution allowed that. With so many elected and appointed officials at all levels of our government: Governors, Senators, Congressman, Judges and Supreme Court Justices, coupled with a list of gleeful surrogates, the likes of Rush Limbaugh, Bill O'Reilly, Sean Hannity and Joe Scarborough, to name just a few, persist with their brutal assault on our political system with relentless resolve. I've listened to their words of disdain and commentary finding little logic, if any at all, on many occasions. I do not believe the Ku Klux Klan could have done much worse.

This Republican Party has attempted to delegitimize our first American President of mixed heritage, half-black and half- white. Notice I didn't say African American? They would have gladly called him African if only they found proof. That evasive birth certificate supporting their claim never appeared.

Where's the proof when a good-old-boy needs some? A Manchurian Candidate has slipped into our country to advance the African and Muslin influences and bring down America too. God almighty, what's a White Christian Nation to do?

President Obama's margin of victory was too wide to steal the election. It worked once before right? So they tried to convince the American people he was not an American but that didn't work either. Why not say he's Muslin, that should do it right? Our great Christian Nation wouldn't stand for such an abomination, but that failed too. Okay, make the government ineffective, let the poor people suffer. They'll be forced to come back, surely that'll do the trick, but even that failed.

Keep that Black President away from our impressionable children, and soon they'll agree and never let this sort of thing happen again in our history. Nope, that didn't work either! He spoke their language and gave them a new vision for America, so different from what they were being taught. Oh my God, what must they try to do? "Take Back Our Country," or "Make America Great Again," two good slogans just might do the trick.

Darn it! They found a slogan that worked. Now all that's needed is someone who knows how to get the people angry, scare the hell out of them and stir up the xenophobia. Besides, who would object to hating Blacks or Mexicans or giving food stamps, free medical care, free education and free cell phones to the needy? What about those Muslins? After all, it costs too much having them around. Besides they're not welcomed in American way anymore since the Taliban brought the towers down.

The Donald has been watching in the wings, just waiting for a chance. Suddenly he rushed in with his announcement; "I'm the one, I can make America Great Again. I'll take it back from the Mexicans, the Muslins, and the

Blacks." Listen, if you think the Jews or Chinese get a pass, think again. So where does all this leave America? Chopping at the bits to do something spectacular right?

Posing as a Republican for the 2016 Presidential Election, there he stood, The Donald. An amoral person, showing no wisdom, justice or temperament for the office; just a promise, "Make America Great Again," and he became the face of the Republican Party. This has gone way past a joke or a TV Reality Show. It's real and should America allow this to happen, there won't be any corner in the world where we'll avoid this embarrassment. A village idiot could take center stage, and we won't be able to recover from this horrific debacle. And to think, during the last eight years, the Republicans have had nothing kind to say about our current President, A Columbia University and Harvard University Graduate, a Nobel Peace Prize Winner, a Christian, a father and faithful husband with only one wife during his lifetime and duly elected twice by a majority of this country's citizens. You compare the two: Donald Trump vs. Barack Hussein Obama. There's no contest, the Donald just don't have what it takes to lead a parade, and certainly not our great nation.

But wait, who are we? Once upon a time, I thought we knew who we were. We're a Christian Nation with deeply held religious values, right? Sure we are flawed, but our moral voice is good enough to be heard around the world. Far from perfect, but we are driven by a noble cause for truth and justice in the world. So who among us can honestly defend the Republican's 2016 Presidential Candidate? Not to a virtuous man or woman; not to another people or nation yearning for a democratic way of life, and certainly not our children who would be given a time-out for most of what The Donald says or does. Can I get a witness?

Even in the face of all of this, I still have hope and here's why. Our young people, some voting for the first time, will save us once again from ourselves. While they've enjoyed the entertainment, they are far too clever to be misled. You see, President Obama knows their language. He knows how to explain things in ways they'll understand. I've been watching and listening. Without him, I'd be worried. I'm certain of this and here's why. Under his leadership, more of our children have advanced their education; more of our children have health care and a balanced food diet. More of our children have been touched by his slogan, "Yes we can." More of our children see the promise of America and its greatness. He has inspired the next generation of leaders who believe in equal justice for all. Making a livable wage; he fought hard for us all. They see the value in treating other people and nations with respect. Walls that divide us will gradually begin to fall.

Thank you, Barack Hussein Obama for your service to our great nation. You honored us with your service. Because of you, I will visit Cuba one day, pass more college educated children on the streets, look in the eyes of more healthy children who benefited from a balanced diet and greet a Muslin or Mexican American on the streets of America and politely say hello. We're a better nation because of him. Now, it's up to us to save our souls.

The Thrill Is Gone

01/20/2017

In a mere six months, perhaps less, the thrill will be gone but when will the pain ever end?

It's 5:00 a.m. and I'm up. Actually, this is a little late for my morning writing session. I'm usually up around 2:00 a.m. Somehow I feel so much better at this time of day. Armed with brain activity on a kaleidoscopic scale, I'm ready to write some amazing things or should I say I try at the very least! I've had so many different ideas of late about the political climate hanging over our country. Of course, I don't wanna bore you with a lot of facts or details on this subject. Obviously, this would be far too mundane or trivial to do much of that. So bear with me for just a few minutes, please.

During the course of my life, I've experienced a few occasions some deep afflictions triggered by several events which were both traumatic and memorable. These events had a profound resonance with lasting consequences for me and perhaps so many other Americans with similar experiences. Here are just a few examples: The assassinations of President John F. Kennedy, Dr. Martin Luther King, Jr, Malcolm X, Medgar Evers, and Robert Kennedy.

As a child, I attended a funeral of a neighbor's son who was killed in the Viet Nam War and that made Southeast Asia a very real place to me. Standing among a small group of kids who integrated a segregated school system in the Deep South amid harsh treatment, included an attempt on my life as well. This crystallized the spiteful or malevolence perpetrated by prejudice in our community. At times this burden seemed too much to bear. After witnessing two stock market crashes, I learned the significance of capitalism and the dangerous role it can play in our lives. 9/11 brought home the relevance of our country's foreign policy and the impact it imposes on other people throughout the world. Finally, the elections of President Obama and subsequently Donald Trump are prime examples of a true antithesis, such a striking contrast that even my fifteen-year-old son noticed.

If you're like me, these memories are indelibly carved in our minds. Seeing people hungry and standing in long food lines in New York City after the 2008 stock market crash was chilling. Equally frightening was watching the World Trade Center Towers fall. I just stood and watched our finest military aircraft patrol the sky around our city protecting us from further harm.

Never before or since 2008 have I ever seen so many people participate in our political process; that was a shining moment for our democracy. So what went wrong? Let me offer a narrative that perhaps you may find of interest.

Our democracy has been hijacked by Donald Trump and the Republican Party. After eight long years of sabotaging the Obama administration, Trump's relentless "Fake News Campaign" declaring that our President was not a U.S. Citizen and finally suppressing voter participation in our election process paid off. Coupled with Congress neglecting the vital needs of our people, this sets the stage for a hostile takeover; capitalism has replaced our democracy in exchange for the promise of jobs for the middle class, no doubt about it. The Republicans starved our great nation into submission. Their tactics worked, and they received the full support of the voters. Now, they control most of the state legislatures, the governorships, congress, the senate and the White House. With their ineffectiveness and poll numbers, how did this happen? Don't you find it rather peculiar that they have been so handsomely rewarded? But oh, six months from now, America will be in crisis again because the fox would have eaten the hens and The Donald's Spell will be broken at last! Here's why we will endure!

On Saturday, January 21, 2017, a powerful Political Tsunami shook the world. The epicenter was Washington, DC where just the day before a new leader took control of the levers of power. His rise was propelled by fear, sexism, racism, bigotry, xenophobia, and greed. Seemingly unstoppable, he promised a new era of change, but darkness and despair were the byproducts of exploitation. The suffering of so many American People hungry for the promise of better jobs was like a gaping wound, crying-out for relief. Our country had grown weary of a political system innately drowning the people they swore to serve. Using brown, black, gender, sexual orientation, immigrants and religion to divide the people, Donald J. Trump assembled enough votes after using questionable tactics to win the presidential election. But on November 09, 2016, the morning after the election, shock and disbelief were the best way to describe the results. So many people were sad, angry and afraid of one man and his message.

Remember the Life Cereal Commercial- Mikey Likes It? Filmed many years ago, it featured three little boys sitting at their breakfast table refusing to eat a new brand of cereal their parents bought without their consent. The two older boys kept saying to one another, "I'm not gonna try it; you try it!" Back and forth they went with no hope of compromise. So finally they looked at Mikey, their younger brother, and decided, "Let's give it to Mikey, he'll eat anything!" Well, I believe that's exactly what happened with Hillary Rodham Clinton's candidacy. So many people, especially white women, defected at the lasts minute for any number of reasons and voted for Donald Trump. With a weak minority vote, especially the black vote in places like Milwaukee, WI, Detroit,

MI, and Philadelphia, PA, the Electoral College was all but given to Donald Trump.

Suddenly, Make America Great Again, President Trump's trademark slogan, didn't feel so great after all. I equated his slogan to mean, the era of All In the Family starring Carroll O'Connor was back in America once again. Norman Lear, a writer in the series, with several others, made history with their poignant social commentary. Archie Bunker, played by O'Connor, was an iconic symbol of a blue collar American defining his vision of America. "Those were the days my friends. We thought they'd never end." These are lyrics from the hit sitcom's theme song which aired on CBS from January 1971 until April 1979. Most Americans couldn't get enough of that show. It yields several spin-offs, including Archie Bunker's Place which was perhaps the most notable after running four seasons following the nine previous years of All In The Family. For me and many others, America wasn't so great then. Segregation, racism, prejudice, being relegated to second-class citizenship and injustice was a stark contrast to so many of us in spite of our pluralistic society comprised of black and brown people, Native Americans, Asians, Latinos, Hispanics, Arabs, women, and Jews.

Now, because of one man, our differences that once united us, now divides us instead. Our consciousness was awakened, and people around the world took notice. Many Americans marched in the streets to demand their voice be heard. Darkness and hate were silenced by love and peace. I felt this in my soul and shared it with a dear friend from New York who traveled to DC to join the march. Thank you, Dee, so much for sharing your personal experience. You and I are now united in a cause greater than one man, the President of the United States. Love and peace will win in the end. I'm certain of it. I feel it in my soul. Don't worry, our numbers will continue to grow, and the world will continue to take notice; change is gonna come, thanks to you and all humanity who shares this common cause.

Peace.

Wait, Hold Up

02/06/2016

When love is tested, take a long deep breath!

It's Saturday, just one day away from game time, Super Bowl 50! I was busy all day, doing work that needed to be done hoping to avoid any unlikely situation interfering with the game. It's hardly a secret who I'm rooting for, the Charlotte Panthers, all the way babe! All week long, I've heard sports commentary influenced by sentiments favorable to Peyton Manning. Well, for all you Manning supporters scratch all of that. Throughout his career, four times to be exact, he's had his chances. I'm not about to concede anything by grandfathering him a final Super Bowl 50 victory. This may be his last game and a Super Bowl win would be good for the record books, sealing a storied career with a Hollywood ending. So, just before sunset, my wife and I went shopping. She bought finger food, selected her drink of preference, and it was time for me to go solo and find my beverage of choice, Miller Genuine Drafts. I must admit, I'm not a frequent consumer of the spirits but one six-pack a year, reserved for the Super Bowl, is good enough for me. I usually have two ice cold Miller Genuine Drafts just before kickoff and one for each quarter. Walla, my six pack for the year.

I must divert from the purpose of this story for a minute please, just one, and share one of my memorable Super Bowl experiences. I'll be brief with my comments I promise; you see, the best-made plans are always subject to an unpredictable anomaly. I believe it was Super Bowl XXV in 1990. My wife and I were watching it together after three short years of a beautiful marriage, but still, this memory and trauma linger. Sharing this experience is comparable to an exorcism of sorts, kinda like expelling a bad demon or memory unworthy of ruining another Super Bowl moment for me or someone else. Who knows, maybe it might just help you with your relationship in one way or another. The game was close with the outcome uncertain. It was the Giants and the Bills; of course, I was rooting for the Giants. I guess you'd say two New York teams playing in the Super Bowl how could we lose, right? After all, the trophy would be in New York, either way, no matter the victor right? Wrong...you would be dead wrong to think such a thing. Because to a true New Yorker, there's New York City and then there's the rest of the state or world for that matter. So our Giants were being tested. Buffalo, with Jim Kelly, was hungry, just starving for a victory. It was the fourth quarter, time for my final beer.

During a commercial break, I made a beeline for the refrigerator. Utter shock upstaged the moment when I couldn't find my beer, the last one mind you. Calling out to my wife, I figured she moved some things around in the frig and surely she would tell me exactly where to look. Before she answered, I had a sudden flashback to a similar situation, not identical but similar. My mind quickly went there, long before of my wife's response. It happened several years ago, but the memory still lingers. On a hot summer afternoon in Northwest Arkansas, it was time to mow the lawn. After procrastinating all week, it was time to get it done. I waited all day for the sun to set wishing for a cool summer breeze, but it wasn't in the cards. It was still hot as h*** just a little bit past six. Finally, I decided to bite the bullet and get it done anyway in spite of the heat! After drinking a little Coke with a stiff shot of Jack Daniel's, my son wanted to join in. I poured him some Coke in an identical glass; at the age of four, he wanted a glass that looked just like his dad's. I suppose it just made him feel older! We sat side by side and had a nice long drink. Just before returning outside, I refilled both glasses and added more Jack Daniel's to mine when he wasn't looking of course. After our break, he went back to play. Once I sat both glasses in the refrigerator, placing his ahead of mine, I headed back to finish the lawn. Sounded reasonable to me, after thinking he'd take the first one he would see. My wife was busy cooking dinner the whole time; little did I think she'd move those glasses around.

About an hour later, I came back inside. Mayhem had taken center stage, the house was under siege. That kid of ours was climbing on everything: the table, sofa, chairs, you name it. Out of control, he was everywhere. Dressed for such an occasion, his Superman suit and cape had propelled him to new heights, and boy oh boy, he thought he could fly. His mother couldn't control him. After watching him for a while, I couldn't understand why he thought he could fly. But I knew it was time to rein him in, especially when he told her to shut up and leave him alone. He was buck-wild! I wanted to take a sip from my glass of Coke and Jack, to cool down a bit. Besides I needed to collect my thoughts before I decided to take him on. Only one glass reminded in the refrigerator, his not mine. When I asked my wife about the second glass, she said he drank all of his quite a while ago. She had moved some things around while cooking and he mistook my glass for his. That kid was lit I'm here to tell you, drunk as a skunk on my Jack and Coke. Oh, my God, I didn't know how to tell my wife what WE had done. It took a while to calm him down, but boy did he have him some fun. Finally, he settled down and took a long, long nap! So now, I'm wondering if my teenage son took my beer like before. He was an instant suspect in my head before my wife finally said.

"Oh, I decided to have one after watching you drink five," was her reply. Trying to control my outrage, I said, "You did what?" Of course, she repeated her unthinkable remarks. My last Miller was gone. What made it worse; she really doesn't drink beer. After taking a few small sips, she put the top on the bottle and safely tucked it away. This totally ruined the game for me, messing up my whole routine in an unthinkable way. A perfect moment had been ruined. I came back to watch the game with dampened enthusiasm as we sat side by side. The Giants won because of a missed Buffalo Bill's field goal attempt, but a victory just wasn't the same because my last Miller had been taken and that was a shame.

I never discussed this with her; it was too upsetting for me to do. However, I broached the subject with a few female friends wondering what they would do. Would they do the same and take their man's last beer doing a Super Bowl Game? Of course, the verdict was resounding NO! It was unanimous from Dominicans, Caribs, West Africans, and I asked a few African American Women for credible representation. One woman, who shall remain nameless, without hesitation suggested next time to buy more beer. Walla, problem solved! Why didn't I think of that?

Now back to the hunt for my twelve-pack of Miller Genuine Drafts. Harlem begins at 110th Street, and I live just two blocks inside of it. I stopped at several stores in my search, finally giving up once I reached 117th. No Miller's to be found. Oh, there was plenty beer but not my brand. Growing up in the south, there was Schlitz Malt Liquor, Country Club, Colt 45 and Budweiser. Lou Rawls promoted Budweiser, Billy Dee Williams did the same for Colt 45 and Windell Middlebrooks for Miller; gone but not forgotten. So what happened? All but one of these brands has disappeared from Harlem. I purchased a twelve pack of Samuel Adams, Boston Lager, at Rite Aid. Not my preference but it'll do.

Within a few blocks from home, I stopped at a corner store on 115th and 7th Avenue in a desperate attempt to find my preferred brand there. Most of the corner stores or bodegas are operated by Persians. So I asked him what's up with this imposed Miller Beer exile from Harlem. He said, "I have some 40oz if you want one but that's it. That's the only Miller Product we sell. What kind did you say?" He kindly repeated. Whoa, I'm not a 40oz Kind of guy I told him. One look at me, he knew it instantly! I'm calling out my dear friend Regenia who retired from Miller a few years ago and moved to Texas. "Homegirl, go back to California and straighten out this mess. I couldn't find a six or twelve pack of Miller Genuine Draft Beer anywhere in Harlem, and that's down right shame."

Schlitz died a slow death in 2013 after being sold. Milwaukee, WI was once synonymous with Schlitz, Detroit, MI had Strohs Brewery, San Antonio, TX brewed Lone Star, and Old Milwaukee was Milwaukee, Wisconsin's infamous beer. Those were the beers back in the day! Now they're all gone. Miller's pitchman, Middlebrooks, was found unconscious in his home in the San Fernando Valley on March 09, 2015; Miller Brewery needs a good replacement to take his place. We miss you man, may you rest in peace!

Go Cam and the Panthers! Folks, enjoy your game.

The Morning After, You Da Man, Period!

02/07/2016

The taste of victory is oh so sweet!

Okay, it's over. The morning after Super Bowl 50 and the party still linger for the winners while the fog of war has yet to clear for most diehard Panthers fans, including me. What can I say? Denver, you won, fair and square. You Da Man, period! Darn, Von Miller and DeMarcus Ware, you didn't let my man Cam breathe the whole freaking game. Did you guys study their playbook?

Before yesterday, he was talking and sounding like a young Muhammad Ali, "floats like a butterfly and sting like a bee; your hands can't hit what your eyes can't see." Dammit Cam, why didn't you run, faster? They showed no mercy in their pursuit. And so, my thoughts are a little scattered this morning about what you could or should have done last night. It's the morning after and Harlem is quiet, but for a brief interruption by my wife's two cats. She calls them Jean-Paul and Madeline. On the other hand, they're Ike and Tina to me. They always fight early in the morning. Jean-Paul is a handsome black male cat who desires special attention from his mate early in the morning, but he doesn't know both of them are supposed to be spayed and/or neutered, at least that's what my wife keeps telling me. Anyway, Madeline ain't feeling it. She routinely fights him off every time, morning, noon or night and especially today. It's the Chinese New Year; year of the Monkey. How ironic because Denver made a complete monkey out of us last night didn't they? I wish all of you who celebrate this holiday God speed toward another good year. My son is home today as are all New York City public school students. He was up late last night on his computer as usual. So I asked, "Shouldn't you be in bed? Tomorrow is a school day after all right?"

"No Dad," he said, "The Chinese New Year is tomorrow." "Well, perfect time for you to brush up on your Cantonese or Mandarin right?" Why shouldn't he? He's benefiting from their holiday, right? Okay, here's wishing all of you peace and prosperity throughout the New Year, especially Jing Hui who called from Manchester, England yesterday and promised to spread the word over there about my novel, Nina Shakes Harlem. Thanks, man, looking forward to seeing you in April when you return to the city. I'm at my computer with headphones on listening to some blues, The Thrill Is Gone; the thrill is gone babe, gone away for good. I'm free CAM, free from your spell, until next year at least.

Just for the record, over 3,900 hundred of you saw or responded to my post, Wait, Hold Up. There are two people in particular that stand out, Eddie and Anna. I just sent both of you invites to my Facebook page, Lawrence E. Crockett, Author. I ain't mad at ya! Hope you're still celebrating. Did you run out of your Tequila, Patron Silver? Don't get me wrong, I wasn't against the Broncos, I was for them before I decided to root for Cam and the Panthers. For five wonderful years, I lived in Denver and Colorado Springs. Went to a lot of the Bronco games at Mile High Stadium and loved every minute of it. As a matter of fact, my son pleaded with me not to move. But it was all about the job; besides, the company I worked for needed me in Atlanta so off we went. However, I still fantasize about the state, Boulder in particular. I miss skiing, hiking, going to Garden of the Gods or Esther's Park. Out of admiration, I would just sit and admire two of God's greatest creations every visit. Darn, I sure do miss that place, but New York City is my home now, been here for over twenty-five years.

I have a confession to make. Remember Super Bowl XXII? It was 1988, San Diego, CA and an epic showdown was built for John Elway and Doug William's Washington Red Skins. Do you remember Denver Bronco fans? Oh, I do. Doug Williams was definitely Da Man that day! It was over at halftime, final score 42-10 Red Skins. Maybe subconsciously I was hoping Cam would remember Doug's performance making this his transformational moment; boy was I ever wrong. Doug was on fire. Superman, that's who he was that day; so Cam, you got the entire off season to watch that game over and over again until you get it right before next season. I'm praying for you man.

I'm going to wrap this up now, but I must give you an update about yesterday. Ended up doing a little work; saw a few clients and my wife had a nice spread prepared for the game. She's my proof reader you know, and she didn't want me sharing the story about her drinking my last beer again. Oh well after twenty-five years of marriage, what's she gonna do? I called my friend to let her know I bought a twelve pack as she had suggested many years ago. Heard from my homegirl who once worked for Miller Brewery and she's gonna have them look into why there are no Miller Genuine Drafts being sold in Harlem. That's a darn shame, and I take it personal! Couldn't drink my third and fourth beers though; it just didn't feel right. This was not the game I expected. Love hearing from all of you guys on my Facebook Page-Lawrence E. Crockett, Author. My novel Nina Shakes Harlem and part 1 of The Dark Side of Fame are selling well, thank you. If you haven't read them, try it. You just might find yourself laughing like a New Yorker. Most of us have a great sense of humor you know. Now there are bad apples in every barrel or city in our case. But on balance, you just might find humor in my writing. Oh, to my Bronco friends, congratulations. You got a whole year to celebrate and wear your crown. Do it with pride and class in the Mile High City! By the way, forgive me if there are any typos in the story. I'm still on punishment from my wife for telling you about her drinking my last beer many years ago during the Super Bowl. She needs to get over it, but for me, it's gonna take another 25 years before I do!

America's Olympic Bluster

08/21/2016

Scratch a lie, find a thief!

On August 05 - August 21, 2016, approximately 11,303 athletes representing 205 countries assembled in Rio de Janeiro, Brazil to compete in 28 sporting events for the Olympic Gold, Silver and Bronze medals. The Olympic Flag proudly flew show-casing the talent from five continents: Africa, America, Asia, Oceania and Europe. Well the games are over, the count is in, and the top five country medal winners are:

United States of America (121)

Great Britain (67)

China (70)

Russia (56)

Germany (42)

Without hesitation, I must say Rio did an outstanding job hosting the games of the XXXI Olympiad. They were up against incredible odds: financial, local crime, environmental issues- especially their polluted water, construction delays, potential terrorist attacks and that dreaded Zika virus. Jesus Christ, somebody scream! Brazil, you guys did a magnificent job in spite of all of this. Had it not been for one American, of course, we don't want to claim him, but after all, he won a medal, Ryan Lochte.

Ryan, you son of a gun! Saying three Hail Mary's during confession or saying I'm sorry just won't cut it bud, not in the least! Oh, you did lose millions in endorsement deals, so once the cameras were off, I'm sure you really cried, seriously. God bless the almighty dollar. Your indecency was too much even for your sponsors: Ralph Lauren, Speedo USA, Syneron Candela and Airweave; amazingly they have limits too, Amen! As a thirty-two-year-old American Olympic Swimmer, you should've known better. Shame on you once for lying especially on camera making disparaging allegations to cover-up your criminal behavior and shame on you twice for leaving Brazil knowing your three young conspirators were still there. It must have been a little embarrassing when the two swimmers were taken off the plane foiling their unsuccessful escape. But you, my friend, left them holding the bag, so much for team spirit huh!

My friend, you are lucky this wasn't Singapore. Remember Michael P. Fay? In case you don't, he's an American who was caught and convicted of theft and vandalism in 1994 while living with his mother and stepfather in Singapore. He was sentenced to four months in jail and six strokes with a half-inch thick rattan cane in public. This is their country's traditional punishment for such mischief. After receiving his punishment, he left and returned to Dayton, OH famous for all the wrong reasons with a scared buttock as proof of punishment for his indiscretion. Unlike you, of course, he didn't have any Olympic medals or commercial endorsements to show for his bad behavior.

Now that I have that bit of housekeeping out of the way let me move on to the reason for my thoughts about this event. The games were rich with talent from all over the world. I don't want to list names because there were so many talented athletes. But I must pay homage to Jamaica's own, Usain Bolt- the world's fastest man! His talent and body are superior to any other athlete in the entire world, and that's a rare combination and blessing. He's done it all these last nine years. What's left for him to do now? Stop climate change and halt global warming maybe? With his speed, he can run around the world spreading the word that the sky is falling; well you get my point. Okay, forgive me; I got a little carried away.

So let me get right to the point. On August 22, 2016, I tuned into the Fox News Channel to watch the O'Reilly Factor. Don't say it; I know already what some of you are thinking. Why right? Just wanted to hear what he was thinking about the games, that's all. Now he laid it on heavy with his Talking Points, and Charles Krauthammer was his invited guest. Of course, he was expected to be a one man cheering squad in total agreement with Bill. If I may, let me paraphrase Bill O'Reilly's point of view:

The United States of America is the only super power left in the world. We're a great nation that produced the most talented athletes. They possess a will to achieve greater than any other nation or culture in the entire world, and this explains why we dominated the Olympic Games by winning more gold, silver and bronze medals. Our American spirit creates more achievers, opportunities, and success than any other nation in the world. And that my friends, makes us exceptional, as such, giving birth to American Exceptionalism- A nation that offers freedom with a strong national character.

Ooh, wee, after making such a proud proclamation, he looked straight into the camera with a big smile and invited Charles Krauthammer to praise him for such a fine analysis of our Olympic victories and standing in the world. Once again I'm paraphrasing, but it was obvious Mr. Krauthammer thought his assessment was replete with riddles and oxymora. He saw no political or philosophical linkage between victory, medals won and American Exceptionalism. Politics had no place in an athlete's performance. Talent, training, and dedication separated the winners from the losers. Whoa Nelly, stop! A gauntlet was used by Charles to crush Bill's Talking Points, and he was visibly stunned. Frankly so was I. Don't they rehearse this B.S. before coming on air? Surely Bill picked Charles because he knew he agreed with his logic, right? So what happened? Maybe Bill's zealous logic was too much even for Charles. Finally, they played nice and agreed to disagree. After all, it's O'Reilly's show.

Here's what I think happened: Bill said he was moved by the USA Olympic Basketball Team. They were a group of twelve African Americans who didn't lose a game, won the gold medals and stood in full attention with their hand covering their heart while our National Anthem played. That was a touching moment he admitted. Makes a grown man like Bill wanna cry!

Now let's deal with his hypocrisy. But first, I must slow down and carefully pick my target. It's hard though, I must admit because this situation is target rich inside their right-wing echo chamber. He knows so little about our African-American Culture, and that explains most of his inept assumptions. Many of us were raised in conservative and traditional homes with parents and in some cases grandparents. As children, most of our households had bibles, a picture of Jesus, John F. Kennedy and Martin Luther King, Jr. Our schools, churches and community organizations, although lacking in resources before integration, began each day or event with the pledge of allegiance to our nation's flag-with our hand covering our heart and singing God Bless America.

So hear my humble cry Bill. America is the land where our fathers and mothers cried; the land where the slaves and natives died from every hilltop and mountain side. Bill O'Reilly may not know this, but America is our country too. For this reason, I love this country with all my heart.

O'Reilly, as you know, is a fervent Donald Trump supporter. So the next day, he had the Donald on his show. He'd been away on vacation during Donald's free fall in the national and some state political polls, and it was time for him to get Donald back on track. Mind you, Donald's themes are: Make America Great Again, we don't win at anything anymore, Obama has destroyed America; black people live in urban areas with poverty, crime, no jobs and can't walk down their streets without getting shot. But vote for him, and he'll fix all that!

Now remember just the day before, Bill was talking about America being a super power and pointing out the fact our athletes are the best in the world. He offered our Olympic medals as proof. Our greatness as a nation offered freedom, unlimited opportunities and success unmatched anywhere else in the entire world. But he embraced the Donald's narrative in spite of what he said the day before; oh what hypocrisy!

Let's take the Olympic Basketball Team as a case in point. Kevin Durant, Carmelo Anthony, and ten other black NBA Stars represented America. They are all millionaires, live in good neighborhoods, can send their children to the best schools in our country and they don't worry about getting shot in the streets, not usually at least. Remember, the Donald's narrative ignores these facts. Many blacks work in major corporations, maybe not any of the Donald's, but so many other companies actually employ black people. There are black entrepreneurs, millionaires, and celebrities. Surely the Donald knows all of this. So why did Bill let him get away with saying otherwise on his show? Simple, there is no limit to their aim to reclaim the White House. The truth is inconsequential; this election must be won or stolen at all cost.

So the next time you see O'Reilly or the Donald, tell it like it is; they're both hypocrites. Twist the truth, scratch a lie or outright lie, say or do anything to achieve, succeed or cash in on a money-making opportunity. It's rumored The Donald is in debt for some 651 million dollars, but in the White House, that kind of debt will soon disappear. After all, that's what American Exceptionalism gives him the freedom to do!

A Black Magic Woman, Part 1
09/17/2016

If your right palm itches, money is coming. But when your left palm itches urgent mail is on its way. If you believe in these things you don't understand, you're likely a voodoo believer, a dreadfully powerful black magic!

Another beautiful autumn day had arrived in Harlem, no doubt about it. It was Saturday morning late September to be exact. My roommate and I woke up, dressed and headed for the Bronx to a scheduled cross country race. We had to be there by nine o'clock sharp. So Charles and I walked over to 110th and 8th Avenue and caught the C train up to 125th Street. After transferring to the A, we were bound for Inwood and 168th Street. Being outdoors on such a fantastic day was perfect and having a chance to watch him run made it all the more spectacular. About a half hour or so later, our train pulled into the station. Practically empty the entire trip, the serenity offered a pleasant respite for a typically long New York commute. Well before nine o'clock, we arrived with several minutes to spare.

The race was in the park, just a few blocks away from our stop. But first, we had to walk through the neighborhood farmers' market to reach our destination. It occupied an entire block. I must say it was a very impressive market and blended quite nicely into the quaint surroundings. Several vendors were neatly aligned along the street bearing lots of fruits and vegetables. Apple cider, baked goods and so much more were included among the specialty items offering a variety of choices for the local consumers. It was a wonderful display of fresh organic produce and goods just waiting to be bought and served too well deserving New Yorkers. Naturally, the people filled the streets carrying their bags with a little bit of everything from the market. Such a pleasant sight it was watching them move about. We admired everyone and everything from a distance while walking. Before long, we were nearly at the end of the market, just a few feet from the park entrance when suddenly I noticed her. Standing behind such an unusual display, her beauty transcended all other merchants previously seen.

Slightly separated from the rest of the market, she stood out and alone at a small table with six baskets neatly displayed. Stunningly beautiful, this tall and rather enchanting woman possessed an exotic look and instantly captured my attention. I've seen all sorts of beautiful women in our city, but this African Woman was different, unlike any other. Her smooth honey brown skin, with black and light tinted hair streaks, were loosely twisted in braids. Wearing a colorful short blue, white and orange dress with beautiful designs assured the chance of being noticed, especially since her long sexy legs were prominently displayed. Well, if her intentions were to be noticed, that dress ensured just that. It was fascinating, to say the least! I couldn't take my eyes off her. She was just strikingly beautiful.

Iconic pictures appeared in each basket filled with glistering white sand, and a decorative bag of tea sat in the middle. As we approached her table, my curiosity continued to grow. It was an unusual yet pleasant display arousing my curiosity even more. A brief glance alerted her of our approach. Not just us, but several other people were walking toward her at a leisurely pace. Maybe she hadn't noticed me specifically. Inauspiciously, I felt our presence was hardly noticed. Nestled among the crowd, my visual obsession was safely hidden from view. Or so I felt. I continued to stare during our approach. But now, with such a short distance from her table, I felt obliged to divert my eyes elsewhere.

Just a few feet away, it was time. I casually pretended to look past her. From the corner of my eye, I saw her sit down. After crossing her legs, she picked up a book and innocently began turning the pages as if she were looking specifically for something to read. Feeling certain we were unnoticed, we slowed our approach hoping for a closer look. Charles noticed my prolong interest. But I just wanted more time to admire her and examine those interesting baskets before passing. Surely you can appreciate the source of my curiosity, can't you? Indeed, if you had seen her and her baskets, perhaps you too would agree how amazingly beautiful and alluring they both were. Instinctively she raised her head as we approached. After looking straight in our direction, she smiled and spoke.

"Well hello,"

Her tone was pleasant, rich in texture, warm and familiar. Surprisingly her voice matched her beauty. It rose above the noisy crowd. The whole time she continued smiling. It felt like she sprinkled magic all over me with the sweetness of her voice and smile. But was I the intended recipient of her charm? Or was it someone else walking nearby? Besides, there were people in front and behind me. I couldn't say for sure if she were speaking to me. Her friendly and personal demeanor surprised me though. It wasn't apparent or expected, and most certainly I hadn't planned to stop or even speak. Then I began to wonder, what if she noticed my stare and was actually smiling and speaking to me? Although unexpected, it's entirely possible.

With people all around us, I had my doubts. Still, the possibility did exist. She certainly could have focused on me without being noticed. Of course, we continued walking toward her table, and then it felt as if she were looking straight at me. I wished like mad, hoping it was true. If only I knew for sure. Then I began to wonder, was my gaze from a distance detected? I couldn't help myself, you understand? After all, I'd had my eyes on her for a while. So elusive, not once did our eyes ever meet. She couldn't have noticed me. I felt sure of that. But then I began to wonder if she was more aware than I previously suspected? My stare was successfully concealed, or had I been discovered? Could I have been cleverly outmatched by someone with far better skills?

Afraid of appearing too awkward or rude, I returned a smile; no match for hers of course. Admittedly, my excitement was noticeable once I learned I was caught. But pleased, I was excited by her discovery. Being the object of her affection was a pleasant surprise. I desperately tried to respond without falling all over myself. A simple hello should be enough.

"Hello...how are you?"

"Fine thank you," she replied with that same smile.

Once we spoke, the ice was broken. I wanted to stop and talk for a while. Instead, we continued walking. After passing her table, I debated my decision. The race would soon start, and my roommate was anxious to get there. A delay would likely have been contested. The thought of stopping, if only for a while, would have been an inconvenience without a doubt. Whether he wanted to or not, I did. Nothing else mattered. I had to figure out a way to turn around and return to her table if only for a while.

"Look," I said to Charles as we approached the park entrance. "Go ahead okay. I'll catch up with you before the race begins." He seemed surprised by the sudden request but at first offered no rebuttal beyond his facial disdain. Unable to hold his tongue as he walked away, he turned toward me with both hands raised above his head and asked.

"Did you come to see me run or meet a girl?"

With a mildly sarcastic tone, he expressed his displeasure. Obviously, he noticed my sudden admiration for the exotic African woman. Of course, he did, how could he not? But I couldn't help myself. How could I hide my interest in such a beautiful woman sitting at a table with six intriguing baskets?

"No, it's not like that at all. I just want to see what she's selling. Is that okay?"

"Sure..." he said after releasing an unpleasant sigh.

"Alright, I promise; I'll see you there before the race begins okay?"

I stood on the sidewalk for a moment and watched as he walked away. Then I turned around and headed back toward the market. Undoubtedly once we walked past her table, she returned to her reading not expecting to see me again. Maybe someone else stopped at her table requiring her attention. But that wasn't the case, she was still sitting alone. After briefly looking up, she saw me walking toward her. If she were really reading, I thought, how could she have noticed me so quickly? Maybe she wasn't reading after all. Maybe she had been watching me the whole time. Whatever the case might have been, she acknowledged my return with another one of her beautiful smiles. This time, the look in her eyes was more intense.

Why was I drawn so to this woman? I could feel something happening inside of me that felt unusual after such a casual and brief greeting. In many ways, it felt a little awkward yet intrinsically familiar. But why I wondered? Searching for something to say, I had to come up with something quick before I found myself standing in front of her looking completely stupid. Come on, think of something, think...; please don't look like an idiot! Wow..., I got it. The words finally came. Now can I say them with poise? Oh well, here goes...

"You look lonely sitting all alone? What are you selling?" She closed her book without breaking eye contact. Once she stood up, we were eye level with one another, all six feet of her. Then she began to speak.

"Well hello again, I wasn't expecting to see you. But I'm glad you came back. I'm Donna, what's your name?"

"Teddy."

"Well, it's nice to meet you, Teddy."

I extended my hand hoping to shake hers. Wow... her hand was incredibly soft, and her fragrance enticed me even more. Holding it longer than I should, perhaps she knew it wasn't just an ordinary hand shake. I wasn't ready to let go, but I had to. It would have been too silly and impolite otherwise. Standing there, while continuing to hold her hand against her will was an unthinkable thought. Unfazed with my unintended foreplay, she kept smiling the whole time. After reclaiming her hand, she began to ask about Charles.

"Where's your friend?"

"You mean my roommate..?"

"Well yes," she said.

"He's at the park getting ready for his race."

"Oh, so he's a runner... What about you?"

"Once upon a time, but not anymore; bad knees put an end to my running pleasure." Not wanting to stare, I continued looking down at her table. "You live in the neighborhood?"

"No..." She said.

"Another borough...?"

"Sort of, but Cape Verde is my home." I didn't notice the music before playing. But on her table were two speakers. Small and sitting near the edge of her table, a song was playing and sounded so familiar to me. I'd heard it many times before but couldn't quite remember the name. It was one of my old girlfriend's favorites. Strange hearing it without her. Carla loved that song.

"What's the name of that song playing?"

"Sodade by Cesaria Evora. Of course, we affectionately call her Cise. How do you know this song?" She appeared a little surprised by my question.

"It was a favorite of a dear friend. She played it a lot." It's sort of nostalgic and felt soothing to my ears hearing it again after all these years.

"Oh, we love Cise."

Then she began to talk more about her country. I knew a lot; perhaps more than most.

"Have you ever been there?" She asked.

"No, but I've heard a lot about the place when I lived in Boston. There are a lot of Cape Verdeans around Boston and Brockton. I guess you could say I've met my fair share of them."

"Oh…, so I don't have to tell you much about us after all, now do I?"

She flashed another one of her beautiful smiles urging me on to share more of what I knew. To be such a small island, her country's culture was fascinating, especially the women. If you've ever met a Cape Verdean, you'd know exactly what I mean; many of them are a mixture of African and Portuguese heritage. They're beautiful people, and the women know just how to love and satisfy their men! That Creole blood is something special. I've met other Creoles from down south in New Orleans and up in New York from Brazil, but they're very different. A Cape Verdean Creoles takes the cake in my humble opinion. I could tell she wanted to know exactly how familiar I was with their culture and their women. But, there wasn't enough time before Charles' race. Besides, there was no need to confide in someone I hardly knew. My intimate experience was personal. Of course, I wanted to hear more about her and her baskets. What was so special about what she was selling?

Here's what I know: Cape Verde is a country of 10 volcanic islands, some of which are uninhabitable, in the Central Atlantic Ocean, just 350 miles off the West Coast Africa. The Portuguese colonized some of these islands in the 16th century, and for years they were a slave port. Once the slave trade was abolished 1875, it took a while, but they finally received their independence in 1975. Tourism and commercial fishing became their primary industries. They have about a half million people, and many of them live in poverty. Their beautiful water and glistering white beaches attract many tourists. With pride she said,

"My baskets are beautiful aren't they?" She just stood there admiring them as if she were a tourist.

"Yes, they are."

"See the pictures and sand in each basket? Oh my..., aren't they beautiful?"

"Yes, they are. You, your baskets and your sand are all beautiful." She was pleased to hear such praise.

"Each picture was taken on some of our best beaches, and the sand came straight from there. Just look at those pictures aren't they gorgeous? "

I didn't want to interrupt, but I was running out of time. So I stopped her in mid-sentence and asked a few direct questions of my own hoping to cut to the chase.

So what are you selling exactly, sand, baskets, tea or vacations to Cape Verde?"

With her auburn brown eyes, she looked straight at me. My, my..., was she trying to stare into my soul? It was a deep penetrating look, and it felt exactly like that. She continued to speak. Her lips were moving, but her words were not in sync. Interrupted by a brief delay, it felt so strange. Finally, her words slowly reached my ears, sort of like reverb expected in music.

"My teas," she explained, "are six of my finest blends. So it's like buying a little bit of Cape Verde with me finely blended inside each bag."

It sounded strange the way she said it and I weren't quite sure what she exactly meant. So I asked,

"What do you mean exactly?" Once again, she pointed toward her baskets and began to explain.

"In each basket, there's a specially blended tea, see the variations in color and the fineness of the blend?"

I moved closer to get a better look at each one. She was right. Some teas were darker than others, and each blend was different.

"Yes, I can see that."

"Unlike any tea, you've ever seen, right?"

"Well, you could say that but what about the taste? Do they all taste the same or different?"

"Of course each one tastes different. I make these teas from an old recipe handed down to me from my mother. She received it from her mother, and my grandmother received it from her mother. These recipes are very special and have been in our family for generations. They're all gone now, leaving me with this awesome task of sharing our family legacy with a charming young man like you. May their spirits continue to rest in peace in São Nicolau. So you see, I'm certain you've never tasted anything like this before. Without saying much more, once you've tried it, you'll understand exactly what I mean. Each bag has magic and possesses an incredible taste. You should try one; but remember, the darker the color, the stronger the tea. These blends are not intended for the faint-hearted. Oh no, not in the least."

I just stood there for a moment, closely examining each bag and trying to decide if I should give it a try. Is it just tea or did she really sprinkle some kind of magic in each bag? Or could this just simply be another New York scam? There's so much of that going on these days. But I was curious, so I kept asking more questions.

"How much do you sell each bag for?" Without hesitation, she replied.

"How much would you like to pay?"

That seemed a bit odd and a most unusual response. "Come again, you can't be serious are you?"

"Of course I am. How much would you like to pay...?"

Okay, living in New York City, I've heard it all. So this was her little tactic; you know, her way of negotiating. I remember once stopping a livery cab on 110th and 8th Avenue. I wanted to go to Columbus Circle, but I refused to get in his car until he quoted a fare. Without a meter, you are at their mercy, and if you refuse to pay, trouble soon ensues. Trust me, that kind of trouble you want to avoid. He asked the same thing she's asking, "What do you normally pay?"

After a few exchanges, no agreement had been reached. I grew tired of this silly game, so I said, "a dollar; one big fat dollar. That's what I usually pay."

He took one long look at me before hitting his gas pedal and sped away. So much for negotiating! But this was different. I didn't want it to end that way. So we continued our little negotiation.

"I don't know exactly. What do you normally sell it for?"

"It depends..." She said.

"On what..?" I asked.

"What you hope your experience to be like once you try it." She replied.

She began to rub her necklace while continuing to look right at me. It was a gold unicorn hanging from a gold chain. For a few seconds, I was mesmerized by her charm. I'm not easily distracted or persuaded, but she had me acting sort of strange. Was she casting a spell? I tried desperately to clear my head, foolish of me to think such silly thoughts. I stood there thinking for a moment; wondering what to do.

"You're not making this easy. I just want to try your tea but how can I if you won't say how much you're selling it for?"

"Well let me help you a bit. The more you pay, the more you play! It's just that simple, and it's all up to you. I will accept whatever you give me, one dollar or two but a gift of fifty would certainly please both you and me."

"Fifty dollars for one bag of tea; you're joking right...?"

"The more you pay, the more you play." She repeated with a smile.

Am I out of my mind considering such a thing? Fifty dollars for one bag of tea, crazy right...? But she wasn't leaning on me at all or trying to pressure me to make her sell.

"Okay, I'll try one bag. Give me your strongest blend. You accept debit cards, right?"

"Of course..."

She reached into her purse, pulled out her phone and attached a device to swipe my card. Once she finished with the payment, she picked up the tea and placed it inside a bag. A card with a picture, just like the one inside the basket, was also included. After picking up a small spoon from her table, she scooped two teaspoons of sand from the same basket the tea once sat. After pouring the sand into a small pouch, she put a string of her hair inside the bag and then used another string to tie it shut.

"Now, here's your tea, two spoonfuls of our glistering white sand and a picture of the island it came from. One of our most beautiful beaches, I must say. I have one more thing to give you; your instructions."

From underneath the basket where the tea once sat, she pulled out a pink card and placed it in my hand.

"Use all of your tea in one serving on this date, September 29th at precisely ten o'clock p.m. After you drink all of your tea, take the pouch of sand and place it under your pillow and repeat these words before falling asleep: Carla mama se so far away...Carla mama se come near... Carla mama se come closer, let me whisper something in your ear. Now let me hold you the way lovers do and let me call your name...! You must follow these instructions precisely as I have given them to you, okay?"

Oh shit, where's the doll? This was some crazy voodoo, plain and simple. My mother believed in this stuff but not me. No way was this crap is real. Once she claimed her cousin had a spell put on her by Mother Ruth down in Greenville, Mississippi. Apparently, her lover suspected she was unfaithful so he took a pair of her worn panties to Mother Ruth and she put a fix on her, at least that's what my mother and her cousin believed. After his visit to Mother Ruth, she never looked at another man. But mind you, he had another girlfriend in his life the whole time and continued seeing her. So if the spell worked so well on her, why didn't she take a pair of his dirty drawls to Greenville and have the same spell put on him? Crazy right...? You'd have to be crazy to believe in this sort of stuff. I never saw any of this coming. But it was too late to turn back now. With considerable misgivings, I took the bag. After all, she had my money, what else could I do?

"Alright, I'll follow your instructions. But what's with all of this hokey pokey stuff? I just wanted some of your tea to drink, you know?"

"What you bought is better than any tea you could possibly buy anywhere in the entire world. Not only that, a dream to die for is included."

"Wow," I thought. I had so much more questions for her, but there wasn't time. I had to go.

"Listen, I gotta get to that race or my roommate will be very unhappy with me. Will you be here later?"

"Maybe," she said, "maybe not. If not, you have everything you need. Just follow the instructions, okay? Remember, a full serving on September 29th at precisely ten o'clock."

This was more than I'd I bargained for but what the hell! It's New York plain and simple. Stranger things have been known to happen. I own it now!

"Okay Donna, I will. I promise. See you later…?"

"Maybe or maybe not, but enjoy the race." With a smile, she shook my hand and said goodbye.

I hurried off to the race with so many unanswered questions bouncing around inside my head. Why of all names was Carla's in the instructions, I wondered? Could it be because she is from Cape Verde? We lost touch when I moved to New York City some five years ago. Such a strange coincidence though. I couldn't think of anything else as I rushed back to the park hoping to see Charles at the start of the race.

The horn sounded, and they were off. It was my good fortune he saw me just before the horn blew. Perfect, I thought, at least he knew I kept my word. I sat on a park bench, close to the trail where they were running. It was a winding course circling the park twice and ending near where I sat. My urge to open the bag was strong causing me to pull her card out after fishing around inside the bag. I searched for her number or address, but the card only had her name printed, Donna, the Dream Merchant. Then I noticed the writing on it, just for you Teddy! Funny thing though, I didn't see her write my name or the message. Besides, she didn't know my name before I returned to her table. Something was really strange about all of this. This must be some kind of voodoo shit! My lord, she looked too beautiful to be a black magic woman but what else could she be?

Approximately twenty minutes later, Charles crossed the finish line. It was a 3.6-mile course, and he was so proud to win his first cross country race. After a brief rest, we headed for the subway. Walking past the space, Donna once occupied now stood empty. She was long gone without a trace. My eyes searched the crowd hoping to catch a glimpse of her, but that was a useless pursuit. My heart felt a profound disappointment. The thought of her mysterious power consumed me. I wanted answers to all the questions bouncing around inside my head.

All that remained of her was inside my bag: one bag of tea, a spoonful of glistering white sand with a string of her hair inside, a picture of an island in Cape Verde, a card with no number or address-just a note written to me, and of course fifty dollars less in my bank account. A sentimental longing for Carla brought an irresistible impulse, and fifty dollars was such a small price to pay for sweet nostalgia. She was quite a woman!

After reaching the subway, we boarded the A train and headed back to Harlem. Charles was in good spirit after the sweet taste of victory. We shared a few good laughs on our way home. I wouldn't dare tell him how much I had paid for the tea or discuss my encounter with a black magic woman. Proof of her origin was evident from the sorted details given in her instructions. In spite of this, the intrigue remained with my purchase as evidence. Crazy right...? Go figure!

Once we reached our apartment, I put the bag on a shelf next to my desk, just a few feet away from my bed. Uncertain what to do with it; at best, it could be a wonderful souvenir-sort of like a fond memory of Carla or a constant reminder of what blowing fifty dollars looked like. I soon dismissed the thought and found more important things to occupy my mind.

A few days passed and September 29th had arrived. For a while, I just ignored the bag. I refused to look at it or inside until I sat at my desk around nine o'clock that evening. It was indeed September 29th just an hour before ten o'clock. Suddenly curiosity got the better of me. What was once easy to ignore seemed no longer possible. Time was quickly approaching for a decision to be made. After paying fifty dollars for that privilege, I pondered and toyed with the notion of getting my money's worth. Without warning, some of those old sayings my mother routinely recited began playing inside my head:

If your right palm itches, money is coming. But when your left palm itches urgent mail is on its way. If your right eye twitches nervously, good news will soon come. But if it's your left eye, bad news surely will come.

This was straight-up voodoo. But my mother swore by these beliefs. Black magic had a hold on her, and she tried for years to convince me of its power.

Carla's favorite song, Sodade, kept playing over and over in my head. Although Cesária Évora sang the song in Portuguese, Carla would gleefully translate while we made love.

"Who will show you this distance? This way to Sao Tome... The longing... the longing for this land of mine, Sao Nicolau..? If you forget me, I will forget you, until the day that you return..." These lyrics had deep meaning to her, and now they have new meaning for me too.

Resist no more, I said to myself; dammit try the tea. After removing it from the bag, I headed to the kitchen determined to boil the water.

Unconsciously humming the song the whole time the water boiled. The suspense began to build even more and more. Once the tea was made, I returned to my room. A found the song on YouTube and began playing it over and over again. It wasn't long before my cup was empty. Placing the bag of white glistering sand with a string of Donna's hair underneath my pillow was the next step just before my final act. I stared at the card for a while before reciting the chant.

Carla mama se so far away...Carla mama se come near... Carla mama se come closer ... let me whisper something in your ear. Now let me hold you the way lovers do and let me call your name...!

My empty cup was placed on the stand next to my bed once the chant was complete. I held a picture of the beach over my heart long before I fell fast to sleep. Was I really asleep? I could hear the song continuing to play. The words were so real to me. "Who will show you this distant way, the longing..." It just kept repeating.

I felt so relaxed. It almost seemed as if I were in a trance. Was it the tea or fatigue from a long day of activity that subdued my restless spirit? My mind and body were lured into a deep, peaceful place. Then it felt like I was falling or flying, I couldn't figure out which. For a moment a deep pain in the pit of my stomach was unbearable. It didn't last for long, peace soon came over me. Once I stopped resisting, the sensation quickly became calm.

I just knew I was traveling somewhere in body and spirit with a destination unknown. Everything was quickly moving around me. If you've ever been near an earthquake or a vortex, you'd know exactly how I felt. I could feel the force of air blowing against my face; it felt and smelled like a cool sea mist. After a while, it all stopped. My eyes were closed for a few minutes, and I struggled to open them again. I could feel the warmness of a summer's sun shining down on my face. The hot sand was pressing against my body. This couldn't possibly be my bed. So I knew I was somewhere other than home. Suddenly a voice spoke to me, "stop fighting, just relax... You're safe. I'll see you soon."

I didn't realize I was fighting this feeling. I suppose when I couldn't open my eyes I began to struggle a bit. It was scary for a minute. But that voice, I recognized. It was Donna's. Clearly, it was no doubt about it. I was sure of it. I heard her again. This time, she whispered, just above the sound of the gentle sea breeze.

"Open your eyes slowly, you are here now."

Just like that, my eyes opened. The sun rays were so intense causing my eyes to squint. Using my hand to block the Sun, I was surrounded by a beautiful beach. It looked identical to the picture I held in my hand just before falling asleep. So far away from home and the farmers' market in Inwood, I stood up and looked as far as my eyes could see. Yes, this was the place, no doubt about it! It was even more beautiful than the picture I once held. Having heard Donna's voice, I expected to see her close by, but she was nowhere to be seen. Feeling a little stiff, I raised my arms and stretched a bit then started walking toward the sparkling blue water. Feeling the glistering white sand underneath my feet and between my toes was incredibly soothing, and the sea breeze was an added bonus. This couldn't be a dream or is it, I wondered? Why did I feel so happy? After all, I was all alone, in a strange place and didn't see a soul, not right away at least. But something inside of me kept telling me to continue walking toward the Sun; so I did. Playing in the water as I walked reminded me of the last time Carla and I went to Martha's Vineyard. Of course, this water was much warmer.

Dressed in white, my shirt and pants were completely soaked. I didn't mind it one bit. I was having fun, all alone on a beautiful beach in Cape Verde, I assumed. After walking a good distance, I decided to sit for a while. A big rock not far from a cliff was the perfect spot to rest. A sea breeze has always relaxed me, and without warning, I drifted off into a light sleep only to be awakened by the sound of music, Sodade. It filled the air with joy and memories of a love I once knew. I sat up and looked around but saw no one. So I decided to follow the sound. It led me to a spot just around a bend from where I was resting. Finally, I got close. Close enough to see someone sitting. They were facing the Sun, and I could only see their back. The music came from there, and I continued to walk toward it. Once I was close, I could see it was a woman, and she was alone, just sitting there on a blanket with a basket of food and wine. Perhaps she and a friend, or better still, a lover was having a romantic moment. But I saw no one else. For a mile at least, I could see no one in sight. Maybe she was waiting, and he would soon return. However, mysteriously I felt drawn to her. Besides, there was no harm in saying hello. The same song, Sodade continued to play. Just a few feet away, I spoke.

"Hello…," she didn't turn around or seem surprised by my approach. Immediately she answered after hearing my voice.

"Join me, I've been expecting you." Such an odd thing to say considering she didn't know me... Without looking back, she held up a glass of wine and said.

"This is for you, just the way you like it."

How could she possibly know that? Anxious to see her face, I hurried toward her. Still holding the glass of wine, raised high above her head, she stood up just before I reached her and turned to face me with a smile.

Shocked by this sudden discovery, I stopped dead in my tracks.

"Carla... how did you get here? Better yet, how did I get here? What's happening here, babe...?"

"I've been waiting for you... Aren't you happy to see me?"

Of course, I was happy to see her. I just didn't know how all of this happened or why for that matter. She had such an expression of joy on her face. But my words dampened her glee...

"Babe, I didn't mean it like that. You know the way it sounded. I just can't believe it's you. How did we get here?"

"Enough with the questions come over here and show me how much you've missed me."

With her arms wide opened, she invited me to come closer. Once our bodies met, we became entangled as one. My lord, my heart began to race with joy. No words could match the emotions I felt inside.

"Can I hold you like this forever?" I whispered in her ear. She said nothing. Her body spoke the language of love and seduction. I realized just how much I really missed her.

"I remember, you know, the way you use to make love. I've missed you. Did you miss me, babe?" If only she knew how much.

"Of course I did. No one has ever loved me the way you do. I'm so sorry babe; I should have never left you. New York is nice, but only you understand me the way I need to be understood."

"Do you have someone else now? I know you don't like being alone." She asked.

"Well yeah, sort of, but they're nothing like you. It's been five years, three months and twelve days since I last saw you. Just love like me like you do! That should tell you just how much you've been missed."

"What are we waiting for?" That was all the encouragement I needed.

Her soft, gentle voice awakened a part of me that had been asleep for years. So tender and so soothing, you couldn't possibly imagine the sensation she ignited inside me.

"I've missed you babe; I've missed you so..." Man her voice felt like a sweet potion.

With my arms around her, we collapsed on the blanket and made passionate love until sunset then fell asleep. Everything was so, so beautiful... If this were a dream, I didn't want it to ever end. Suddenly I sat up in pain. My stomach was on fire. Carla was awakened by my uncontrollable moans.

"Babe, what's wrong?"

"My stomach is on fire. The pain is unbearable... What's happening to me?"

I could see the tears in her eyes. She sat up and put her arms around me as if she knew. Holding me close soothed my pain until the next one came much stronger than before. She began to cry.

"It's time for you to return. That's the only way your pain will stop."

"What are you talking about babe?"

"Donna couldn't tell you this, but she's a dream merchant I hired. I paid her to find you and for our dream. Our time is up, and you must return that's the only way to stop the pain. She's pulling you back and the more you fight it, the stronger the pain. You must return before the pain kills you."

"I don't want to. I want to stay here with you, forever. What can we do? I don't want to leave. Oh God, this pain is killing me. Carla, help me, babe, please..."

By now the pain was excruciating, I was struggling to breathe. My body was consumed by a painful metamorphosis, worse than before. But then I didn't fight it. I fell back into Carla's arms as my body began to transition into something unrecognizable. Feeling like I was falling or flying, I couldn't tell which.

"Carla... Carla...help me please!"

Touched By An Angel

12/22/2016

No one or nothing can knock you down or keep you down if you know how to get up!

Unafraid, she moved innocently across the room. Each step brought her closer to us as we were no more than fifteen feet away. Wondering out loud, was she an acquaintance of mine or my friend? Perhaps Di knew her, but I'd never seen her before. Rather odd, somehow it felt as if I recognized something familiar about her as she slowly approached us. We were at a repast for an old childhood friend. Standing in the serving area surrounded by good food and talking with Di while she sat at a table eating her meal allowed a few moments for us to get reacquainted. So much time had passed since our last encounter, and it felt good seeing her again. But that charming little girl caused a brief pause in our conversation bringing a new purpose to the moment.

Funerals sometimes bring friends, families, and strangers together orchestrating fortuitous encounters that under normal circumstances rarely occur. At best she was about three years old. Wearing a cute dress, her long braided black hair and adorable eyes created a presence which caused her to stand out among the crowd. I couldn't help but notice her as she walked toward us smiling, bearing a gift; a cap meant for someone but certainly not me. After all, how could she possibly know me? Finally, she stopped in front of me. Without uttering one word, she raised her hand and offered the cap. Somewhat surprised by her gesture, my reluctance was tossed aside once I kneeled down to accept her offering. Alone in a room full of strangers or so it seemed, that was the least I could do. Yet something led her to me, but what? Surely I didn't know her nor could she possibly know me. No chance of that I thought. But for reasons unknown someone or something brought us to an incredible intersection allowing us to meet. Maybe the gift was meant for my friend, but she showed little interest in a cap if any at all. Nonetheless, she could be the intended recipient I still insisted. Then again, unlikely I thought, after giving further thought to the situation. Di said nothing, casting, even more, doubt of the little girl's true identity or intentions. So I felt compelled to say something as she stood there looking at me with those adorable eyes.

"Well hello, what's your name?" Not once did she take her eyes off me. With a beautiful smile, she offered no words, just her gift which she insisted on giving. I reached for the cap and said,

"Thank you, but I'm sure this belongs to someone else. Where did you get it from?" She pointed across the room in the direction from which she came. Against the wall, an empty chair appeared to have been the last known place of origin. So I said, "that's so sweet of you but this belongs to someone else do you know who? We should return it, don't you think?" Once again she just continued looking at me with her adorable smile. The look in her eyes was so innocent, disarming and familiar but how could this be? For sure, I was certain I'd never seen her before; yet, she had the presence of an old friend coming over to say hello and catch up on what's happened in my life since we last met. As we approached the empty chair, a man I recognized from the church pulpit was passing and appeared to be looking for something previously left there. Once again I asked the little girl if she knew whose cap it was. Finally, she spoke.

"That's Paw Paw's cap." He heard her and replied, "It sure is." Part of the mystery had been solved. I exchanged a few pleasant words with her grandfather and said goodbye to her. Not expecting to see her again, I headed for the exit after briefly stopping along the way to say goodbye to a few more friends I hadn't seen in years. My brother and I had come together, so I joined him near the exit and waited for our departure. But once again the little girl reappeared. Pulling on my hand for attention, she spoke with urgency.

"I'm thirsty. I want some water."

There was a water fountain nearby. So I led her there and raised her high enough for her to have a drink. She was definitely thirsty, but once she had enough, she raised her head from the streaming water. I felt compelled to ask another question.

"Where is your mother or Paw Paw?"

She turned and pointed back into the room where we first met.

"Oh, I see. Take me to them." I wanted to meet her mother. I didn't think it was safe for her to be alone so close to the exit.

Without saying anything, she led me to her mother. After our introduction, I said goodbye to her and her daughter and left. A day later her spirit evoked such curiosity inside of me. Searching for answers, I called Di, and she seemed a little surprised by my quandary. After listening for a while, she began to share her thoughts.

"You haven't figured it out yet?"

"Well frankly no I haven't. But it sounds to me like you have."

"That little girl reminded me of your mother the moment I laid eyes on her. Her hair and skin color are just like yours. I'm surprised you didn't put that together."

Wow, I was speechless, but she was right after some serious reflection. But why would my mother's spirit be present in that little girl? She couldn't possibly be drawn to me for any other reason than my mother's spirit drawing her near. Not knowing why I just stored my thoughts and cherished the encounter. The feeling was peaceful, comforting, touching and special. A few days later, my mother's first cousin passed away. Her name was Aldonia Baldwin-Lashley, a very close relative and a cornerstone in so many of our lives in the Turner and Baldwin Family, especially mines. She was a shining light in my life for many years, and I feel an irresistible urge to share her with you.

Her picture is sitting in front of me. When I look at her, I remember all the reasons why I love her. Since birth, I've known her love and her love for our family. Think back to a moment during your childhood and imagine a cold night and feeling all alone, wondering if anyone could possibly love you so much that just having them hold you close, so close you feel the heat from their body and the love from their heart so intense that it calms your soul, ends your loneliness and chase all of the world's coldness away. That perfectly describes our Aunt Aldonia. She offered us shelter from all of the darkness and apprehensions this old world possesses and created such an everlasting memory for so many of us. That's what she meant to me and so many others in our family.

Her time ended on earth December 11, 2016, and I felt horrible and empty inside. When the news of her passing reached me my tears endless flowed. My heart was full and crying uncontrollably was all I could do. Sorrow consumed my soul, and I found myself struggling, trying to cope with her loss. I began to call on our ancestors.

Lucy Turner: her son and his wife (Joshua Turner Sr. and Phoebe Carter-Turner), her grandson and his wife (Joshua Turner Jr. and Anna Brown-Turner) and her great granddaughter, Ivelia Turner-Baldwin who is the daughter of Joshua Jr and Anna Brown-Turner. They represent three generations of Lucy's blood line. Now she is with them, including my mother, Charlotte "Shirley"

Watson-Crockett who reached out to me through that little girl to prepare me for Aldonia's transition. Oh lord, thank you so much for that God-sent blessing.

Aunt Ivelia, at last, you now have all of your children with you: Aldonia, Eddie, Eula Mae, and Maurice. She is your eldest child and longest living offspring who brought honor to you and your memory. When we were hungry, she fed us. When we were lonely, she comforted us. When we strayed from the path of righteousness, she counseled us. When no one else believed in us, she praised and encouraged us. Her love was like chocolate, sweet and rich with so much heartfelt joy. I will never ever get over missing her!

In spite of it all, she never complained, although many times there were reasons to do so. She never spoke ill of anyone or forsaken her faith. Unlike some, she never brought dishonor to our family. Your death during child birth left her behind with many challenges, but she never complained. Her belief in God sustained her. So please welcome her with open arms and let her find peace and everlasting love once again, the kind of love that only a mother can give to her child. No one or nothing knocked her down or keep her down because she knew how to get up! Amen...

I just returned from a two-month hiatus; being separated from my writing for such a long time in many ways felt unnatural and traumatic. My fingers endured such loneliness. Longing for the intimacy and passion felt with every key stroke was incredibly overwhelming. Should I admit I missed sharing my thoughts with you? At times, it was unbearable. I'm up again at 2 a.m. just a few days from Christmas; couldn't sleep, so I found my way to my computer. After losing someone I love, I just had to share her with you.

There is so much love between us...thanks for allowing me to indulge and share my thoughts with you for a few moments.

In loving memory of Aldonia Baldwin-Lashley, a mother, wife, grandmother, great grandmother, cousin, in-law and friend

October 24, 1924 - December 11, 2016

Benjie

07/10/2017

For days, I've tried to write his story. Trapped inside an emotional maze, I waited and waited until his spirit came to guide me through this endless loop. Oh, how I prayed..!

Oh, my Lord, it was one restless night of struggle, desperately trying to sleep. Restlessness overpowered me without much warning before finally succumbing to sleep. It was so unusual being deep in thought as tired as I was. Fatigue had claimed my mind. There wasn't much left of me just before bedtime. But an endless treasure buried inside of me was unleashed bringing a wonderful dream that included Benjie and me. Recalling all those memories first brought pain but at long last joy. Oh, what a dream it was! Joyous, so much joy filled my heart. After all, it was his birthday. Another year had come and gone without him in life, compounding the loss incurred some thirty-eight years ago.

Remembering all the time we spent laughing and talking about so many silly things brought pure ecstasy to some moments in my dream. He was special to me; after all, we are kin. Mm, I remember still, the anguished heartaches during our youth. Endless pain and despair chronicled a few of our careless love affairs. Of course, I remember, and his spirit does too. Maybe that explains why it came so late that long lonely night. Our last conversation was so long ago. Filled with so much uncertainty, I still hold his words close, very close. Anguish is what I remember most from his last call.

"Lawrence," he said. Man, we need to talk!" Oh, I still remember his voice. It was in early October of 1979. A long time perhaps for some, but his words still remain trapped inside my mind. It sounds every bit the twenty-three year old he was back then. I could sense something was wrong. After listening to his voice, I was certain there was serious trouble locked inside his heart.

"What's wrong?" I asked. He hesitated for a while before speaking again. I felt his heart inside mine. There was too much sincerity in his voice for him to hide. What trouble was he in? What circumstance prevented him from speaking the truth? His mind was under siege, and the love in his heart led him to me. Could he, I wondered, fight through his pain and win the struggle for peace?

"Are you okay?" I asked. I often wondered about him, sometimes more than most! A sudden decision to enlist in the Army came as an enormous surprise.

"Yea man but I'll call you later, I promise and we can talk some more, okay?" Those were his last words. Little did I know that would be our last chance to speak; just the thought of this still hurts, so deep. He didn't make it, and we never again spoke! A few weeks later his battle was lost, death was the victor. But in my dreams, he's alive still, happy and playful the way he used to be.

Lying in bed, the painful thought of his death just wouldn't let me rest. Reliving the moment when we last spoke is very hard. Could I have said something that touched his heart, forever sparing the pain his tragic death now cause?

My wife tried so hard to console me. But when my heart is full the tears uncontrollably flows. Nothing could stop the pain I felt inside. My spirit felt so much stress. There was no chance for peace until his spirit relinquished its hold on me.

His spirit awakened something so real. Once dormant but now my heart was a raging sea. A restless spirit is awfully powerful. No peace will be found until a blanket of love surrounds your heart and calmly settles your spirit down. In May, just four months before his death, we were together with our families in Northwest Arkansas before moving to Denver, Colorado. A job offer separated us. A month or so later he enlisted in the Army. Like his father, Jacob Benjamin Caruthers, he became a proud Army man. Would you mind if I took just a few minutes to tell you a few things about Ben?

He was born on July 10, 1956, in Paris, France to my mother's sister, Era Mae Turner-Caruthers and JB, a career serviceman and proud dad. He was their eldest son. I often teased him about being a lefty. But his left hand packed one hell of a punch. A brief boxing experience demonstrated that. He loved music, baseball and eventually girls. A late bloomer was he, but he found the love of his life in short order. For a while, he and Denise were inseparable. True love is what I saw in both of them. After listening to so much Isaac Hayes, he developed a convincing rap! Every album Isaac Hayes released soon found its way to Ben's musical shelf. I loved hearing him laugh. His heart was always jolly and full. Perhaps that explains why I miss him still.

Whenever I watch a baseball game or go the stadium, I think of him. For several seasons he worked the concessions for the Cardinal's farm team, The Arkansas Travelers in Little Rock. We went to our first concert together at the Barton's Coliseum in the summer of 1967. For ninety-nine cent, we saw James Brown, The Stable Singers, Bobby Womack and the Emotions. Well, it really cost me a dollar, because I tipped the pretty woman at the ticket booth. That dollar was hard earned. We spent an entire day mowing lawns to earn it!

Born in France, his first language was French, not English. It was evident each time he called his sisters names: Angie, America, and Denise. Whenever he said "Mommy," it sounded so French to me. Ever so quiet and gentle, just like his dad, until you pushed the wrong button; then a fist full of hell quickly came.

Whenever I heard the name or saw a Shoney's Big Boy Restaurant, I thought of him. He worked there for several years as a cook. Because of Ben, I'm addicted to fried shrimp. Such an unwelcome gift, if his athlete's feet were a fair exchange. In a rush one day, I briefly wore his shoes but once was enough. Thanks, Ben. Each day I'm reminded of you.

Benjie's life abruptly ended long before expected on October 23, 1979, at an Army base in Fort Polk, Louisiana. He was just twenty-three years young. To this day his death remains an unsolved mystery. Surrounded by darkness, this tragedy brought such pain to the hearts of so many of his loved ones. All I know is what was said. He was found shot with one bullet to his head.

So what triggered that late night visit from him? A longing perhaps or maybe he just wanted to say hello. But that night, oh how I cried. Why I wondered why? This wasn't his first visit. His spirit has come a few times before. Through the years he comes while I'm in a deep sleep. Usually, when I awaken, I remember bits and pieces. Reminders of his visits are all around. Evidence carefully placed to let me know he came.

Now before you dismiss my experience, I have a secret to share. There's a place inside our heads that holds all precious memories and thoughts. It's such a unique treasure we share without a doubt. I can't prove this with any science, just words and thoughts. But I know it's there. A place hidden so deep inside our head and beyond any man's reach; only God holds power allowing us to see. Could it be his secret workshop where he comes and dwells? Coming and going from time to time, checking in and out repairing our mind and heart when we're so full of doubt? Easing our troubles and offering guidance too, he comes and goes after fixing all things broken inside of you and me. There's nothing routine about this place; our time is sacred because of his grace. On special occasions, we're allowed to go inside and use some of the gifts he's left behind. Unbound by any earthly restraints, we're allowed to enter once we receive his holy grace.

Somewhere in the universe, the path God traveled is clear, and when our time expires on earth, we will travel the same route. It'll seem so familiar, the path he once took. Oh, this journey is unlike any other experience we've ever had. It's real alright. Where else does a spirit go? Our memories are proof. Why can't we explain all things we see or hear? The reason is he, the one we call Jesus our Christ and savior in thee.

Ben was quite a character, and indeed I love him so, all five feet eight inches of him. A dark complexion with long black curly hair, the kind Barry White would have killed for; he stood tall. Perhaps his hair was a gift from our great-grandfather Joshua Turner, known for having a good head of black curly hair. Ben's spirit roams free among the stars. When a cool summer breeze caresses my face, I imagine he's saying hello. I'm not ashamed to cry when my heart is full. And when Ben comes in my dreams, My Cup Runneth Over because it's so full!

In loving memory of my dear cousin, who was also a brother, uncle, father, husband, and friend

Benjamin Darnell Caruthers

July 10, 1956 - October 23, 1979

Prince

04/21/2016

Even a genius can succumb to addiction!

Another giant tree among us has fallen leaving a huge space for humanity to fill. He shall be remembered simply as Prince and associated with a magnificent identifiable color-purple; not black, brown or white, just purple. Rightly so, I think, because he defied conventional labels: Black, White, Person of Color, Colored, African-American, Negro, and even a symbol. None of these names fit. This gifted soul rose above all traditional and trivial coded languages relegating him to a category or class beneath his talent. He refused to let them control or limit his value and worth. Oh how beautiful and blessed we were to be entertained and educated by perhaps one of God's finest works.

I never met him or saw one of his concert's live. But I listened to his music, watched his performances from afar and quickly began to take notice. Loving music as I do, I saw many influences in his musical style and presentation. You see, I like to juxtapose unexpected artists and find similarities in their talent and work. Of course, there are so many contemporaries to compare him with, including the great legends. Oh, Prince had talent, but even he was influenced by others before him like Little Richard, Jimi Hendrix, James Brown and Elton John. Could there be others? Of course, I'm certain of it, but this four artist standout. Skillfully blending Rock, Pop, Jazz, and R&B into a musical fusion like no other; he became a master chef with each new creation. Quite often, we didn't know what to call what we were listening to. We just loved it. That was his gift; his musical genius. Surely this made him special. Oh sure, others have tried, even Miles Davis but few have had the magical success of Prince.

Upon his death, I heard someone say, "He was one of a kind. There will never be another like him." Well, they might be right but I think there's someone among us or will eventually come, anointed with talent and devoted to their musical genius and craft. They'll find a spot in the forest of humanity, rise up and grow to new heights. Once again we'll take notice; their talent will deserve no less. When you might ask? Only God knows for sure, but at their appointed time they'll come. Patience is required. God is not through with humanity yet. But I must confess, watching a video of Lenny Kravitz and Prince on stage performing American Women is a thrill!

Farewell Prince Rogers Nelson. I wish you peace and safe passage on your journey as you work your way through the darkness toward the light of glory and eternal life. Offer our savior a color, not just any color but purple. He'll explain, you won't have too, but I wondered why purple of all colors was chosen by you. Perhaps he'll explain.

"Purple is the color most often associated with royalty, magic, mystery, and piety my son. Only the most religious or reverent should wear. You have chosen wisely. Come and play a song for me. I've prepared a place for you; you see?"

Prince Rogers Nelson
June 07, 1958- April 21, 2016

A Tribute to Michael Joseph Jackson

06/14/2017

"Momma, Momma...Me Be Bad Too!

Several years ago while watching a Michael Jackson Video, I noticed an adorable little kid standing alongside his mom. Five years of age at the most, Michael's music connected him to something larger than his little body. We were both drawn to Michael's talent. This was nothing new for me, having watched him many times throughout the years. But for this little fellow, it was different. It was a new experience, and his response was uninhibited, absent of any decorum.

Michael at his best, it doesn't get much better than that. The song could've been any one of his many hits. But on this occasion, it was BAD! With several orchestra punches, a slamming bass line and drums locking in the groove, within eight bars, he instantly had us hooked. And then he began to sing:

"Your butt is mine, gonna take you right.

Just show your face in broad daylight.

I'm telling you, on how I feel.

Gonna hurt your mind, don't shoot to kill.

Come on, Come on...

Lay it on me All right..."

Michael's genius was too much... The little boy couldn't contain his jubilance. He began to move, bounce and weave. Oh, it was a joyful sight to see, mimicking Michael's every move with a few original steps of his own. Four minutes and fourteen seconds later, he was covered with sweat. His mom reached for him to wipe it all away. A mere five years of age with incredible rhythm too, he was hooked on Michael. Such pleasure it was, watching a man many times the little boy's age skillfully communicate through music, song, and dance. It was magical just watching. An anointed talent, Michael expressed God's grace with amazing ease. The envy of so many world leaders: political, religious, business and social alike. It didn't matter, as long as he honored God, Allah, El Elyon, Jehovah, Elohim, El-Shaddai, and Immanuel, just to mention a few. So many people were touched by his genius. His memory lingers still.

As we approach June 25th, eight years since his untimely death, I paused for a moment of reflection. In the words of the little boy consumed with such adulation. As he jumped into his mother's arms, he said. "Me Be Bad too, momma, Me Be Bad Too.

Michael your gift was a bright light in a world with too much darkness. Your music offered peace and understanding throughout this planet. Such an anointment you had, God chose wisely when he selected you. Rest in heavenly peace Michael, you earned the right!

Michael Joseph Jackson
August 29, 1958 – June 25, 2009

Hello Cousin

10/18/2015

A connection of a lifetime to the loveliest Rose of all...

"Hello cousin," this was her customary greeting each time we spoke for many years. Fourteen years older than my deceased mother, I'm thankful for our blessed relationship. She became an important link to the memory of our grandfather, Ben Watson, after her mother's death. Her mother, also my Aunt, was my mother's big sister, the only connection she ever had with their deceased father of whom she never met. On October 18, 2015, she took her last breath and joined her parents and husband. Surely they were awaiting her in heaven, there must have been so many, especially her parents- Annie Mae Watson Williams and Samuel Williams and Walter L. Sutton, Sr. her beloved husband for many years.

Cousin Sammie, as I affectionately called her, was a beautiful rose in a magnificent garden of life. She had a full and enriching journey on earth. An only child, a successful and motivated educator, a devoted Christian, wife and mother, Bishop College couldn't have trained a better teacher. She loved her city, Marshall, Texas and couldn't imagine living anywhere else. Her presence was felt in her community during her Christian Fellowship and service at Bethesda Missionary Baptist Church and the Karnack and Marshall School Systems for over thirty-two years.

A fervent member of Upsilon Zeta Chapter, Zeta Phi Beta Sorority for years, she brought a renewed spirit to their motto: A Community-Conscious, action-oriented organization. Their flower is a Rose. Oh how appropriate, for she was the finest Rose of all!

Seldom, if ever, did she complain. That just wasn't her way. Her strong faith brought her so much joy and comfort. Her voice, gentle and caring, was full of love and compassion as she never failed to ask how my family was making out in a busy place like New York City. She never stopped being a teacher you know. Always willing to listen and share her wisdom with anyone who needed it so; of course that included me as well from time to time. Her unsolicited advice was almost never imposed, not a usual act from such a gentle soul. If you're wondering about my feelings for her, you need not wonder no more. I truly loved her with all my heart and soul.

I must say, she had a full life which she shared with a loving and devoted husband, son, extended family and friends. The career she chose was truly a perfect fix. She wore it so well with pride and dignity. Marshall, Texas she really loved you. During her brief time away, she never failed to say how anxious she wanted to return. She just hated being away from friends and her church. It meant the world to her.

I'm so disappointed I cannot be with her friends and family to say my final goodbye. A true Christian Servant and Child of God deserved a wonderful home-going, no less. A heartfelt celebration of her life and being among all of her loved ones would be like standing in a beautiful meadow full of Roses and Sunflowers during the rise of a beautiful morning Sun. A radiant beauty would be reflected for the entire world to see. The lives she touched, the countless acts of kindness and the sacrifices made in the name of Jesus was noticed and praised. Right now the only thing that brings me solace is my belief that she is in our father's house in heaven in fellowship with family and friends who preceded her in death. Imagine the conversation she's having with the Lord about her work. Surely he will listen and say with such love and care, "Welcome home my child. You have earned your place in paradise, and I'm all too pleased to share. Well done my faithful servant now comes rest a spell." In Christ name, I pray... Amen.

In Loving Memory of
Sammie Mae Williams Sutton
March 06, 1922 – October 18, 2015

Hello Fella

05/29/2016

If this story is too different from all the rest, forgive me for I feel eternally grateful and blessed.

"Hello, fella!" Once upon a time, this was such an enduring greeting from a very special man, our Uncle. He was our mother's brother and in many ways a father figure too, all rolled into one person, most affectionately called Uncle Charles, Sonny and Dad. Their love for one another was strong and true. Oh, we could tell, anytime his name was mentioned or whenever he came to visit for a spell. Regrettably, she never knew her father. But every time she spoke of her brother, her unscarred heart showed no effects from an unknown father and his neglect. Her brother Charles gleefully saw to that. The pride of having an uncle like that boasted the love for our family even more with no regrets.

We grew up anticipating his summer visits with reverence; add a beautiful wife and five kids that made it even better. The joy they brought to our lives was sweet compensation for a love our mother treasured for so many years. Although on vacation, Uncle Charles walked through our door looking for things to fix, leaving a trace of his presence long after their annual visits. Many years have long since passed, but I still remember the joy it brought to our hearts and home. The cool Watermelons we ate one after the next, on those hot July summer days, were an endless treat. The sweet melon juice tasted so delicious to drink. After we'd dispensed a mouth full of seeds, nothing felt better than a good Arkansas melon's juice, dripping from our mouths once we were through. No spoon, knife or fork was required, just our hands and a good set of teeth. In my mouth, the taste of melons lingers still. The long memories of laughter bring joyful tears to my eyes. This prize I treasure and keep locked deep down inside.

My grandmother, Virgie Lee Turner, had seven children: Curtis, Clinton, Era Mae, Charles, Charlotte, Benny Fred and Joe. As you can see, she had a thing for the letter, C. Curtis, Clinton, and Charles began with perhaps her favorite letter of all. Her first daughter, Era Mae changed her name to Erone, Charlotte-my mother, changed hers to Shirley Ann, Benny Fred became Melvin or Mel, and Joe became Robert. If our grandmother had an aversion to these changes, I never heard her say, or for that matter, no one else I knew. But Charles was the only one known by a nickname, not one but two: Sonny and Dad. His brother Clint often referred to him in our conversations as Dad. One day out of curiosity I asked my uncle why? After a few chuckles, he cleared his throat and began to explain.

"Your Uncle Curtis and I were raised by our grandparents, Joshua Turner, Jr and Anna Brown-Turner. That made Sonny the eldest male figure in our mother's house in Shreveport, Louisiana where they lived. She moved there with Cousin Neely after her divorce from Cousin Punch, our grandmother's nephew. The way he carried himself always seemed to me like he was the man of the house. They lived a pretty good piece away from us. We rarely saw them. Our mother didn't have a husband most of Sonny's life, so he was the only dad Era, your mother and our two younger brothers knew. He always worked and looked out for everyone, especially your mother, Charlotte, Mel, and Joe. Curtis and I started calling him dad; in a way, he was their brother and the dad of the house."

Well I never learned where the name Sonny came from but I suspect Uncle Curtis pinned that name on him, and it stuck; that was just his way. It seemed to fit because of his disposition. He was an upbeat and affable fella. Besides, Sonny was a very common and enduring name people used back then. If you didn't know someone's name, you could call them Sonny. He was an easy going lovable guy with an infectious laugh and smile. Calling his Sonny made perfect sense.

Born on August 01, 1931 in Shreveport, Louisiana he embraced their traditional food and culture. They cooked rice for breakfast, Rice Pudding for dessert and lots of beans and rice with most meals. In spite of their close proximity to Arkansas, where most of his immediate family lived, Shreveport was his preferred spot to call home. Their schools were better, and so were the opportunities for work. But at the age of ten, they moved back to Baxter, Arkansas after a previous trip home when Sonny was about five and our mother, Charlotte was less than a year old. In 1941, their grandparents, two brothers-Curtis and Clint, and extended family welcomed their return.

In Arkansas, they were mostly farmers, a step down from the career path Sonny felt destined for. Shreveport was a thriving city with a demand for skilled laborers. He was good with his hands, a quick study and loved working with electrical and plumbing material. All he needed was to see something fixed once, maybe twice; after that, he knew next time what to do. When he came for a visit, that's exactly what he did. Once discovered, he'd find a way to fix it right away. He wouldn't rest until the repair was made. Making himself useful was his way of expressing his love you see.

Quickly adjusting to their move to Arkansas, he soon found a local repairman, RC Bins. Becoming an apprentice made up for the life he left behind. Once he was older, a local distributor, Silver Nickels offered him a better job. My mother fondly spoke of him buying her dress for Easter Sunday

Service. She loved that dress! It was new and beautiful, but more importantly, her big brother bought it for her. Just like a dad, the only dad she ever knew.

After completing high school, he enlisted in the Army. Our country needed so many men like him willing to serve during the Korean Conflict. War was never declared, but our soldiers fought and died with valor and a sense of duty. When his enlistment ended, he returned to Arkansas looking for work and to form his family. His first child, Ruth and her mother, Janie were waiting. But there were no jobs; migrating north was the obvious and only choice. After stops in St. Louis, Chicago and finally Milwaukee, he found work and started his family after marrying Jessie Marie, his beloved wife.

One peaceful night, not so long ago, he came to me in a dream. Since his death, it's been an awfully long wait, but he finally came. Driving a green Buick Station Wagon, he once owned, in a heated rush he arrived. Looking pretty much the same since the last time I saw him alive, nearly thirteen years ago and shortly before he died. Bearing a message unlike any I'd expect to hear, with power and emotions, his presence was so consuming and sincere. It's become a defining moment which I hold so dear because a few days later, his eldest daughter passed away. He came to tell me, but I thought it was only a dream.

I'm a grown man, and I don't like being too emotional, especially when I awaken from a dream in tears. Sometimes my heart gets so full just thinking about that moment because it feels so real. Writing about it brings back so many emotions I must embrace. So strong and moving but I guess I'm okay. However, this story is not so easy to write. When you deeply love someone, you feel a part of them, and their death can leave a hole in your heart that never seems to heal. Unfortunately, there's no cure for the loneliness and pain we must endure, but every once in a while their spirit reaches back to wipe away our tears. Temporary relief does ease the pain from sadness once their spirit touches our heart again. If this story is too different from all the rest, forgive me for I feel eternally grateful and blessed.

To his wife, Jessie Marie Smith-Turner and five children: Ruth, Ronald, Anthony, Darlene and Belinda, thanks for sharing your dad with us! Charles Elord Turner, sleep in heavenly peace. You're gone but not forgotten. There's so much love from me...

In loving Memory of Charles Elord Turner aka Sonny and Dad
August 01, 1931- February 24, 2003

Anybody Seen Benny?

05/25/2016

I've known Benny for about ten years. He's kinda like family.

It will soon be the first of the month, time to party at least for Benny and his friends! He usually gets his pension and Social Security Checks by the third of each month. Of course, it's no secret where he lives or how he spends his time. Each month like clockwork an entourage of social hangers-on rushes to his side with dry throats and a huge desire to party. Okay, I'm being polite. They're straight-up alcoholics, all five of them and they convene for about one, maybe two days to celebrate until all the money is either gone or their bottles are completely empty with no chance for a refill. They call their gathering a communion of sorts minus the mental and spiritual aspects. However, they drink from dusk 'til dawn passing the bottle around from one set of lips to the next. Using a glass or paper cup would be quite pointless. They're a lively bunch with an opinion about most things. Their long stories from years ago about what they once did, a camera and microphone would record one hell of a show. The things they say they did are hard to believe.

Who knows for sure if there's a thread of truth in anything they say. If you ask me, they tell nothing but tall tales about themselves while passing the time away. Too many empty bottles of alcohol are in their past it seems. That's my proof which cast some doubt, a huge shadow looms.

But to Benny, they are his best friends, or he thinks so for a few days each month at least. Once they run through his stash, they quickly abandon him and flee. In search of the next watering hole, off they go to look. But during those few days of each month, Benny is their star. Beneath it all, that's enough for him; it really means a lot. Oh, he walks through the projects on First Avenue and 99th Street like he owns the place giving away his money and sharing freely. All it takes is giving him the slightest attention, and he'll gladly accommodate your wish; a drink or a few dollars and maybe a drug or two. Despite the pretense, a few dollars can go a long way. Cop some drugs or a drink to pass some time away. Oh, he's an alkie for sure, but that's as far as he goes. Drugs, he doesn't touch, that's not how he rolls. But he's cool with that if that's someone else thang; after all, they're his friends, and Benny just loves his fame.

I've known Benny for about ten years. He's kinda like family to me. With a big heart and a warm personality, it's hard not to like him so. Single with no kids, he feels the same way about me. Actually, he reminds me of my brother. He's an alky too. Their lifestyles are so similar, doing the things they do. After working over in Jersey for years as a janitor, he retired once he started having health problems. That, plus the commute, got the best of old Benny. Once he learned how much pension and Social Security he could draw, his working days were done. So at the age of 66, he retired. Years of drinking all that alcohol, some good but mostly bad, finally did him in, but old Benny couldn't give it up. His liver is shot. Someone put a notion in his head about his Social Security Benefits, but it backfired, really bad.

During all those years of working in New Jersey while living in the projects of New York City, he never filed a New York State Personal Income Tax Return. He worked in Jersey, liked their low taxes and felt proud of his annual state refunds. Someone told him to declare New York State as his residence for all those years because his Social Security Benefits would be much more when it came time for cost of living adjustment each year. Sounded good to Benny, so he went and applied; after all, it was all about getting more money and put a sparkle in his eyes.

Now Benny doesn't know much about computers or technology. But once he lied, The Social Security Administration printed out his earnings for twenty some odd years and sent it to New York State Taxation and Finance. They took one look at his earnings for all those years, saw he had never filed a Personal New York State Income Tax Return, and this opened a can of worms. They calculated his New York tax liability for each year and sent him a letter demanding a response. Well, he did what most alkies do; if it's not about the alcohol, or receiving more money, they just ignore.

That was a big mistake! It took a while, but they found out where he banked and cleaned out his savings and checking account, every penny he had. That's how we met; he came looking for some help. A friend brought him to me, and old Benny was completely broke. Well, there wasn't much I could do. Once they take your money, it's hard to get it back. Besides, with penalties, interest and tax liabilities for New York State and City, that was the end of that. Without money, he couldn't pay his rent, buy any food or liquor. He could accept being a few months behind on his rent and not having any food in the house but taking his bottle was just too much.

So Benny went underground. No one saw or heard from him for days, including me. I went looking for him. Turns out he was hiding in his apartment. He wouldn't answer his door. So I called his super, and with a set of keys, we opened Benny's door. Oh, it was a mess in that apartment. His shades were completely shut. His cell phone service was cut off, and with no electricity in the place, it was dark as hell. Thank you very much ConEdison, old Benny was in the dark, no food except for a few honey buns and potato chip bags on the stand next to his bed. Old Benny was depressed, in a real bad fix.

I went all out for him. Filed his New York State Personal Tax Returns, all twenty-five of them, and called the taxing authority to plead his case. Out of pity, they gave him enough money to pay his rent, buy a little food and pay his ConEdison bill. He'd be in a shelter on their dime without a little help. So they did the most humane thing. Besides, it was cheaper for the state to help rather than take care of him. We got a payment plan agreement, and Benny was back in business within thirty days.

The following month Benny's world was restored to normal, just like before. He was back in business, a rock star once more. His entourage returned much like the ducks in Central Park, just in time for feeding. All was forgiven by Benny's friends once the liquor returned. Benny is back in the high life again. Oh well, just like I said, "He's family."

One Strong Memory

04/03/2016

Unforgettable ... he truly is.

He had such an infectious smile with a beautiful disposition at an earlier age. Corey Jermaine Hale was really something special. An only child, his mother Carolyn was quite a mother. Hardly relevant to say how we met, but I've opened my heart to share his story. For many years, he remained in my heart since his death thirty-four-years ago. Somehow, I feel compelled to introduce his spirit to you because I loved him so. I don't usually talk about him much but this moment feels right.

It was 1982 when life was very different then, so different from the life I now live. One night, I had a taste for a good bottle of wine, and after a long day's work, I just needed something to take the edge off my day. A nice meal and a good bottle of wine felt like the perfect ending to a beautiful evening in Colorado Springs. I lived there for three and a half years. Back then, it was a big military town undergoing a small tech boom. I'd received a decent job offer from a promising company there, so I accepted the offer and relocated, leaving Denver, Colorado behind. Man, I sure hated leaving Denver even though it was just shy of a few hours away. God was full of himself when he composed the geological character of that city. The snow Crest Mountains and crispy clean air elevated one mile above sea level with a speculator view is nothing short of a perfect oasis. It's a beautiful city with charm and quite seductive too. Once you've seen it, oh well, let's just say you'd understand what I mean and find it almost impossible to forget, much less leave.

So let me get back to the wine and liquor store. I went there in search of a good bottle of wine and met a very nice friend. It appeared we both were looking for the same thing that evening. Hey, I've never enjoyed drinking alone so given that I'm a pretty good cook, I invited her over for dinner, and we shared a lovely bottle of Chardonnay. After that evening, we developed a very good friendship and whenever we spoke she always talked about her nephew, Corey. Single with no children of her own, he was her pride and joy. Her sister Carolyn didn't seem to mind sharing him with her big sister. So after a few weeks of dating, I insisted on meeting him. He was about five or so at the time with an incredible personality. He'd never met a stranger. Always the conversationalist, his communication skills were well beyond his age. So friendly and fun loving, we quickly became friends. I was quite impressed with him, and with each encounter, we grew close. I learned to love him even more. He was just that sort of kid. Whenever his aunt and I made plans, we had to include him. Truth be told, I started to feel like he was part of my family too. His IQ was probably off the charts with his curious mind. He was surely destined for greatness. But one day that abruptly changed. A horrible accident tragically took his life.

A routine visit to the dentist office to get his teeth cleaned, but a few cavities were discovered and needed to be filled. No one knew he was allergic to Novocain. While his mother sat a few feet away, just outside the room, the dentist ignored all of the distress signals from a bad allergic reaction. With force, he strapped little Corey tightly in that chair. With all his might Corey fought hard to hold onto his life. His teeth were cleaned and cavities filled without much delay. Once the work was finished, motionless Corey laid. A fatal Novocain reaction took Corey's life that day. Strapped in that chair, this precious little child fought with all his might.

It devastated his mother and everyone who knew him. Five years old, a mouthful of clean teeth and a couple of cavities filled but dead! The dentist probably was more concerned about being compensated for service rendered rather than Corey's health. He was a Medicaid patient, and if the work weren't complete, there would likely be no payment. What other reason would the dentist have to treat Corey this way? No other reason explains this horrible outcome. I've thought about this many times before. Why else would he overpower this defenseless child? But for money for service provided ignoring Corey's distress?

His funeral was one of the saddest I've ever attended. We all took his death hard. His mother grief stricken and in shock, I still hear her moans from thirty-four years ago. To see her pain and tears touched my heart so. His death deeply affected me. I don't think I've ever spoken of him to anyone or about the incident until now. After all these years, I couldn't help myself. I just had to share this with you. The pain, so much of it, has been penned up inside. You can't imagine my struggle just thinking about how he died. Oh, what a joy he would have been if he were alive. Watching him grow up would have been a joy. I count myself among this lot. I imagine him in heaven having a conversation with God:

"You know God, you took me too soon. My mother misses me. I've heard her crying through the years. Sometimes I feel her grief all the way up here. Don't you think she needed me more? I would have done some great things down there for you. Why God, why did you take me so soon?"

I can imagine God listening to Corey as he pleaded his case and after reflection, for a bit, he responded to Corey. "My son," he likely said, "Come, I want to show you something. Look over there; see that bright shining star? So magnificent isn't it? That's all because of you. The world needed you more.

Your inspiration is seen everywhere. This was your purpose. You'll see your mother again. She and your loved ones will all join you soon. They'll appreciate the work you've done here, and your mother will especially be proud to call you son."

Corey, I know God couldn't let you go once he saw you. After all these years, I remember and understand why. One day, we'll meet again. But today is your birthday, and I just wanted the rest of the world to hear how special you are.

Carolyn, your son, was one incredible human being. Although we lost contact with one another many years ago; wherever you are, I hope life has treated you with kindness and mended your broken heart with love.

Peace and Love for one incredible and unforgettable kid...
Corey Jermaine Hale
April 03, 1977 – July 20, 1982

Thinking of Home
07/24/2016

We did the impossible with meager resources. It's hard to imagine how we made it this far.

Nostalgia is such a sweet and appropriate word to describe sentiments held so deep inside of my heart and head. Whenever I think of home, family or friends, it's simply nostalgic. Seems like so many years ago since I've felt that special feeling home, sweet home once evoked. Those precious memories I still hold close. When my parents were alive, it always brought joy going home to visit a while. Of course, life has a way of changing all of that. Time plays such an important role with our memories and circumstance. Sometimes memories are altered by time. What was once crystal clear can easily be changed or lost with each passing week, month or year. So what was once like so, will never be anymore.

I was born and raised in Dermott, a little town in Southeastern Arkansas just a few miles shy of the Mississippi and Louisiana State lines. During my childhood, Dermott was a typical segregated southern town with lots of manual labor, low wages and even fewer educational opportunities for our youth. But what it lacked in opportunities somehow was balanced with its rich conservative culture and entrenched values. We were all taught how to work, wash and clean. A good education was part of most of our dreams.

Most of what we did was very hard work. Working in the fields, agriculture shaped our minds and spirits of so many of our youth. A good education was revered, and many of the town's black high school graduates went straight to AM&N, a historically black college in Pine Bluff, Arkansas just sixty miles away. Money was always tight, but somehow family and friends found ways to send their aspiring children on to college. Dr. Lawrence Davis, the college president, rarely if ever turned any deserving student away. That's just how it was back then, during those days.

In the spring of 1914, at the age of seven, my father and his family left McCall Creek and headed to the closest train station. Once they reached Brookhaven, they boarded a northwest bound train desperate to leave Mississippi. A prominent plantation overseer met their train in Winchester, Arkansas, a little town in Desha County. A new life was assured if you owned a mule or plow. Sharecroppers were an instant hire. There was such a hot demand.

After several years of farming, my father found permanent work with the Missouri Pacific Railroad as a common laborer. Except for a brief enlistment period with the United States Navy, he returned to Arkansas and bought a farm in a nearby neighboring county, Desha. Eventually, he settled in Dermott. For many years he was a railroad man, and Dermott was the perfect spot to call home and raise his family.

My mother's grandparents came from Starkville, Mississippi in 1916 searching for a better life than what they left behind in that horrific state. By train and wagon, they made their way to Baxter, Arkansas in Drew County. Back then, the only thing worse than Mississippi was death. The conditions were harsh, unlike anything imaginable today. My great-grandparents with his two brothers and a sister started a new life in Arkansas. Up until 1979, Arkansas was my home as well.

Although life was hard for most blacks, Jim Crow Laws made it even harder. But that little town of three thousand people or so was my home, and for me, it felt solid like a rock during my adolescent years. We owned our home, most people did, and a farm with livestock: lots of chickens, pigs, and a cow. Our community at best was tolerable for blacks living in the south. If you knew your place and didn't challenge those dreadful Jim Crow laws, you could scratch out a living. Those horrible laws and ways cast a large shadow over our existence but allowed us to earn a meager living among the white people who ran the town.

We had separate schools, churches, cemeteries and the same could be said for all of the public accommodations in our small town. There were two schools for the blacks, Chicot County Elementary and High School, and Morris Booker Memorial College which was affiliated with the Southern Baptist Churches. It was the flagship for religious training in our community. Each summer, we routinely had two weeks of Vacation Bible School whether we wanted it or not. Rev. York Williams saw to that for sure. There was a separate school for whites, and as a child, my encounters with them were both brief and unusual.

During my adolescent years, I attended all three schools in Dermott including Ms. Hall's kindergarten. It was my first stop in the beginning of my formal training. It was unthinkable for any neighborhood kid to skip her legendary preparation. She was a retired and devoted elementary school teacher who built a small classroom in her home and opened up a two-year kindergarten program for the community. So at the age of four, my education began. My parents felt that was the best ten cents a week they ever spent on my education, and frankly, after all these years, I fervently agree.

Since my parent's death, I seldom go home for a visit. But a few weeks ago, I went to Arkansas to see family and take care of a few things that required my attention. In so doing, I met Robert Fulford, an old family friend.

He and one of my brother's share a passion for gospel music. Our encounter sparked a lot of fun memories, and I'd like to share a few of with you.

Long before I left the south, my palate was influenced by the infamous Slick Robinson's barbeque, Rose Café's fried barbequed chicken sandwiches, Susie Townsend T-Bone Sandwiches, Ms. Ora's hot tamales, fresh garden vegetables my mother routinely cooked, fresh local fruit straight their trees and vines, homemade ice cream, and of course, my mother's favorite Sunday desserts- peach clobber and banana pudding. Oh my, my, I didn't know what fast food tasted like until I left home for college. There's nothing quite like the taste of fresh pears, figs, grapes, plums, berries, Watermelons and apricots after they ripen on the trees or vines. Never have I tasted anything sweeter than honeysuckles. We simply had the very best fruit and nuts in the entire south.

Robert reminded me of our humble beginnings and the struggle he endured while growing up on a plantation nearby just a few miles north of Lake Village, Arkansas. His journey was more difficult than mines, but we both benefited from the same system that produced our desire to succeed in life in spite of our struggle. So much joy came to my heart when he shared his success of writing about his experiences. Sometimes he visits the local schools and shares his stories with an enthusiastic young audience. I love his spirit, and his music is amazing. His courage and hunger are unmatched by anything I've encountered since leaving the south many years ago. We fought for everything including the right to our education. The black schools were inherently unequal. We routinely received old books from the white school once they received the latest editions. But that didn't deter our hunger for learning. Our teachers, usually black, saw to that in our schools, churches and community organizations making sure we learned what was needed to advance our education while motivating us to make something of ourselves.

Robert has published some of his colorful stories in two books entitled, Dark Days of the South, before and After Segregation and A Collection of Anecdotes During my Childhood While Living on Yellow Bayou Plantation. His website is www.mrrobertfulford.com. I encourage you to check him out.

Just the other day, I shared some of this with my daughter while proudly naming my most important mentors, Daisy Matthews, Evangeline Kate Brown, Rev. Taylor, Rev. Williams and Mr. and Mrs. Wadlow. Oh, how awesome they were especially Ms. Brown. As a teacher and community activist, she touched so many of our lives, including mines. A retired tenth grade English teacher, she taught me how to write, communicate and prepared me for college. Without her mentorship, my journey would have been quite different. Ever so vigilant, she would correct my writing and speech anytime I was in her presence. Poor grammar was unacceptable, and she demanded this from everyone, especially me. I spent many years under her guidance learning to read, write and communicate correctly. Out of envy, some of my peers made fun of my transformation. That didn't seem to bother me much. But for my father, mother, and uncle, no one has ever been more given or a better teacher than she.

Oh, we had our share of colorful character also: Boot Mosley, Charlie Sly Hone, Pab Moore, Old Howard, Helicopter, Partner, Preacher, Shaky, Snow Davis and much more. There are so many wonderful stories associated with each name. One day I just might write about some of this for you.

Looking back over the years, working on our farm and using my hands early in life was valuable. Learning how to solve problems at an early age, taught me so much about life. I learned so much from these experiences.

Working the land, raising animals and fellowshipping with nature is an awesome experience, unmatched by anything else in my life.

We did the impossible with meager resources. It's hard to imagine how we made it this far. My parents and several siblings are deceased now, but the memories and love remain. The town has changed. Those legendary figures in our community have long since passed, forever changing the face and character of our small town. However, I see traces of their existence. We were enriched by their wisdom. Traditions and culture are the keepers of their secrets. Time brought about change forging new ways and opportunities for a few.

I'm convinced we need to reclaim and hold on to the things we learned during our struggle. I saw this in Robert, and I see it in myself too. Our spirits were formed in the way that steel is made, strong and everlasting in a very special way. Our families were more resilient, and our children were more determined to succeed. Our faith guided us and helped us understand.

Going home will never be what it once was, but it sure feels good knowing that home is still a part of me. I carry it in my heart with every wonderful memory. Every word I write has been touched by a deep memory from that part of my life. One day, I believe it'll be soon, I'll return home, and joy will be in my heart, the way it was back then. But first I must reconcile the change that time has brought and embraced a new spirit that I hold within.

Oh, we knew so little about drugs, massive gun violence or crime at today's level. The black-on-black crime was a figment of our imagination. Dysfunctional families and welfare were handled by grandparents or other family and friends. Ineffective schools were fixed by the local PTA within the community. We found the answers to many of our problems. Between our churches and community organizations, a solution was often found. So where did we go wrong? I think we changed too many of the old ways for the new. Our schools, churches and community organizations were either abandoned or drastically changed. One day, I hope real soon, we'll get back on track again. We must shape the next generation of our youth. I'm hopeful. What about you?

The Strangest Thing

09/02/2016

One Incredible moment!

After all these years, I still remember so well one of the strangest experiences I've ever had. Never before or since has anything ever happened quite like this. Fresh in my memory, like it was just a few years ago, but actually it happened so long ago. It was spring break during my freshman year of college. I was home visiting my family. Such a joyous occasion it was; my parents and siblings were all well and happy to have me back home for a while. I was equally pleased to be in their company too. The house was busy as usual. School was in session for my younger siblings, daily chores had to be done, and with beautiful weather, it was unthinkable to waste one minute of a perfect day.

Daddy was gone somewhere, working no doubt, leaving just my mother and me home alone in the middle of the day. She was busy in the kitchen preparing the next meal. It would be dinner time soon, and everyone would be home expecting to eat at the usual time, around six o'clock. Fully dressed but feeling mental fatigue from the academic demands college finals imposed, I felt tired. So I settled into a comfortable chair in our Livingroom expecting to take a short nap. Suddenly, I drifted off into a deep sleep. Can't say for sure how long I was asleep but it felt like forever. Have you ever felt so tired before falling asleep, and once it happened, you lost track of time?

That was my experience in the middle of the day. Usually after a heavy rain or being near the ocean, so close that an incredible sea breeze lures me into a deep sleep. I sleep so soundly and wake-up so refreshed. Nothing like that was the case that day. I was home. It hadn't rained while I was there and Arkansas is nowhere near a sea or ocean. Without any such inducements, I hardly expected to sleep so soundly, but I did.

All at once, a sudden impulse came over me, urging me to awake. Now, this is where the strangeness begins. Mentally alert and fully conscious, I had no control over my body. I could think and hear but had no ability to move, open my eyes or speak. Feeling trapped inside myself was very frightening. What do you do when you experience a level of consciousness but unable to move? For several minutes, I struggled to open my eyes, move my body or speak. It was impossible to do any of those things. With each passing minute, and after several failed attempts, my frustration rapidly grew. If only I could call out to my mother, surely she would know what to do. But I couldn't utter a sound. Momma... was what I wanted to say and I could hear myself calling her name inside my head, but I couldn't open my mouth. I kept trying over and over again. Finally, I heard myself mumbling, but she was too far away to hear. Louder, I demanded. I must do it again but louder. My next attempt was, but still too low for her to hear. Then suddenly I knew I had to scream her name and hope it would come out with the imagined intensity held inside my head. Talking to myself, I counted in my mind, 1... 2... 3, breathe, now take a deep breath and scream Momma as loud as you can. Okay here goes, MOMMA..., finally it was loud enough. I heard her call out to me as she rushed through the house. She made her way to our Livingroom as fast as she could. It must have been such an alarming and distressful cry for help. But I intended for it to be. I was in desperate need of help.

"What's wrong?" She asked. I could hear the fright in her voice. My eyes finally opened at the sound of her voice. She was standing over me with a look of concern in her eyes. "Lawrence, what's wrong?"

I was trying so hard to gather my thoughts before speaking. "I'm okay. I don't know what happened to me. I couldn't wake-up, speak or move but I'm fine now."

"You sure..?" She asked. "Yes momma, I'm fine." I didn't want her to worry, so I concealed the fear raging inside. It was such a chilling moment. Never have I experienced anything like this since. She returned to the kitchen to finish dinner, and I stood up and decided to go for a walk. Thinking a little fresh air was just what I needed.

While writing this story, one of my dear friends called to say hello. I shared my experience with her, and she had one of her own to share. In her case, she was home visiting her mother in Wisconsin. Asleep in her bed, she suddenly woke up and began to meditate. She felt her spirit separating from her body after meditating for a while.

"My spirit left my body, and babe, that scared the shit out of me. It went into the kitchen where my mother was. I kept trying to get back inside my body, and it took a while, but I got back in. I'll never do that again. I was through with meditating, that did it for me."

Like me, her experience was powerful and memorable. A fearsome struggle like ours leaves an indelible memory. As strange as all of this sound, it was real nonetheless, at least for her and me. If not true, that's one bad dream I don't care to repeat. Experiences like these are hard to believe much less share with someone else, especially to write and publish. But if you've never had a similar experience it might be required before becoming a believer. I'm not particularly a superstitious person; seldom do I believe the unthinkable but my experience happened. There are things in life that seem hard to believe unless it was you who had the experience. Such is the case with my encounter, and maybe my friend's too.

Ms. Ora's Hot Tamales

01/12/2017

A secret recipe to die for!

Ooh wee, do you remember eating Ms. Ora's hot tamales? Of course, I do, but how about you? What, you can't remember...? Oh my, how could you? You must be under fifty, way too young you see, to remember the bundles she once sold for four bits in exchange for three. How could you possibly miss what you never had? What if I told you? What would you say? Should I try, you know, to write something that takes you back to yesterday? Why should I impose such an enticing feat? Never, I mean never, will you ever taste anything so succulent or sweet; her hot tamales were such an insatiable treat. A legacy tied to her name, just vanished forever; oh what a shame. Replicate her recipe, you must be insane! Countless attempts could fry your brain. I wouldn't dare admit or recount my disdain. Perfect, yes it was; each bundle brought incredible joy. Memories, sweet memories are all that remains of a local delicacy associated with her name. Rare, so rare, you'll never find anything like hers. Whoa... don't even think about it; you shouldn't dare! Without her recipe or one single clue, no one will ever duplicate what she used to do!

No, not yet at least, but my friend Jerry repeatedly asked for that coveted recipe. Refusal after refusal she stood firm; vowing never to reveal any part of her precious secret. Not even a little boy who loved to cook could convince her to let him take one quick look. He promised never to reveal any part of her crown jewel. After all, it was he and his family who freely supplied some of those incredible corn shucks. But why, oh why wouldn't she share? Was it tradition or a promise she swore to keep? Even though he lived just up the street, she still refused to give him one little peep. The corner of School and Willow was only one block away, separating him from a coveted secret she took to her grave. She guarded her recipe with vigilance and pride, never once disclosing any ingredients inside. On to the next life where new and old customers await, a line so long filled with countless appetites that hardly could wait. Maybe her kitchen held all the ingredients there. Oh, the excitement must have been overwhelming, especially for her new clientele. Surely her arrival was greeted with a long standing ovation, so many wildly waited with such anticipation. Her recipe is legendary; of course, you must know this by now. Not hard to imagine once you've tasted just one somehow. After licking the spicy red juice from her tasty corn shuck, you'd surely say, good God almighty Ms. Ora, you sure know your stuff. Oh, how busy she must be, making each bundle with such joy and glee. There's no bragging here, just the plain truth. I offer the finest testimony you'll ever hear.

So allow me to proceed without pretense or delay. My suspicions or theories can't be debated or swayed. If you never had her tamales with that spicy red juice, you wouldn't know how delicious her soaked shucks were so yummy through and through. Just let me try to tell what I remember most. It's hard to describe if you really don't know. Oh what a shame, how could it come to this? I'm not exaggerating, not one little bit. Well maybe a little, my palate has been tempered by time. So with that said I'm willing to try, to take a stroll, way back in time. Will you come with me? Only you can decide. Do you want to continue reading this story or will you toss it aside? Decide...have you yet? Oh, I see you're still here; so you must hear the rest. Okay, I'll try my best. Do forgive any relapse in memory should I stumble or fall. Don't get too impatient. I won't take too long. Just a few minutes will do. Maybe, just maybe reminiscing is a good thing for us to do. No matter what, when, how or why, I love these memories; keep them? Of course, I will; always and maybe forever or until I cease to breathe. Or better still, until my spirit becomes motionless, but when it rises and takes flight again, I surely know where I'd go. Direct to Ms. Ora's kitchen no matter where she resides. Buzzing with excitement, it won't be too hard to find. Her customers will be standing in a long, long line. Oh, she'll gladly work overtime.

Ms. Ora was a quiet light brown skin woman with lots of black moles decorating her face; so odd and peculiar in such a strange sort of way. Her long black hair occasionally worn down revealed her beauty and charm, once plentiful for all to see. But usually, she wore her hair pinned in a bun, giving her face a different look to me. As a child, she looked old, old enough to be my grandmother. Her kind ways cast her in a maternal light; that's where her spirit remains, in my heart, never too far from sight. Soft spoken with a love for cats; ten or twenty maybe she had more than that. I knew no others in our small town who wanted more than a couple to constantly keep around. She didn't work outside her home; at least I never saw that. After so many years of running a restaurant, she grew tired from all of that. But come Friday and Saturday of each week during her twilight years, the aroma from her kitchen filled the air in our streets. With no air conditioning, her windows and doors were constantly wide open, freely advertising her bundles she gleefully made with pride.

Her first name is the only name I ever knew. Seems a little funny how in our culture the things we still say and do. Like using the first name as a surname of sorts, accompanied by a Mr. or Ms. to show proper respect of course. Don't recall ever hearing anyone say her middle or surname, and while nicknames were common, no one ever used one. The same could be said for her companion, Mr. Jimmy no less. Occasionally I'd hear someone refer to him as Black Jimmy, not to his face of course; that would've been too disrespectful, making an enemy of a man who seemed too invaluable to offend.

She and Mr. Jimmy lived in a big white house on Norwood and Willow, just one block away from where we stayed. Our house stood on the corner of Norwood and Pine, so close we smelled her hot tamales cooking each weekend every single time. Their house had plenty room for two; with no kids, they were quiet, kind and sort of neighborly too. Although they could have been married, I never knew for sure. They seemed to be a couple to me at least, but who really knew? That was a conversation for grown-ups alone, not a child like me. No child would dare be so forward to ask; besides, Ms. Ora was a legend and Mr. Jimmy too. When you're famous a first name will do. He was known all over town as the one who carried a pail and sold her tamales from sunup to sundown. That tall, thin, dark skinned man faithfully worked every Friday and Saturday Night. Bundle after bundle, up and down, back and forth he went, stopping at every joint or parked car along the way. Skid Row was lively, and he left no place unchecked.

From Alberta Sims Blue Front Café, an iconic local entertainment spot of sorts, to Dole's Barber Shop, every single place of business he stopped; even Gales, Rose, and Susie Townsend's Café didn't escape a weekend visit from old Jimmy, no way. He and his pail had no limits. Not even Slick Robinson's bar-b-que or Ms. Ayers Hot Tamales too could compete with him and his infamous pail. Anytime he ran out, he returned minutes later with more hot tamales to sell. Ms. Ora's kitchen was working at full-throttle no time to rest a spell. An incredible pace was needed to keep the men and women with plenty to eat. They whined and complained if Mr. Jimmy didn't have any; back and forth he came until their tummies had plenty. He made so much money; a bundle bringing four bits at a time. His pail was full making so much loose change. Ms. Ora probably counted each bit, twelve and a half cent at a time, because each one of her bundles cost a mere fifty cent.

I never had many occasions to visit her much, unless I made and saved some money running errands during the week. She sold singles to kids just like me. I went to her house with pennies, nickels, and dimes. In a good week, I saved enough for her delicious treat. Fifty cents would buy a bundle, and of course, I'd share maybe one with a brother or sister, only if they swore not to tell. I didn't have enough for everyone. There were too many of us to feed. But it was a proud moment handing Ms. Ora two quarters or a half dollar piece. A fair trade, I thought coming straight from me, especially after a long hard week. Her smile signaled her approval, and oh she had such a lovely smile. She knew I must have done something good and special during the week. My good deed was rewarded, entitling me to a little bit of her recipe. I felt mighty proud once our little transaction was complete. After a hand shake and smile, I stood there holding my treat.

Occasionally, a situation here or there sometimes jeopardized our coveted transactions. Back then telephone lines were shared between two neighbors. Of course, not everyone had a phone during the fifties and sixties, especially in Dermott, Arkansas. Having a phone was a rare amenity. If you were fortunate enough to have one, it was understood. You and your neighbors were obliged to share. Two customers for every phone line was the way it used to be. In our case, one long ring meant a call for Ms. Ora and two short rings was for us. With a house full of kids, like ours, and neighbors frequently coming over to make or receive a call, our phone was always busy many times blocking Ms. Ora's calls.

One summer, my brother James found love for the very first time with a girl right up the street. Consequently, their late night phone romance presented a big problem for me! Once they were on the phone, the other party couldn't make or receive a call. Without interrupting a call in progress, a neighbor's line would remain busy until the call was complete. Ms. Ora and Mr. Jimmy were too polite you see, to interfere with a budding romance James had with Rosa Lee. Quite often, Ms. Ora was agitated by their romance. Of all the neighbors in town, why would Southwestern Bell cause such trouble for me? Did they not know of her recipe and the problems this posed for little old me? Sometimes she would let me know, and I certainly didn't want anything coming between her and me. For heaven sakes, I tried to keep the peace! After all, she had the upper hand, as far as I could see. Her powerful monopoly was too enormous resting in her gifted hands. What if she cut me off and refused to sell her hot tamales to me? Just because of my brother's love affair with Rosa Lee. Oh, what a crisis this was for me.

All summer long, once daddy and momma went to sleep, ten o'clock each night, shortly after the nightly news, their late night romance began, not one minute too soon. After waiting all day long to hear her sexy voice, James could hardly wait to make that late night call. A passionate love like theirs was hardly suitable for a party line. But he poured his heart out wooing the love of his young life. Of course, this made it impossible for Ms. Ora or Mr. Jimmy to make or receive a call if only from a neighbor they wished to say good night or good morning with a local call. Well, they were just out of luck until their thirst for love was filled. Faculty 44113, our phone number, shut down Ms. Ora's service until my brother and Rosa Lee was done. Besides, I hardly remember them receiving many calls. Her kitchen and those cats were the centers of their universe after all. Very little time was spent socializing with neighbors or talking on the phone. Her recipe and cats were all the company she needed. Those cats, oh she had plenty; I mean plenty!

Sometimes for enjoyment, we occasionally listened in. A neighbor's conversation was fair play on a party line. Always a sure bet for hearing the latest gossip too. Without ever leaving our home, it was so easy to do. Perhaps this explains how nearly everyone knew about their neighbor's affairs, every little detail from all over town. There were no secrets safe if spoken over the phone. Good neighborly gossip was always a welcome treat. Long before the internet, reality shows, soap operas, late night TV and endless channels to watch, that was all the entertainment we had. There was nothing else to do. But all of this was insignificant come Friday and Saturday Night. This was a sacred time for Ms. Ora and Mr. Jimmy, the main attraction for two full days. Her kitchen was open for business! Those fresh spicy hot tamales quickly left her table. Always selling out, it was necessary to quickly conduct my business before too late during the day.

Armed with diplomacy, come Friday or Saturday Night, I made my way to her Kitchen door, prepared to settle any dispute, including our phone use. If we let too many neighbors use our phone during the week, I had an answer for that. If James and Rosa Lee's romance got on her last nerve, I was obliged to apologize for that. You see, a good neighbor was always allowed to make a friendly call. But my brother's heart was under siege, and he was the biggest culprit of all!

All day long beginning Friday morning or maybe the night before, she would perform magic, a culinary, artistic feast. Fit for our President Obama or maybe royalty too, Ms. Ora's hot tamales could compete with the best! I long for her hot and spicy juice, unlike anything I've ever tasted, and to think I had it first in the most unlikely of places. Dermott, the place I call home.

I just can't believe it. I've traveled far and wide hoping to find some hot tamale that could compete with Ms. Ora's culinary prize. After so many years of search, I gave up long ago. Why I've often wondered, were her hot tamales so delicious and so tasty to me? But then again it wasn't only me, from the old to the young, the verdict was the same. It was good, so good the taste still remains. In my heart and in mind, after all these years it remains unchanged. Just thinking about eating one bundle awakens my palate lured from a deep long sleep.

At long last, I now know her name, Ora Lee Bryant. With no children or close family left alive, her recipe is safely buried with her, resting by her side.

Ms. Ora, it has taken many years to recognize just how special and remarkable you were. You touched the palates of so many people spicing up their lives with such a wonderful treat. Had I been blessed with wisdom beyond my youth, surely I would have said thank you for your kindness and culinary skills to boot. I find it necessary to share my memories of you with so many others who wished they'd met you or maybe someone like you. Your sweet and gentle touch made a difference in a world that lacks what you freely gave, and gave so much to us.

A magnificent love wrapped inside an ordinary corn shuck, with meat and corn meal delicately marinated and tucked. Soaked in your special red spicy juice, just the thought alone unleashes my hunger within causing me to salivate after so many years. Oh, how I miss you so! So often and so deep, on and on, maybe endlessly, or until my mind drifts back to when you lived just up the street. I could hardly wait to eat once the aroma from your kitchen filled the air in our streets. The thought of eating just one more bundle still excites me. You are remembered now and forever, always, until...!

Special thanks to Dorothy Mae Davis-Duren, Thelma Davis, Nora Nita Turner-Briggs and of course, Matthew "Peaches" Davis-Strickland of Strickland Funeral Home of Dermott, Arkansas.

In Loving Memory of Ms. Ora Lee Bryant
February 22, 1899 - June 11, 1981

Are You My Daddy?

06/12/2015

"Are you my daddy?" "No," I said, "but I'd be mighty proud if I was."

A few years ago, I was in Arkansas helping my brother move a tenant into one of his rental properties. She was a young single mother with a few kids and expecting a new arrival within a few months. There were so many kids hanging around, I didn't know which ones were actually hers. But there was a little boy about five years old or so that just seemed to stand-out from the rest. He had a special glow about him. I sensed greatness within him if only there were someone in his life willing to guide him toward it. Full of energy, I made good use of his eagerness to help by giving him little things to carry back and forth to the truck.

He responded so well to receiving directions. Frankly, I enjoyed having him around. All he wanted was a little attention and interaction with anyone who treated him with kindness and respect. I saw a little bit of myself in him at that age. As we were getting ready to drive away, he turned toward me with a smile and asked,

"Are you my daddy?"

With a youthful, exuberant look in his eyes, I knew he was serious. Startled by such an unusual question, I needed a moment of composure myself. Before long I had to respond.

"No," I said, "but I'd be mighty proud if I was." He flashed a big smile after hearing such kindness and praise. As we drove away, I began to think. I couldn't imagine going through life not knowing who my father was. Just thinking about such a thing rocks my world. Growing up in a household with a mother and father I just took it for granted. Each one of my parents contributed to my growth and development. But my father taught me how to be a man, a father, and husband. He was forty-eight years old at the time of my birth.

My mother was his third marriage. After marrying his first wife in his early twenties, it was over inside a year. She wanted out of the South. So she did what most blacks in the south did at the time, moved north. Without his consent, she moved to Chicago after saving money for her ticket. Shortly after her arrival, she found work and promptly sent money for him to come. Of course, he refused to go for two reasons: He was not a city person, and he didn't have an education beyond the ninth grade. He couldn't see his way clear making a living in a big city like that. Besides, she left him and expected him to follow her. His hubris just wouldn't allow that. Over time, I understood and respected his decision. He would often say,

"I've never seen any food growing on a sidewalk. In the south, we had land. I always had plenty to eat with livestock and a garden. So even if I was broke, I had plenty food, maybe not everything I wanted but I was never hungry."

That made perfect sense to me and my training from him was built around this logic, self-reliance. Common sense was my first degree earned in life. Conferred upon me by my fifteenth birthday, my father was an excellent teacher. He taught me how to work the land which included driving tractors, trucks, handling all sort of tools and guns. It was hard work, and I learned a lot. Many days were spent working in the fields or with animals including cows, pigs, and chickens. When I wasn't doing farm work, I found other work to do. As long as there was a head of hair to cut, or carpentry, or a plumbing job to do, I always kept a little extra money in my pocket. We were constantly working, from one job to the next, and I learned so much from my father's training method and beliefs.

Before my birth, he bought a farm in a neighboring county not far from where we lived. He lived on the farm once, during his second marriage that lasted nineteen years. Tuberculosis nearly destroyed his family, killing his wife and two sons. Of their seven children, only two survived, twin girls, who became my big sisters.

By the time he met our mother, he had seen so much death and hardship including the Influenza in the fall of 1918 which killed all but two of his siblings. His experiences in life had given him so much to share with us, and my life was shaped by these experiences.

All of this was missing from that little fellow's life, and my heart felt his pain. I can only hope he finds his way and learns how one day to become a father, husband, and man. Maybe, just maybe, he finally found his daddy or someone who believes in him. Someone willing to shape his future and helped him become a man.

Youthful Innocence

06/30/2016

You've got your hands in the Lion's mouth, so work hard to get it out!

As a parent, it's an incredible challenge raising a child in an environment where few rules seem to apply, and sometimes common sense is dismissed in the interest of individual freedom or compromise. Living in a so-called pluralistic society, balancing diversity, nested in equality, requires vigilance and tolerance. In New York City where we live, the true measure of our melting pot is on display and tested daily. A little bit of the entire world seems to be represented here, bringing different cultures, beliefs, and values to our community. Having said this let me get to my point.

We have a teenage son. He's quiet, studious, and most of the time, a very responsible fifteen-year-old kid. Last spring, it was time to upgrade his cell phone. My wife and I allowed him to express his preferences in the selection process; because after all, it would be his phone for at least the next two or three years. However, I did express a few obvious concerns regarding the purchase. Like his father, his safety is always paramount. A teenager with a highly desirable cell phone on the streets of New York City carries inherent risk. After his selection and before we made the purchase, I reiterated my concerns in light of his choice, a Galaxy Note 3. Under the wrong circumstances, I told him, his choice could draw unwarranted attention from nefarious characters, in other words, a predator looking for their next victim. He said he understood but would be cautious while using his phone and promised to protect himself from the thieves and all the rest.

A few months ago during his summer break, my concerns were realized when his phone was stolen on a playground in the city. It was June 25th to be exact. He removed it from his pocket for a brief period to make a call or perhaps play one of his favorite games. In doing so, another teenage saw his phone. Unaware, little did he know a predator had quickly set his sights on that phone! Using an excuse of needing to call his mom, he approached our son and asked if he could make a call home. At first, our son said no, but the young man's persistence and bully-like manner prevailed. Once the phone was in his hands, he jumped on his bike and fled. He headed for the projects, nearby where he lived.

Ill-advised and certainly impulsive, our son pursued him still. Following him to his building and getting his apartment number was brave, maybe stupid, but he did. With this information, he found his mother to inform her of what happened. Of course, they reported the phone stolen to our service provider and then filed a police report. A few hours later, my son called me with the bad news.

"Hi dad," he said.

"Well hello, son how is it going?"

"Not good, I have bad news. Are you going to be upset with me?" Although I was out of town on business, I received a text alert from Verizon notifying me the moment he reported his phone stolen and requested a service suspension. "Let me guess," I said. "Someone stole your phone, right?" He got real quiet, as a matter of fact, for a brief moment he was speechless.

"How do you know?" Of course, I didn't want to tell him exactly. So I said, "A father knows things like this son. It comes with the job of being a good dad!"

"So are you mad with me?" I could hear the anxiety in his voice, and a scornful word from me wouldn't make him feel any worse than what he already felt. Recognizing this was a teachable moment, I wanted to find some good in all of this for him.

"No son, I'm not, but this is a matter for the police now, let them do their job. That's how it works you know. Have you and your mom filed a police report?"

"Not yet." He said.

"Well that's the next step now, and the sooner you do this, the more likely you are to get your phone back." I spoke with my wife and encouraged her to take him to the local precinct. It was important that he participate in the process. At the age of fifteen, it would be his first encounter with them; a far different experience than mine growing up in the south during the sixties and seventies. When I was his age, I was arrested by a police officer who felt it was the appropriate time and his solemn duty to teach me a thing or two about the law and how the world really worked for a young black teenager growing up in the south.

In the fall of 1971, my brother invited me up for a weekend visit to his place in Pine Bluff, Arkansas just an hour's drive from Dermott, our hometown. When he and a friend met me at the bus station, four of my friends were with me and needed a ride as well. Unwilling to say no, we piled into his back seat, all of us, three boys and two girls. After we got into the car, a white Police Officer, more like a John Wayne wannabe just welcomed an opportunity to flex his muscles. He stopped us within a block or two from the bus station and questioned my brother about having seven people in his Volts Wagon Beetle. Although his car had mounted exterior mirrors on each door, obstructing the driver's view was the offense. As the owner of the car, my brother was arrested and so was his friend who was driving. Not having his driver's license with him while operating a vehicle was the offense and that got my brother a second charge, letting an unauthorized person operate his vehicle. Trust me; I'm not making this stuff up. That's just how things were back then. The police officer was rude and showed little consideration toward us while performing his duties with a white audience standing nearby in front of a tavern cheering him on. I felt so bad about everything because this was largely my fault and the officer visibly saw my disapproval of his conduct. At best, a ticket was warranted, but an arrest seemed to be harsh and heavy handed. In retrospect, his tactics were consistent with the times.

As I attempted to leave the station, he followed me down the hall. Why I wondered? Cautiously looking around, he wanted to catch me alone and well beyond the reach of any witness; a witness would have spoiled his plan. Before I opened the door, he called out to me, "Boy, you're not going anywhere; I'm putting your ass in jail too." A false claim of verbal assault on a police officer was the charge; he claimed I called him a white Mothafucker, oh please! But without a witness, there was no proof. Without a defense, my arrest and conviction were imminent. Until then, I'd never seen such blatant abuse of power. Mrs. Brown, Attorney Howard, my mother, and father came to our aid, paid a bail bondsman, and we were released within a day.

As a minor, I was required to stand trial. Standing in front of the judge a few weeks later, he clearly saw the injustice but sided with the police officer nonetheless. After listening to our testimony, even he found it unlikely. Oh please, the thought of me cursing a police officer was unconscionable but alleged. The judge rendered his verdict. "Guilty as charged with a ten dollar fine." So much for ninth grade civics; civil rights, the Bill of Rights and our Constitution weren't being practiced the way we were taught in high school, that's for sure. And to think, I only asked the officer for directions to my brother's home. Of course, he refused so I reminded him of his civic duties as a public servant in the state of Arkansas. After all, my daddy's property taxes help pay his salary. Naturally, he took offense to my logic and expectations of assistance.

Unlike mine, I wanted a different experience for our son. A positive and professional one would be preferred, creating a good and lasting first impression of our law enforcement service whose motto is "Courtesy, Professionalism, and Respect." Over forty-five years have passed; besides, we live in New York City with one of the finest Police Departments in the world. Surely they'll demonstrate this and more, setting a fine example with well-trained professional law enforcement personnel.

After two months of waiting, my son's case is still unsolved. In spite of two visits to the precinct, several calls to the detective and providing a picture of the suspect, with his address, his Facebook name and spotting a phone identical to our son's in the hands of one of his friends in a Facebook post, no arrest has been made. So far, our son's technical savvy has produced more results than New York City's finest Police Department. He even sat at one of their computers and showed the detective how through the use of Wi-Fi and GPS, the phone could be located. Oh well, at least our son is learning from his experience. I'm convinced moving forward he'll benefit greatly from this costly lesson. However, some of his youthful innocence has been lost, bringing him one step closer to becoming a man.

Hire Me Please

08/18/2016

Lord, help me, Jesus, please...!

On any given day, I can walk up or down Lenox or Seventh Avenue which are very busy streets in Harlem and see food lines in front of several food pantries. So many people are hungry and want something to eat. With little or no income, they get food anywhere or wherever they can. Quite often young men are hanging around in front of buildings or on the sideways, talking loud and shooting dice. Many of them are jobless with nothing but time on their hands with no special place to go. Sometimes I'm close enough to hear portions of their conversations and observe their manner and style. The clothing they wear in many instances reflects who they are. Can I be blunt and honest for a few minutes and just speak the truth? Would you hire any of them if you had a job to fill? Is your answer a yes, no or maybe so? Oh really, I know I'm not the only one who's thinking these sort of thoughts. I'm hoping you said yes. If not, we're in deep, deep trouble because probably no one else would either. I repeat no one will if not you or I won't. So would you? For some, their appearance and manner would be a troublesome fact, but everyone deserves a chance when it truly matters after all.

For some time now, unemployment has been a systemic problem in America, especially among the poorly skilled, marginally educated or displaced workers. Usually, this means a disproportionate number of black or brown Americans. Global markets, international conglomerations, technology, and greed, have become the new standard by which wealth is generated and controlled. After all, we live in a capitalistic system. Allow me a few minutes to share one of my favorite fairy tales because there are striking similarities hidden in this fictional account of Washington Irving's short story, Rip Van Winkle.

Irving, a Birmingham, England born writer, wrote Rip Van Winkle in 1819 after a failed business venture forced him to file bankruptcy. In defeat, he turned to writing. Rip Van Winkle, one of his fictional characters, lived near the foot of New York's Catskill Mountains in a beautiful Dutch Village. He was loved by all, especially the children for the stories he told and the toys he gave. The wilderness was his refuge. He would often slip away to avoid work. His wife's constant demands for him to earn income for their family were a persistent complaint.

One autumn day, he wandered into the wilderness and headed for the mountains. To his surprise, he saw a man carrying a keg of moonshine up the mountain, and it was obvious he needed help. After they had reached their destination, he saw a group of men oddly dressed and playing a game. They knew him and made him welcome. But how did they know him he wondered, especially his name? After all, he certainly hadn't seen any of them ever before. Their moonshine was irresistible, and before long, he began to drink a lot. Perhaps too much, because after consuming so much alcohol, he fell into a deep sleep. Twenty years later he woke up and discovered while sleeping the world had changed. But for the generosity of his grown children who still remained in the village after their mother's death, he would have been homeless and likely starve to death.

Our moonshine was a Vietnam War, rampant drugs abuse throughout our inner cities and our schools suffered from neglect to pay for a costly war. The war was actually called a conflict. Although nearly 60,000 American Soldiers lost their lives, the war was never declared or won. A lot of our men returned home physically wounded, mental trauma, hooked on drugs, and our national spirit was deeply scarred. Once the war ended, President Nixon and Secretary Kissinger wasted little time normalizing relations with China, our biggest adversary. Remember, China was North Vietnam's ally during our twenty-year war, from November 1, 1955-April 30, 1975. Without China's support, we would have crushed North Vietnam. So what were we fighting for? A new trading partner apparently, thanks to our soldiers and all those bombs dropped from the belly of our B52 Bombers in North Vietnam, Laos and Cambodia. With our schools and communities showing the cost of war, the suffering among the people finally took its toll.

Once we established a diplomatic relationship with China, our markets were flooded with their cheap goods. U.S. based companies gained access to cheap Chinese labor. Wage exploitation was taken to a new level. In the seventies and eighties, all of our top business schools were promoting the concept of the U.S. being a dominate Financial Global Power. The U.S. Dollar remained the preferred currencies for worldwide trade. We were clearly a global force once again. Largely because of cheap Chinese labor, there was a drastic reduction in union labor for our economy to thrive and grow. We marched toward global prosperity leaving the poor and middle class behind.

Why bother with American Workers, when the Chinese would work longer and harder for less? Absent of those high U.S. wages, troublesome environmental and labor laws, corporations and the wealthy made their money unencumbered with few restrictions if any at all. All of those federal relegations protecting worker's pensions, benefits, and our environment were casually dismissed. Corporate profits became paramount with this new plan. Something had to be done putting an end to sharing the money. So the race began to outsource U.S. factory jobs to China and India with dire consequences. Now, look at where we landed?

While President Ronald Reagan was in office, huge tax incentives were given to the remaining manufacturing companies allowing them to automate their plants at very low and attractive tax rates. The goal was to increase production with fewer workers and yield greater profits.

President Reagan accelerated the decline of our unions and the middle class. Remember the Air Traffic Controller Strike? He destroyed that union with haste! Once President Bill Clinton put the final nail in our heart, NAFTA was the final blow that tore our lives apart. The U.S. Manufacturing base was decimated by the North American Free Trade Agreement. Hello, Mexico and goodbye to the middle class!

Why might you ask? Money and lots of it was likely given to our political apparatus. No matter the party affiliation, they all got paid at the expense of the middle class. You see, the reality is the United States of America is a mature market. They can only sell so many cars, television, cell phones, refrigerators, washers and dryers in America. Far short of their production capacity; besides, most of us have plenty of this stuff already, and with maxed-out credit, we're simply tapped out. But all of those exported jobs to China, parts of Asia-especially India and Mexico brought new customers with new demands for those same products. That's where the growth is now, China, India, and Mexico. There are millions, maybe billions, of new customers with good credit, nice paying jobs, many of which, were imported from America and they're jumping at the chance to have what we Americans have in our homes and driveways. I can't be the only one who sees this unfolding right in front of us; am I? It's time to wake up from our long twenty-year nap. Hello Rip Van Winkle, we're like you, behind in time and lost, but finally waking up.

Our world changed while we were sleep. So what should we do now? Realize a couple of things first. In capitalism, there are three levels: a bottom, middle and a top. We commonly refer to these three groups as poor, middle class and upper class, especially the Top One Percent. This is unlikely to change in our lifetime. There are acceptable levels of unemployment in our system, usually around five percent or so. The sooner we educate our children to this reality, the better off they'll be. Without skills and a relevant education, they will be permanently trapped at the bottom.

Because of sports and entertainment, there are more black and brown millionaires in America than any other place in the world. Did you know that? A West African friend pointed this out to me several years ago. We've maxed out this niche. Have you noticed the NBA, NFL, MLB or Hollywood lately? There's very little expansion left, just replacing the old with the new seems to be the pattern nowadays. So education and entrepreneurial opportunities are the new frontiers. Science, math, engineering, and self-employment is the future for our kids. The belief that someone is going to hire all of our children is a myth. Their children are well ahead of us and rightly so. They own most of the businesses. Be honest, wouldn't you hire your child first before hiring someone else?

I remember all too well, in the sixties, when Malcolm X and the Civil Rights Movement, namely Martin Luther King debated this issue. Before then it was W.E.B. Du Boise and Booker T. Washington. Nearly 50 years later, I now see the consequences of the choices we made. Many of our businesses were destroyed, jobs were lost, and black commerce never recovered after integration. President Nixon threw us a few crumbs with the Small Business Administration, but we weren't ready for that.

This transition won't be easy. A case in point, my daughter recently graduated from a good college with a Bachelor's Degree in Communications. She and I have had long conversations about her career along the way, dating back to high school. I shared my early experiences as a Director of Career, Planning, and Placement at a college down south. That experience was an incredible up close look at industry. It can be a daunting task finding a job straight out of school. For so many college graduates, without much experience, your first professional job can be hard to find. Of course, I shared all of this with her. She politely listened, but I see no clear evidence that she has taken any action or understand the importance of my advice. Over 180,000 dollars spent, a degree with good grades does not guarantee a job!

Oh, she has her own ideas about her future, and that's what troubles me the most. Her understanding and expectations, like so many of her peers, are rather idealistic, perhaps too much so. Your education or skills, experience, character, judgment, and ambition, are all needed assets. Personal appearance, self-discipline, willingness to accept direction and constructive criticism are all essential qualities too if you want to be a professional and have a good career. More importantly, having good instincts and the will to work toward something you love to do require discipline, especially for our kids. She, like so many others, just seems so unwilling to accept the simple facts. Lord, help me, Jesus, please...!

Well, I believe you feel the frustration in our struggle. All we can do is pray. Twenty years of sleeping is quite a long, long nap!

Peace.

Music and the Business

09/10/2016

Let the music play...oh, it will. Long after the shady side of the business is gone.

Above the noise of our time, music has always stood tall. Politics, social unrest, wars, recessions, the ups and downs of life, all of these things mattered less, as long as good music continued to play. Nothing stops our appetite for it. Collectively, we've embraced the magic held in these seven wonderful notes, played in all sorts of variations- naturals, sharps, and flats. Somehow, life is a little easier just because of that. The music makes us feel better, much happier it seems. Do you miss some of the legends like I do? Marvin Gaye, Barry White, Etta James, Michael Jackson, Luther Vandross, Whitney Houston, James Brown, Ray Charles, Teddy Pendergrass, and of course Prince, they were among the best doing it just right. Once upon a time, the list was longer, the talent seemed endless, and we were better because of it. Then darkness came, bringing despair, death, and change. Suddenly the music began to slowly die, forever changing the landscape of our lives. We will never be the same again, never. But an occasional song reminds us of what we once had.

Have you noticed the harshness of our rhetoric lately? This new language is far more vicious than ever. Lyrics, the good ones, once so meaningful and inspiring have all but disappeared. A good love song is so rare these days, hope and inspiration have been lost somewhere between time, and a new era has begun without our consent! Well, certainly without mines. The origin of R&B is deeply rooted in Gospel Music; kill the church and the music dies. Sounds like quite a stretch but think about it for a moment. So much talent came straight from the church; singing in the choir marked the humble beginnings for many legendary singers. Now, so few young people go to church, like we once did, following the path laid for many, many years.

YouTube is a godsend for music. I'm lost without it. My earphones are like an umbilical cord connecting me to the music I love so dear. Without a doubt, it's therapeutic and feels like a nurturing source of hope and inspiration. I don't remember exactly when I first fell in love with it. Too long it seems to remember exactly when, but like a favorite pair of shoes, the comfort and security lingers on.

Oh yeah, now I remember. I was around ten or eleven years old, in the fifth grade, and had an enormous desire to play the saxophone. Junior Walker was one of my favorite musicians at the time. Too young to join the school band, I lost hope of playing an instrument but not my love music. It has a special place in my heart. I wrote my first song around fourteen or fifteen and sent it to Nashville, Tennessee. For weeks on end, I hoped someone would take notice of my talent. Talent, what talent for writing a beautiful song? Well, my love at least was there, but not one break came along. Sad to say, that opportunity never came. But I don't understand; how could they not see me, a diamond in the rough? Years later, I moved to New York City after many years of working several jobs without passion. So I decided to give it just one more try and write a few good songs. My passion still ran deep.

I joined the songwriter's guild, The American Society of Composers, Authors and Publishers (ASCAP) and started writing songs. Collaborated with a couple of good musicians and wrote a pretty decent tune. We received quite a bit of interest in the studio while recording; I was so happy. Finally, my first song had been produced, and I stood tall with pride. I thought we were on to something! After spending time and so much of my hard earned money, I had a song to shop, hoping someone would take notice and give me a shot. In the music business, that wasn't an easy job.

Have you ever seen any of the Behind the Music episodes or Unsung, a TV One? Each episode is a documentary telling the stories of the artists behind the music. Oh boy, were my eyes ever opened! Hard to imagine a successful business, like music, could have such a dark and dreadful past, but it does. Careers have been ruined, lives destroyed fueled by greed, drugs, and exploitation. If you venture into this business without a strong constitution, you'll certainly be eaten alive. For some and perhaps me in particular, it felt like taking a lamb to slaughter, of course, I was the lamb!

All sort of nefarious and greedy characters were just waiting for the next raw, naïve talent to walk through the door. Yet with unending expectations, most would certainly be quickly devoured or exploited becoming the next prey. Once inside, contracts are presented and signed, sometimes without receiving one dime. For so many, this experience is nothing more than legalized slavery, but desperate souls sign regardless hoping to renegotiate a better deal in the future. I met them all: representatives of record labels, producers, publishers, straight-up bull-shitters, and other fellow song writers. The list was endless, and this brutal orientation robbed me of my joy until one day I met a lawyer. He had connections to a major record label. We scheduled a meeting, and I went to his office hopeful I had finally found someone willing to broker a fair deal for me and my song. His office was nice, located on Park Avenue, not too far from Times Square.

I arrived at his office a little early, didn't want to risk any chance of being late. His secretary greeted me; she seemed really nice. After making me feel welcome, she returned to her clerical duties. It wasn't long before she told me,

"Mr. Pearl is ready to see you now." Of course, I can't say his real name, but Pearl is close enough.

My heart began to race slightly. That moment, I had long for since childhood finally had arrived. I had the scars to show for this heartfelt struggle, not to mention, the thousands of dollars spent in pursuit of my dream. He had a nice spacious office with decorations clearly suggesting he was making money from his roster of clients he represented. My background includes many skills like marketing, sales and contract negotiations. Little did I know these skills would render me unsuitable for what I was about to hear.

"Good Morning Larry, have a seat." Once he stood up to shake my hand, he was much shorter than I imagined. From our conversation over the phone, his voice sounded strong and firm, very matter of fact; likes a tall, aggressive athlete brash with lots of fame.

His interest in the song was apparent. It was a first rate production I must admit. But there's always a catch. He wanted me to sign over the copyright to him without compensation. With a straight face, he insisted that was a great deal and my only path into the music business. Of course, I bit my tongue holding back my disdain. In spite of this, I kept my poker face intact. I inquired about his family, their lifestyle, and opulence. Oh, he was living a good life. So after listening long enough, I had to ask, "Why would you expect me to want anything less for my wife and kids?"

Oh, that was a deal breaker. What else could he say after that? He reminded me that was just how things worked in that world. Well, I decided to create my own world. It's taken longer, but I'm doing pretty good I must say. I'm sure a lot happier!

Talent can't be replaced. Eventually, good music will return. Technology has created new opportunities for success. Thank God for that! So I say let the music play; oh it will. Long after the shady side of the business is gone.

Peace.

The Internal Revenue Service Scam

08/30/2016

Don't hang up, this is an important call.

"Hello...," Don't hang up, this is an important call. "Who is this?" My name is Mr. Watson; a revenue agent with the Internal Revenue Service, my badge number is 1000843241. Your case has been assigned to me for nonpayment of your Personal Income Taxes for 2014 and 2015, and if you don't cooperate with me today, you will be arrested. I see here you have an outstanding balance of $2,504.25 and this amount must be paid in full, or we'll come to your home and arrest you for sure!

Her heart began to race, giving new meaning to panic, but she composed herself before speaking. "I don't have that kind of money; I'm not working now." Upset and frightened she knew she was in trouble and needed help. Some good advice or representation was necessary because IRS trouble was a matter she had lived without. So she decided to stall him and get help. "Give me your number, and I'll call you back."

No, you can't hang up until this matter is fully resolved or at least make a payment of some kind today to avoid your imminent arrest. Against his stern instructions, she hung up anyway. Besides, his phone number appeared on her caller ID, and after speaking to someone, she intended to call him back.

Ava was frantic when she called. "Larry," she said, "the IRS just called me and said if I hung up my phone without paying $2,504.25 they would come to my home today and arrest me. Can they do that?" She was so upset I had to calm her down before I could explain anything. "You know I'm not working now and I don't have the money. What am I'm going to do?"

"Calm down Ava, this is America, not Ethiopia. The IRS won't call you like that demanding a payment over the phone." Although she has legally lived in America for several years, any call from our government, especially the IRS, struck fear in her heart. After I had convinced her there was no chance of the IRS coming to her home to arrest her, she began telling me all about this mysterious call. Not one word spoken by this man was true. He wasn't a revenue agent or an Internal Revenue Service employee. It was a scam plain and simple. He kept calling her until we did a three-way call with him. After we were finished with him that put an end to his calls.

In May of 2015, the Internal Revenue Service was a victim of a massive data breach. Hackers penetrated the IRS Computer System. Their Website's Online Automated Service was hacked. Using their Get Your Transcript Program, they stole information on more than 724,000 taxpayers. Names, social security numbers, date of births, dependents, filing status, addresses, phone numbers and account status were taken. It was all over the news. Perhaps you may have heard about this.

While the IRS has made many attempts to alert taxpayers with letters and information posted on their website, the thieves seem to be a step ahead of their efforts, at least in some cases. Here's how they work: They usually target victims with surnames that sound foreign or tax returns with Individual Taxpayer Identification Numbers (ITIN), low-income taxpayers were a perfect target for Earn Income Tax and Child Tax Credits and the elderly. Calls are placed from outside the United States, out of reach for U.S. law enforcement agencies. Usually, the number that appears on your caller ID frequently shows a Washington, D.C. Area Code, 202. If you try to call back using that number, it's difficult, if not impossible, to reach anyone. Quite often the caller has a foreign accent.

They're using this stolen information to file fraudulent tax returns, claim your dependents, secure loans, and credit cards as well as shake down easily intimidated victims. Over the last year, I've talked to several people who have received these illegal calls. Actually, they even called me one day. Naturally, I had a great time playing along with the scammer. Once he finished telling me how much I owed and what would happen if I didn't pay, I agreed to pay him cash and told him where we should meet. It was my local New York City Police Precinct, the 28th. Once he realized this, the next sound I heard was click!

However, one of my friends wasn't so fortunate. She's from the Ukraine, and her last name was a dead giveaway. Once they got her on the phone, they really got to her. They insisted she go immediately to her bank and withdraw over two thousand dollars. She was instructed to purchase pre-paid debit cards, put her money on it and give the card numbers to them. They kept her on the phone the entire time. She called me within minutes once she hung up. We tried to place a block on the cards because she thought they were not activated. Regrettably, we weren't successful. Within minutes of receiving the card numbers, they withdrew every cent. She lost all of her money with no hope of ever getting any of it back.

I was right in the middle of writing this piece when I received a call from Eddie. Just minutes before, he was on the phone with someone posing as an IRS Agent. With an Indian accent, he referenced case number, RF93271DF0268 after identifying himself as an agent with the Department of the Treasury. Eddie was given two choices: Settle with them or face legal action in court which would likely mean a tax levy against his bank account and all of his personal assets. He was a savvy New Yorker and wasn't fooled a bit. He knew it was a scam. He kept them talking until he got all the information he needed to call me and ask a few questions. But they tried to get whatever they could out of him before he hung up. Before he ended the conversation, they told him a mere two hundred dollars would be a show of good faith. He could pay the remaining balance with a payment arrangement. Oh how nice of them, right? So he called me.

"Larry, I just got off the phone with this guy impersonating an IRS Agent. What's going on and how did he get my information?" Once I told him what I knew about the scam and the millions they have stolen from taxpayers all over the country, he knew he had done the right thing. Fortunately for him, they didn't get one red cent of his money. By the way, the call came from a 202 Area Code. We tried to call them back with no success of course.

Now, if you think you've been a victim of identity theft, go to the IRS Website or call them and request an Identity Protection PIN. This six digit PIN can save you from a lot of trouble. Your personal information will be protected by the IRS, and no one can file a fraudulent tax return using your information without your IP PIN. Check your credit report and make sure there isn't any recent activity on your account.

Remember, this whole thing is a scam, and as long as it works, they'll continue calling. I hope you have not been victimized by these unscrupulous people. So spread the word and help shut these horrible people down.

From Me to You, I'm Just Saying...
09/14/2016

Water seeks its own level!

Usually, when I rise in the morning, an endless flow of random thoughts are shooting like sparks from a lingering campfire inside my head. From the day before or influenced by something, I'm currently thinking, the origin doesn't seem to matter as much. This activity offers a constant source of stimulation which is always good for my brain. Occasionally an incredible dream from the night before, or during the wee hours of the morning just before dawn, fascinates me beyond any predictable expectations. Sometimes my morning run can be just as thought provoking. So when I can't quite decide what to do with all of these thoughts, I just let them sit inside my head until I find a useful purpose or place for them to go. If I can't let go of it, the need to express my thoughts and sentiments become too overwhelming to ignore. These moments pose a challenge for an occasional procrastinator like me. Today I decided not to let them linger. Reticence will no longer hold these thoughts captive. I've found the perfect place for them; sharing them with you. So let me begin:

My First Thought

"Nothing is more powerful than an idea whose time has come."

Those words were eloquently spoken by a French poet and novelist, Victor Hugo many years ago during his life between February 26, 1802-May 22, 1885. Somehow my mind fixated on his powerful words while watching a brief segment of The O'Reilly Factor last night. Three profound issues were raised in my mind, but of course, in haste Bill O'Reilly's narrowly focused on the obvious red meat needed to feed his audience, disrespecting our flag while the national anthem is played during an NFL Game. Blinded by hypocrisy, the time has come to challenge him and others who think like him because America is diverse, not homogeneous.

O'Reilly, a zealous right-wing personality on the Fox Cable Channel is concerned about preserving the integrity of the American Flag, the National Anthem and upholding a long standing tradition of the inclusion of both of these relics at major sporting events in America and throughout the world when our athletes compete and win. Colin Kaepernick, a San Francisco 49er Quarterback, is now the focus of his disdain causing him to throw down the gauntlet and draw a red line before anyone else foolishly crosses and follows Colin's deplorable example. As some of you know, Colin, a black man, has decided to exercise his constitutional rights, of free speech and peaceful protest against some of the police for their inappropriate conduct in the line of duty. Simply stated, in some cases, a few have unjustly used deadly force against young black men and teenagers in our country, and this has sparked his outrage like so many other Americans. Colin has a guaranteed right under our Constitution to peacefully protest, and this right is afforded to all Americans, regardless of race, creed or color. But a footnote is required here. Some believe these rights were originally intended for Caucasians only. Maybe at first, the founding fathers intended it this way. Most of them owned slaves and perhaps never considered equal protection under the law for people of Asian, African or Native American decent. Our flag represents our nation and its constitutional values. So when Colin refuses to stand while the national anthem is played, this is viewed by O'Reilly and others like him as disrespectful. But is this a fair assessment? For example, in the preamble to our Constitution it states:

"We the People of the United States, in Order to form a more perfect Union, establish Justice, insure domestic Tranquility, provide for the common defence, promote the general Welfare, and secure the Blessings of Liberty to ourselves and our Posterity, do ordain and establish this Constitution for the United States of America."

Now let me get right to my point, do you see the first word, "We"? Of course, you do, right? But what you or I don't see is "US," the blacks, browns or any other variation thereof. We're not included, period. Why? Well because our founding fathers didn't view us as full citizens and therefore excluded us when they crafted the Constitution. Therein belie the hypocrisy. Another case in point let's take a closer look at our national anthem, The Star Spangled Banner. It was written by Francis Scott Key, a lawyer, author, amateur poet, and slave owner who witnessed The Battle of Baltimore on September 13, 1814, between the British and the American Colonies during The War of 1812. After watching the battle during the night from behind enemy lines, the next day he penned a poem that later became a song. In 1931 our Congress proclaimed this song to be our national anthem.

The Star Spangled Banner has four verses. However, the first verse is the only one we're accustomed to routinely hearing performed. We are mentioned as slaves or hirelings in the third verse.

> *"And where is that band who so vauntingly swore*
>
> *that the havoc of war and the battle's confusion*
>
> *A home and a country should leave us no more?*
>
> *Their blood has wash'd out their foul footsteps' pollution.*
>
> *No refuge could save the hireling and slave*
>
> *From the terror of flight or the gloom of the grave:*

And the star-spangled banner in triumph doth wave

O'er the land of the free and the home of the brave."

What exactly does Key mean here? I refuse to assume anything regarding his intent.

Back to Bill and his guest, Charles Krauthammer was asked to join in the discussion after showing a clip from a morning news show featuring him promoting his latest book, Killing The Rising Sun. In the clip, Bill challenged Colin Kaepernick to read a free copy of his book. Of course, he offered to send it to him. He was certain once Colin read it, he would have a better understanding for respecting our flag and patriotism for our country. Truthfully, he couldn't resist pursuing a little controversy to promote his book free of charge. Have you no shame sir?

Now Bill believes we should accept his premise and version of our history and tradition without reviewing the facts for ourselves. Our country has an interesting past. Applying today's standards would ruin everything and change forever the lofty image of our founding fathers and their well-kept secret, the total exclusion of women, Africans, Asians, Hispanics, Latinos and Native Americans from our Constitution. He fears if the people really knew the truth about our esteemed founders, no one would consciously embrace singing our national anthem or salute our flag after learning the truth. He may have a point and here's why.

The hypocrisy is too obvious to ignore and, "Nothing is more powerful than an idea whose time has come." The idea of a slave master talking about freedom and democracy is the height of hypocrisy and just doesn't ring true anymore. We've fought World Wars, imposed our will on other sovereign nations in the name of freedom and democracy without first looking in the mirror and correcting our historical mistakes. Sure we've changed some but largely because people like Colin shined a light on injustice. People of African, Asian, Hispanic, Latino and Native American descent love this country as much, if not more than some Caucasians, but for different reasons. We suffered and died for just and unjust causes throughout our nation's history; long before the same rights were given to us. Can you imagine fighting for someone's freedom when you're not free? The flag and constitution may not mean as much to us as you, but the soil, water and the air we breathe does. Like you, our deceased loved one's bodies are mixed in the soil we fight to protect and defend. And so, I proudly say, God, bless America, the land that I love. Stand beside her and guide her, through the night with light from above.

To Colin and all the other protesters I say; "Don't just protest the police injustice. When a senseless killing occurs in our country, we all should protest their wrongful death as well regardless of color or the killer. Remember the promise of our Constitution, "life, liberty and the pursuit of happiness." This is no less important than the second amendment to the Constitution, "the right of the people to keep and bear Arms shall not be infringed."

So who should we condemn, the sin or the sinner? Maybe both, you decide, but a system built on injustice will not survive!

My Second Thought

By all accounts, this thought seems somewhat juvenile, but yet so prevalent. Routinely I see and hear so many people, young and old, begging for money. When I first moved to Harlem, I was shocked by the ease with which a mere stranger would approach someone and ask for spare change, as they call it or swipe from your MetroCard to enter the Subway Station. Never stopping to engage in a conversation, sometimes I reach into my pocket and give my change. Many of them look able enough to work a job, but begging seemed natural. Eventually, I learned that most of them need some sort of counseling or mental assistance. They come inside businesses, restaurants and on the Subway looking for someone willing to give. If they feel ignored, some of them will lash out with some of the worse language used. Sometimes you see them in front of a liquor store, on a corner, sitting or sleeping on a bench, the sidewalk or on the steps of a building after they use their drugs. For some, the spare change they collect supports their habit.

One afternoon, I stopped at a bodega on the corner near where I live. As usual, there was a line. Standing at the back of the line, a teenager was holding a bag of chips. From her appearance, she didn't seem to be a typical panhandler. Oh so clever was she, as a matter of fact, she was good. She turned to me and said she was hungry and didn't have enough money to pay for a bag of chips. Her request seemed genuine and innocent enough for me to help. Once I got some change, I gave her a dollar to make her purchase. After all, it was for food, and she said she was hungry.

After I'd given her the money, she returned back to the line. I should have paid for her chips while at the counter like I sometimes do. But on this occasion, I believed she was really hungry. So few young mothers cook a full meal these days, and she could have been telling the truth.

After a few seconds, I found a spot to observe her without being noticed. I was curious and wanted to see if she would pay for the chips. She didn't notice me watching her as she returned her bag of chips before leaving the store. She needed money, not food. But she was real smooth and convincing; one darn good actress I might add. I just shook my head, laughed and walked away. One more lesson learned in the streets of Harlem!

My Third and Final Thought

It was September, a week or so after Labor Day, and the children were back in school after a long summer vacation. I remember this time in my life although it was many years ago. The city issues Metro Cards to each student who lives beyond walking distance to their school. Twice a day, in the mornings between 7:30 am and 8:30 and afternoons between 2:30 pm and 4:00 the Subway is packed with students. Full of energy, some might say uncontrollably, they make their way to and from school. For some, their loud conversations and horseplay quickly change the atmosphere on the trains.

Some commuters elect to avoid using the Subway and Bus Service altogether during this time of day and here's why:

I can't distinguish the difference between their horseplay and a fight. They play so rough with one another. In most cases, civility is lacking from their interaction.

I've noticed owners of the corner stores hire extra security and limit the number of students in their store together. Theft is an obvious concern.

Truancy Officers are position around the schools urging the students to leave the premises before a crowd gathers, increasing the likely chance of violence and sometimes I do see an occasional fight.

Upon reflection, I began to wonder about ideas I've had for a while. What if we required our children to commit to community service, starting with their freshman year of high school? The work should be meaningful, with structured supervision, for at least a couple hours a day, maybe two to three days a week. So many of our children could benefit from structure and expose them to situations of learning. Mentorship should promote civility. It's long overdue. I firmly believe it could make a difference in some of their lives too. Enough said it's just a thought.

On balance I truly believe there's good in everyone. Sometimes we're blinded by unseemly behavior too powerful to ignore. I'll continue to hope and pray my good deeds will come through each and every day. I just love life and living, and I pray you do too!

Peace,

"Every single day I wake up with the thought of one thousand ways or more to fail, but my day begins once I find one good way to succeed!"

Lawrence E. Crockett, Sr.

May 2017

Facebook, Google+, E-mails, Twitter, Text Messages and Direct Mail

Over one million social media views and here are a few comments from some of you:

KW: Wow! This is absolutely OUTSTANDING! I'm speechless Larry, long overdue...!

ACB: I just finished reading your tribute to Benjie. It's beautiful, touching and deeply moving. I'm sure he has that big beautiful smile on his face. He loved you so!

JA: Well stated and certainly something to remember. Congrats, again!

KW: Speechless.....You are a genius. I can only think of one word to describe you...Amazing!

NJ: One of few influential people in my life is my Author friend Larry Crockett. I'm in love with his mind and his ambition. Please take a moment to read an excerpt from his latest collection. Much continued success, My Sunshine... Wow!!! I felt like you were writing about me :-) I can't wait to read the finished project.

ACJ: Truly, every beat of my heart and feelings! God has blessed you Lawrence with the power of heartfelt compassion and words. Thank you, I know this, and all of your love and research brings so much joy to all of our ancestors and to our forever cherished Aldonia, we called Aunt Aldonia, having joined the family already in heaven. God bless you! God bless our loved ones in their reunion and continued journey in the spiritual world! And they are still with us; though not visibly present in this mundane world they are ever present. Blessings to you! Truly beautiful! Thank you for sharing! Love, peace, and prosperity to you and family!

SG: Thanks for sharing, very interesting enjoyable reading.

ALJ: I love to find myself stuck for 10 minutes reading this story. I like what the Author stated- "Let the world admire God's creation." Personally, I considered myself as 'perfectly created by God' thus I'm trying to seek that perfection not really physically but spiritually.

ADT: So touching. I know your brother; may he Rest in Peace, hears you.

GM: Thanks for sharing

AG: I love this story

SL: I like the story

JCS: This story was indeed amazing.

RC: Amen

MPC: Nice story

BC: It was incredible

SJ: Great job, Lawrence! I'm just getting the memo; however, I'm elated to know you are doing great things!

JB: Great work class mate, keep it coming. Continue to take care

PS: Keep doing what you do!!!!

BW: So proud of you Lawrence, MUCH LOVE!!!!

RJJ: Very nice, you are a talented young man

SG: Hi Larry, this is a great tribute. I enjoyed reading it. Thanks for sharing.

OW: Heartfelt, my cup runs over...thankyou

LS: If you haven't already, start writing articles or op-ed pieces for newspapers and magazines.

BJJ: That was so nice. I enjoyed reading it

DD: Very Very inspiring Lawrence!

MD: Great story, the old man wins.

WS: Peace and Love to you Larry.

JC: Very nice...I luv those words of heart.

AG: Berry nice.

JJMP: Bravo

LR: Amen

JO: Amen

LS: Great. And, much-continued success.

JM: Well said, Lawrence

LK: I really enjoyed reading Nina Shakes Harlem! Can't wait for the sequel!

SB: WOW...it's on my list...congrats

NSG: I got my copy, can't wait to get started!! Thank you for the kind words!!

GRS: Awesome, Happy for you!

JR: Very nice...I luv those words of heart.

OA: Wow can't wait for release how are you it has been a long time? I'm good.

NS: Can't wait if I can get it on my kindle

JDH: Amen...touched my heart...

JE: Thank you for my autographed copy which is so good!!

JCS: This story was indeed amazing.

REW: Well said..., love it

GM: Well done!!

MP: Praying for you keep up the good work.

ZMP: Love it

RF: This is a beautiful tribute to President Obama. A Job well-done Larry!!!!

GL: Very well said!!!!!!

MC: Well said, thanks

DB: Your stories are amazing. Have read them all, and am looking forward to more from your prolific pen.

DB: Gorgeous tribute to an inspiring day.

PT: Beautiful picture, the writing is awesome looking forward to reading the article that will follow. Thanks for sharing. God bless and keep you all.

EDB: Larry, keep on writing. Time doesn't wait as you state in your Valentine's Day story. One word at a time and before you know it, your stories will reflect your efforts and time.

MC: That was a good thought.

AJ: Thank you, Larry! I love the cover! I can't wait to dig in and read this fabulous book!!!!

VSP: Awesome

SS: You said it perfectly, "we lost him in body, but not in spirit." Your brother sounds like an amazing person, happy belated birthday to him. Great read!

SH: You are a great author (and yarn spinner...), and people are surely expecting many more gems like that. If I may, I am lending this masterpiece to a friend who is my Citibank's branch manager (and I think, originally from Harlem} Enjoy a Great Weekend.

SM: Oh my . . . what can you possibly add to that? Your writing makes me cry. Listening to you and how well you articulate is nothing new to me; I've done it for 42 years. Reading you on paper is a different experience. I haven't even started "Nina Shakes Harlem" because I'm afraid of the emotions that it will pull out of me.

DD: AMAZING, Great! I am still searching for your Short Stories.

MPDS: You have good diction; you can't teach talent. You're born with it.

MJ: GOOD STUFF AS ALWAYS! SORRY I DIDN'T GET MY BOOK WHILE YOU WERE HERE

KL: Larry, it was great to visit with you today. Thanks for making the time.

NGCC: COOL

SEM: Cool

SBBB: Adan

SAMLF: Nice

BTWC: Nice

SK: cool

SPLP: Nice, Nice, and Nice

WS: Your words Larry are lovely and inspiring! Thank you and God bless you and your family. Peace and Love

RF: Just finished your book. I really enjoyed it. I'm ready for the sequel. Can't wait to see what happens to old Preacher!

AG: amazing story Larry ... the sky is the limit for you ... At the end of the tunnel there is a light waiting so the whole world can read the stories and will have great enjoyment.

KW: Wow!!! The way that you put your words together is an incredible gift that only the Man up above could have giving you. That piece is such a true depiction of the hypocrisy that exists in this country. I regard you with the deepest admiration and respect. Nice job my friend.

SG: As usual that was exceptional. You are always on point. Thank you, about to download your book to my iPad.

KW: WOW!!! I am absolutely SPEECHLESS! Now that was incredible Larry.

AD: Wow! Very touching and at the same time very educative.

GA: Wow, u amazingly hit me bull's eye.

HE: Great read Larry.

CCM: Keep me proud!

LM: Mr. Crockett you sold me again with your Awesome Words... I can tell your Daughter has not fallen too far off of your Tree! Congratulations Sir, many blessings to you and your Family.

DB: Wow Larry, I love reading your essays. You move seamlessly from point to point, and always have clever observations and enlightening perspectives. They entertain because you embed them in this informed, folksy style that makes the reader feel like part of a conversation on the porch over a beer. Keep them coming! Great work!

CG: I loved this piece! Amazing how our thoughts can be an integral factor in our lives.

DB: As usual, such vivid prose, Larry.

CP: I have often heard that God works in unusual ways in our daily lives. It truly was great to hear how he touched your life by revealing your mother's spirit in a little child. Sometimes we get involved in everyday activities and forget our past. Keep up the good work and I know your parents are smiling.

VPN: Dermott, Arkansas the town where the family, church & community shaped our character. We share a deep legacy. Praises to God & honor to our ancestors! So proud of you!

SJ: We love you, and you'll be always our guide to lofty skies and a path to noble deeds. Chicot County High School will always be dear to my heart!

WS: May your journey ahead be joined by the spirits of Mr. James Baldwin, Dr. Maya Angelou, and the incomparable, Zora Neale Hurston to name a few. We salute you, Larry!!

SG: You are amazing keep up the great writing so happy and proud of you.

DT: Aww... that last sentence touched my heart.

JN: You are awesome Larry. Love your amazing writing always.

From my heart to yours, thank you guys so much, especially:

Arkansas, California, Connecticut, Georgia, Louisiana, Maryland, Minnesota, Mississippi, New Jersey, New York, South Carolina, Texas, Wisconsin, Washington, DC, The Philippines, Mali, Senegal, Nigeria, Zimbabwe, South Africa, Pakistan, the Dominican Republic, and of course, Harlem, NY. Because of you, a new joy is in my life!

Biography

Lawrence E. Crockett, Author

www.facebook.com

Lawrence grew up in a large family with his parents and fourteen siblings working their family farm in Southeastern Arkansas, near Dermott where he was born and raised. Upon graduating from high school, he attended the University of Arkansas-Fayetteville Campus and graduated with a Bachelor's Degree in Business Administration. After working in Student Services at the University, he pursued a career in human resources, sales, and tax preparation. He's worked with several corporations including AT&T, Digital Equipment Corporation, Block Buster Video and H&R Block.

For several years he lived in Colorado, Georgia, New Hampshire and Massachusetts before moving to New York City in 1990 with his family. New York City has been his home for over twenty-seven years. Writing has always been his passion, but publishing his first novel wasn't realized until June of 2015. Nina Shakes Harlem was his first, and he hasn't stopped writing since. Having so many enriching experiences along the way included managing his son's career. BJ Crockett had many successes with TV Commercials, voice overs, theater, television, and films. His son found success working with so many accomplished actors such as: Rafe Fines, Sam Waterston, Dan Aykroyd, Denzel Washington, Patrick Wilson, Whitney Huston, Courtney Vance, Chris Noth, Chris Webber, Jennifer Holliday, Anna Marie Horsford, Arthur French and many others.

While managing his son's career, Lawrence pursued his evolving interest as a songwriter. As a songwriter and producer, many opportunities to meet and work with several successful artists included Leila Florentino, Harry Whitaker, Burnis Stubbs, Johnny Kemp and Clifton Weeks. Finally, writing has now found a permanent place in his life. Comparing it to a rebirth, he feels rejuvenated and blessed.

Armed with a feeling and thought is how it all begins. I've never felt so good. There are so many amazing and beautiful things all around us to write about. It only requires a good eye and ear to appreciate it. God if you're listening, thank you for such a beautiful world. This precious gift you've given us is beyond any measure! Pick up one of my novels and began to read; you won't be disappointed. As a matter of fact, you just might find yourself laughing and remembering relatable experiences life has offered you.

Other Related Links

https://twitter.com/Crockett312

https://www.amazon.com/s/ref=nb_sb_noss_2?url=search-alias%3Daps&field-keywords=Lawrence+E.+Crockett

https://plus.google.com/u/0/102232157011441233436

https://about.me/larry.crockett4/edit

https://www.amazon.com/s/ref=nb_sb_noss?url=search-alias%3Daps&field-keywords=Lawrence+E.+Crockett&rh=i%3Aaps%2Ck%3ALawrence+E.+Crockett

https://www.facebook.com/NinaShakesHarlem/?fref=ts

https://itunes.apple.com/us/book/nina-shakes-harlem/id1003567866?mt=11

https://www.smashwords.com/profile/view/Crockett44

https://www.youtube.com/channel/UCNy7I5iISDgXEv5W_Odkncw

Other Releases:

Coming Soon...

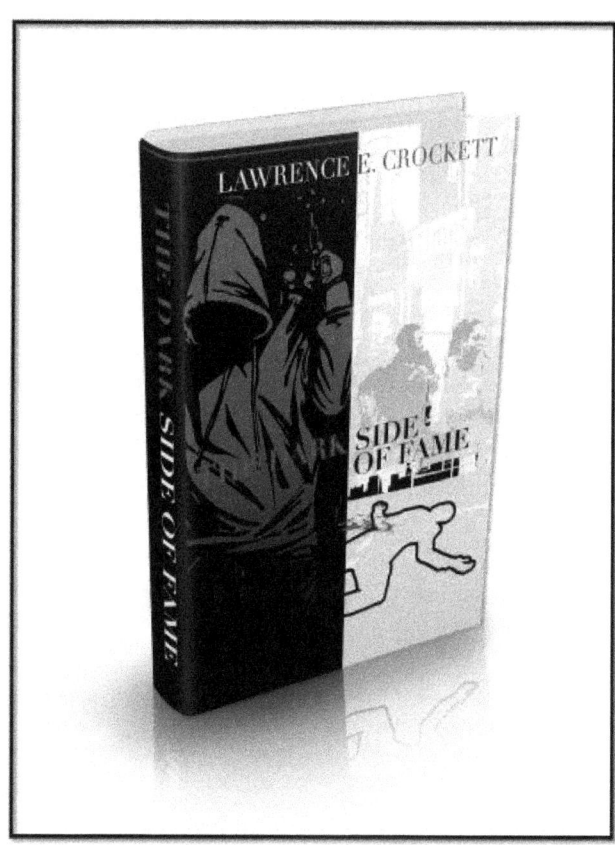

www.ingramcontent.com/pod-product-compliance
Lightning Source LLC
LaVergne TN
LVHW041611070426
835507LV00008B/190